Learn Electronics with Raspberry Pi

Physical Computing with Circuits, Sensors, Outputs, and Projects

Second Edition

Stewart Watkiss

Apress®

Learn Electronics with Raspberry Pi: Physical Computing with Circuits, Sensors, Outputs, and Projects

Stewart Watkiss
Redditch, UK

ISBN-13 (pbk): 978-1-4842-6347-1   ISBN-13 (electronic): 978-1-4842-6348-8
https://doi.org/10.1007/978-1-4842-6348-8

Managing Director, Apress Media LLC: Welmoed Spahr
Acquisitions Editor: Aaron Black
Development Editor: James Markham
Coordinating Editor: Jessica Vakili

Distributed to the book trade worldwide by Springer Science+Business Media New York, 1 NY Plaza, New York, NY 10014. Phone 1-800-SPRINGER, fax (201) 348-4505, e-mail orders-ny@springer-sbm.com, or visit www.springeronline.com. Apress Media, LLC is a California LLC and the sole member (owner) is Springer Science + Business Media Finance Inc (SSBM Finance Inc). SSBM Finance Inc is a **Delaware** corporation.

For information on translations, please e-mail booktranslations@springernature.com; for reprint, paperback, or audio rights, please e-mail bookpermissions@springernature.com.

Apress titles may be purchased in bulk for academic, corporate, or promotional use. eBook versions and licenses are also available for most titles. For more information, reference our Print and eBook Bulk Sales web page at http://www.apress.com/bulk-sales.

Any source code or other supplementary material referenced by the author in this book is available to readers on GitHub via the book's product page, located at www.apress.com/9781484263471. For more detailed information, please visit http://www.apress.com/source-code.

Printed on acid-free paper

For my wife Sarah.

Thank you for all the support you have given me whilst writing.

Table of Contents

About the Author

Stewart Watkiss has been a keen electronics hobbyist and maker since the early 1990s. He has a master's degree in electronic engineering from the University of Hull and a master's degree in Computer Science from Georgia Institute of Technology.

His interest in electronics was revitalized thanks in part to the Raspberry Pi and Stewart has created several projects some of which have been featured on the Raspberry Pi blog and The MagPi magazine. He particularly enjoys creating physical computing projects and projects which involve his two children including their current garden railway project.

He has created numerous projects many of which are explained on his website www.penguintutor.com or on the PenguinTutor YouTube channel.

Stewart also volunteers as a STEM ambassador, going into local schools to help support teachers and teach programming and physical computing to teachers and children.

About the Technical Reviewer

Sai Yamanoor is an embedded systems engineer working for an industrial gases company in Buffalo, NY. His interests, deeply rooted in DIY and Open Source Hardware, include developing gadgets that aid behavior modification. He has published two books with his brother, and in his spare time, he likes to contribute to build things that improve quality of life. You can find his project portfolio at `http://saiyamanoor.com`.

Acknowledgments

My family have been very supportive during the writing of this book. Thank you to my wife Sarah for her support and especially to my children Amelia and Oliver who have been both a source of inspiration and enthusiastic testers of the games and activities.

I'd also like to thank the team behind the Raspberry Pi including the Raspberry Pi foundation and the community that has grown around it. The Raspberry Pi has reinvigorated my love of electronics making it possible to interact with hobby electronics projects in a way that I'd only dreamed about before. Raspberry Jams and community events have been a great way to meet the team behind the Raspberry Pi as well as other members of the community which has encouraged me to pursue this further.

My thanks those that have bought the previous version and particularly those that have left useful comments through reviews and social media.

There have been many other people have helped in the making of this book. Special thanks to the technical reviewer Sai Yamanoor who tested the projects, and all the team at Apress.

Introduction

Learning computer programming is fun in itself, but when the computer is connected to external sensors and outputs, then your computer programs can interact with the real world. This is known as physical computing, and it opens up the opportunity to create some fun projects.

I am a big fan of learning by doing. It's much easier to learn when you get to make the projects rather than just reading about what other people have done. It's even better when those projects are fun. This book covers simple projects that you can make at home to make games, control toys, create your own films, or just have fun.

The Raspberry Pi computer is great for learning physical computing thanks to special pins that provide access to ports on the processor itself. These 40 pins (or 26 on earlier versions) provide a simple way to extend computing into the physical world. The circuits in this book are adding sensors, outputs, and electronic circuits to a Raspberry Pi. With a little bit of programming, these can be made to do some pretty amazing things.

We will start with some simple circuits which can be controlled from Scratch, but then move up to Python and some more complicated circuits. By the end of the book, we will have covered enough so you can start designing your own circuits.

Most of the circuits can be created by plugging wires into a solderless breadboard, but there are tips on how to solder, which opens the possibilities further. It then goes on to explain how to design custom circuit boards and looking at how we can use some of the common Raspberry Pi add-on boards and HATs.

Updates to the Second Edition

The electronic theory that you will learn in this book is something that will stay consistent for many years, but there have been some changes to the implementation and interaction with the Raspberry Pi.

Since the first edition of the book, there have been several changes to the Raspberry Pi. These include new hardware including the new Raspberry Pi 4, software updates to Raspberry Pi OS and Scratch, and changes to some of the libraries used. The new edition has provided an opportunity to update those and bring the book up to date.

Reviewing the book also gave me an opportunity to think about other electronics that I'd like to include. I have therefore added an extra chapter looking at digital logic circuits. Although creating circuits out of the standard logic integrated circuits is less prevalent these days, it is an important step in understanding how digital computers work. I have added a related practical project in driving 7-segment LED displays which is related to this topic to provide a practical application.

Who Is This Book For?

This book is for anyone who wants to learn about electronics and have fun in the process. This book focuses on fun projects, so it's great for older children and young adults. My eight-year-old son helped with some of the easier projects, so young children could have a go with adult help. While the fun aspect appeals to younger adults, there's no maximum age for having fun, so this is just as useful for adults of any age who want to learn about electronic circuits and connecting to the Raspberry Pi.

You don't need to know anything about electronic circuits before you start. Having a basic knowledge about computers and computer programming will be useful but is not required as it will be explained as we go. We'll be using Scratch and Python as they are good programming languages for those learning programming, but the electronic circuits can be controlled using any programming language that can communicate with the GPIO ports.

Making the Circuits

As with many books, you can read this book from cover to cover, or you can jump straight to the project that you find most interesting. The book introduces new concepts and components in each chapter. The first few chapters start with simple circuits and work through to more complicated circuits. There is an explanation of each circuit as we go, so for the first few chapters, you will find it most useful to follow in order, making the circuits as you go. Most of the circuits in these first few chapters are based around low-cost components, which should be within the reach of most readers.

Most of the projects are contained within a single chapter, but some are based on concepts explained in later chapters and so are split between the chapters. The notes explain which chapter you will need to refer to for the rest of the project.

Some of the later projects do use more expensive components or add-on boards for the Raspberry Pi or are designed to interact with more expensive toys. Where possible boards have been chosen to keep costs as low as possible, you may want to just read about how the circuit works or look for the suggestions on how these can be adapted for use with cheaper components or items you may already own.

Creating the examples in this book should not be considered the end. I hope that the information in this book will provide the inspiration and knowledge for you to go on to learn more about electronics and design your own circuits.

After working through the projects, it's useful to have a summary of the components so that you can refer to the book when designing your own circuits. To make it easier to refer to, I've added a summary of some of the components in the appendix along with some extra technical details which are useful when designing your own circuits.

Is Soldering Required?

When talking to teachers and students about electronic projects, I am often asked the question whether soldering is required. Unfortunately, I think that this is something that puts some people off from learning electronics, and I don't think it should.

Firstly, there is a lot that can be learned through creating circuits that don't need any soldering. Many of the projects in the first few chapters, and in some of the subsequent chapters, are designed to be made without any soldering. These are usually using solderless breadboards, but some can also be made using crocodile clips or with an inexpensive crimp tool. There are however some components that are not suitable for use on a breadboard or that need a small amount of soldering so that they can be used with a breadboard. In fact, many "breadboard-friendly" components may need headers to be soldered on to them first.

The second point I'd like to make is that soldering is not as hard, expensive, or dangerous as some people have been led to believe. Chapter 12 explains about soldering and will hopefully dispel some of the myths about soldering. If you are still uncertain, then see if you have a local maker club or Hackspace where you can speak to someone experienced in soldering.

Buying a Raspberry Pi

If you are reading this book, then there is a good chance that you have already got a Raspberry Pi. Since the Raspberry Pi was first released in 2012 there have been several different versions, some have had only minor changes, but one of the bigger changes was increasing the size of the GPIO connectors from 26 to 40. This was introduced with the Raspberry Pi B+ and the larger connector has been used on all new models since, including the Pi Zero and Raspberry Pi 2, 3 and 4 models. If you don't have a Raspberry Pi or only have an original version with 26 pins on the connector then, I recommend buying a Raspberry Pi 3 or later with the 64-bit processor and built-in Wi-Fi and Bluetooth. You don't need the extra processor power for the projects in this book, but it does make it possible to use the computer for other things. After all, nobody ever says, "This computer is too fast!" The exception is where low power is important such as when running on batteries, where the Pi Zero uses less power.

The official Raspberry Pi suppliers are listed on the Raspberry Pi website, but they are also widely stocked by various electronics and hobbyist suppliers so you shouldn't have a problem finding a supplier.

Buying the Components

Obviously for a book about making electronic circuits to follow the instructions will need some electronic components. There is no single kit that will provide all the items required, which will depend upon which circuits you decide to make as well as the suggested variations. Details of the main components required for each project are listed in Appendix A. One thing that is worth stocking up on is a variety of different resistors; you may want to say buy either an E6 or E12 series resistor multipack (see Appendix C for an explanation of the resistor series).

Most of the components are common and can be bought from any good electronics retailer. There are several retailers that are specifically geared toward makers; in the United States, there are companies such as Adafruit and SparkFun, or in the United Kingdom, two popular suppliers are CPC Farnell and Cool Components. You may also want to look at Raspberry Pi retailers, many of whom have an increasing range of electronic sensors and other components. Pimoroni has created several add-on boards and HATs specifically for the Raspberry Pi, and for those fortunate to live near

Cambridge, there is an official Raspberry Pi store. There are also international electronic retailers such as RS and Farnell or many smaller independent suppliers located around the world.

One thing about electronic components is that a device with an almost identical name may work differently. It may be possible to substitute a similar product, but where a specific component is required, I've tried to list the specific part number to help find the correct one. Watch out for codes that are almost the same but may have different electrical properties.

Installing Raspberry Pi OS

The official operating system for the Raspberry Pi is Raspberry Pi OS. It is based upon Debian Linux, but has been customized for the Raspberry Pi and comes with some additional software. The operating system needs to be loaded onto an SD card before it can run. The easiest way to install the Raspberry Pi OS is through the Raspberry Pi imager which is available at: `https://www.raspberrypi.org/downloads/`. When running the imager, it defaults to a recommended version with only certain software installed. To follow the projects in this book you will need some additional software which is included in the full install which is under Raspberry Pi OS (other). Alternatively, the additional software can be installed through either the recommended software application or the command line apt program.

It is usually a good idea to update to the latest version. In the event of minor updates to the operating system then it is normally sufficient to run an upgrade to update to the latest version of the installed software. To do this, launch the terminal which is under the accessories category of the start menu. Once you are in the terminal shell, enter the following commands:

```
sudo apt update
sudo apt upgrade
```

If the version is much older, or it has been a long time since your last update then it is recommended that you download a new version of using the imager. The new image can then be installed onto the SD card.

Software Required

All the software required in this book is available for free and mostly available as open source software. This does include some libraries that have been created by others where links have been provided to the original location.

The source code used within the book can be typed in manually or downloaded from the Internet. For most short examples, I believe you can learn more through typing and experimentation, although downloads can be useful when trying to get a circuit working or when the amount of typing is enough to make your fingers ache. You can download the source code and media files from github at `https://github.com/Apress/Learn-Electronics-with-Raspberry-Pi`. When you download the file, it will be called `Learn-Electronics-with-Raspberry-Pi-master.zip`. This is quite lengthy so after unzipping you may want to rename it to something shorter. This can be unzipped using the following commands:

```
unzip Learn-Electronics-with-Raspberry-Pi-master.zip
mv Learn-Electronics-with-Raspberry-Pi-master learnelectronics
```

The first command unzips the file, and the second command renames the directory to learnelectronics. The files are then contained in the relevant subdirectories for each chapter.

You are free to use the software source code and circuit designs that I have provided in your own projects, but some of the accompanying files or suggested downloads may come under a different license.

Safety Information

All the circuits in this book are designed to run at a low voltage and as long as an appropriate power supply is used in terms of personal safety they will be safe to touch them, although you could damage sensitive components. To make these projects permanent then it may involve the use of power tools where the safety information related to the power tools need to be followed.

Some of the projects use bright LED lights which can be used to flash on and off. Some people may be sensitive to high-frequency flashing lights which in some circumstances may cause seizures. This is more likely if the flash rate is increased beyond that used in the supplied code. Please take this into consideration when modifying the source code especially if using the lights in a public space. You should also avoid looking directly into any bright light including the LED lights used.

More Electronics

The projects in this book should be considered a starting point when learning electronics and the Raspberry Pi. At the end of each chapter, there is a section which gives a summary of the key points in the chapter and provides suggestions on how the projects could be improved or ideas for related projects. These have been left as an exercise for the reader. I hope that this will result in future projects inspired from this book, and I look forward to seeing some on the Internet in the future.

CHAPTER 1

Getting Started with Electronic Circuits

Most of this book is going to involve connecting circuits to a Raspberry Pi, but before we plug anything into the Raspberry Pi, you will need a basic understanding of electronic circuits. This is going to be a gentle introduction, so if you already know how to build your own simple circuits and would like to jump straight in to connecting into the Raspberry Pi, then feel free to jump to Chapter 2.

An electronic circuit combines individual electronic components to perform a specific function. This could be as simple as a light circuit in a torch that turns on when the on switch is pressed or incredibly complex such as the circuitry inside a laptop computer. Electronic circuits are all built around the same principles.

The most basic principle is the concept that an electronic circuit must make a complete physical circuit. For a circuit including a battery, there must be a complete path starting from the positive (+) side of the battery, through any components (such as a switch and buzzer), and then back to the negative (–) side of the battery. This is shown in the circuit in Figure 1-1.

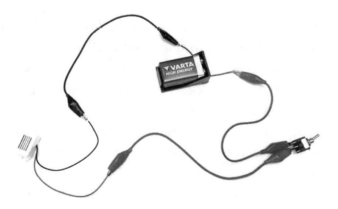

Figure 1-1. *Switch and buzzer circuit*

© Stewart Watkiss 2020
S. Watkiss, *Learn Electronics with Raspberry Pi*, https://doi.org/10.1007/978-1-4842-6348-8_1

This is a simple circuit connected using crocodile clip leads. The circuit has a buzzer and a switch which can turn the buzzer on and off. When the switch is closed, the contacts inside the switch come together completing the circuit, which allows current to flow around the circuit making the buzzer sound. When the switch is open, there is a gap between the connections inside the switch preventing the current flow, causing the buzzer to stop.

Obviously, this is a very basic circuit, but it's also the basis of almost all the circuits we make. We will replace the mechanical switch with an electronic component and use different sensors to turn the switch on and off. We will also use different outputs including LEDs and motors.

Voltage, Current, and Resistance

I'm going to keep the theory as simple as possible, but these are some terms that we are going to refer to throughout the book, which will be explained in this chapter. Understanding how the circuit works and the math involved is going to be important by the time you get to the stage where you are designing your own circuit. I have avoided putting too much math into the projects, but there are some examples where we need to perform some calculations.

The **voltage** is the difference in energy between two terminals or points in a circuit. It is measured in volts indicated by a letter V. If you had a 9V PP3 battery (such as the one used in the buzzer circuit in Figure 1-1) then the battery has a difference of 9 volts between its positive and negative terminals. We would consider the negative terminal to be at 0 volts and the positive terminal at 9 volts. Although the battery is designed for 9V, the actual voltage may vary depending upon how much charge is in the battery and what load is connected to it.

The **current** is the flow of electric charge around a circuit which is measured in amperes. This is normally abbreviated to amps and is indicated by a letter A. The current is related to the voltage as the higher the voltage of the power supply, the more current can flow through the circuit, although it also depends upon what other components are in the circuit. Using conventional electric current, we say that the current flows from the more positive to the negative terminal. In the electronic circuits we create, most currents will be small and so will normally be measured in milliamps, mA, where 1mA = 0.001A.

The electrical **resistance** is a measure of how difficult it is for the current to flow around a circuit. It is measured in ohms, which is represented by the Greek omega character Ω. There is resistance in all components of a circuit, but we can normally disregard the small amount of resistance in a good conductor such as a wire. The resistors we will be using normally range from around 200 ohms to several thousand ohms ($k\Omega$).

Note   This book uses conventional current where the electrical current is considered to flow from positive to negative terminals. This is based on an incorrect assumption from early electrical theory. We now know that current is a flow of electrons from the negative to the positive terminal, but for circuit design, conventional current is used.

Ohm's Law

When creating advanced circuits, some of the math can get quite complicated; fortunately, we don't need to do many calculations for most of the circuits in this book. There are still some basic calculations that we will need to do. In particular, for some of the circuits, we will need to work out a suitable resistor size to ensure that the current cannot damage any components while ensuring that there is sufficient current to allow the circuit to work.

To do this, we use a single formula, which is almost certainly the most important formula used in electronics. It's also one of the simplest. This relationship was discovered by German scientist Georg Ohm and is known as Ohm's law.

The basic formula is

$$I = V / R$$

As you may expect, V represents voltage and R represents resistance, but I is not so obvious. I is used to indicate current based on the phrase intensité de courant based on research by French scientist André-Marie Ampère.

This formula says that to find the current through a circuit, divide the voltage by the resistance. This can be rearranged to find the voltage using the formula

$$V = I \times R$$

To calculate the required resistor size, you can use

$$R = V / I$$

An easy way to remember this is using the Ohm's law triangle shown in Figure 1-2.

Figure 1-2. *Ohm's law triangle*

To use the triangle, hide the value you want to calculate and read remaining entries. To find the voltage, hide the letter V, leaving I and R. Multiply the current and resistance to find the voltage. To find the required resistor size, hide the letter R, which leaves V above I. Divide the voltage by the current to get the required resistor size.

Electrical Safety

Electricity can be dangerous. All the projects in this book are designed to work at low voltages up to 12V, and as long as an appropriate safe power supply (such as a wall wart or plug-in low-voltage power supply) is used, there is no risk of electrocution. The same does not apply to the high voltage present in the mains electricity supply.

In fact, it's not the voltage that's dangerous but the amount of current that can flow through the body. Electric fences used for farm animals give a shock of several thousand volts, but while they give a nasty shock, they are considered safe for use near people as they limit to short bursts of very low current (although should still be avoided particularly by children or those with heart conditions). The mains electricity to your house is between about 100V and 250V (depending upon which country you live in) and is very dangerous as it can supply enough current to be fatal. As a rule, to avoid any risk of electrocution, I recommend only working with circuits designed for 24V or less unless you are 100% sure you know what you are doing.

It's not only electrocution that poses a risk though. Even at much lower voltages, too much current can create a lot of heat and potentially start a fire. This is particularly important when using low-voltage (12V) electrical lighting or car batteries, which can provide very high currents in the event of a short circuit. I recommend only using power supplies with short circuit and overcurrent protection and consider adding a fuse (this is explained later in the disco light project).

Caution   Do not try and connect any of these circuits to the mains electricity in your home, except using the appropriate power supply adapter.

Analog vs. Digital

The world we live in is varied. If we take sound as an example, we may use various words to describe the amount of sound something is making from saying that someone is very quiet or that the MP3 player is very loud or even that a pneumatic drill is being deafening. We don't normally know or care about the actual values of the sound (measured in decibels), but we do know if we want it to be loader or quieter. A computer does not understand these terms. It only deals in actual values. In fact, at a most basic level, it only thinks of things being on and off, but it can compare against different levels to interpret this as a more accurate value.

An analog circuit is one that can interpret any number of variations of the input. Perhaps one of the few remaining purely analog circuits you will find at home today is a simple amplifier built into a set of speakers. Here, as you turn the volume control, the volume changes smoothly, increasing the volume compared to the input signal. Compare this to a modern TV where you press the volume button on the remote control and the volume moves up a fixed amount, say, between 1 and 40.

Most electronic circuits are now digital, and in fact, most include a microprocessor, either a full computer such as a Raspberry Pi or a more basic microcontroller such as the ATmega microcontrollers used in the Arduino. The real world continues to be analog so there is often an analog sensor or output and a conversion between analog and digital and vice versa.

Breadboard

Many of the circuits in this book will be built on a solderless breadboard, sometimes called a plugboard. A breadboard is a good way of creating temporary circuits to allow testing prior to committing with solder. They consist of a plastic board with a matrix of holes. The holes are then connected in small rows so that components plugged into the same section are connected together.

Breadboards are very easy to use and don't damage the components, so it's easy to change the circuit and experiment with different components. If you don't want the circuit anymore, then the components can be removed, and both the breadboard and the components can be used again for another circuit. Integrated circuits (ICs) can also be inserted and wired to other components. To connect wires to a breadboard, you should use solid core wire or special jumper wires which have a solid end that can be plugged into the breadboard. The alternative type of wire is known as multi-stranded wire, which is more flexible and so more popular with soldered circuits but doesn't plug into the board properly.

Breadboards are available in a variety of different sizes from small ones with 170 holes to large boards with multiple breadboards mounted onto a single panel. You can also connect multiple boards together which slot together. Unfortunately, there is no standard for how the boards slot together, so this may only work if using the same manufacturer. A selection of different breadboards is shown in Figure 1-3.

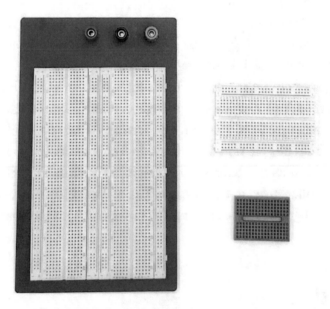

Figure 1-3. *A selection of different breadboards*

Each size of breadboard has a set of circumstances where it works best, from the smallest which can be included in a small box to the large one which is great for larger circuits. Some breadboards include connectors that are useful for plugging banana plugs from an external power supply.

For most of the circuits in this book, half-size breadboard is an ideal size. It's about the same size as the Raspberry Pi and is a good compromise between the space taken up and the amount of space for connecting circuits. An example half-size breadboard layout is shown in Figure 1-4.

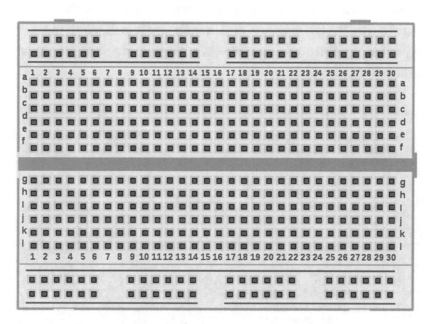

Figure 1-4. *A half-size breadboard*

The main central area consists of columns numbered 1–30 and rows from a to l. Each of the columns is connected, with a break down the center. So, for column 1, positions a to f are connected and then positions g to l. There are then two rows at the top and bottom of the breadboard, which depending upon the manufacturer may be included or as an optional extra. These rows are normally used for the main power rails with the blue row used as ground (0V) and the red row used for the positive rail. Also note that on this example the red line covers 12 holes with there being a break in the line between the next 12. This indicates that there is also a break in the track at that point, so if using a single supply voltage, you may want to use a short wire to connect these together. This very much depends upon manufacturer, so you should check the ones that you have. It's frustrating trying to understand why your circuit isn't working and then finding out it's because your breadboard has a gap in the power rail.

You may also notice that some breadboards have a slightly different number of pins (many have only ten rows between a and j) and are numbered in a different direction. The actual positioning doesn't matter as long as the same pins are connected.

A useful addition is a mounting plate that allows a Raspberry Pi and a half-size breadboard next to each other. An example is shown in Figure 1-5. The mounting plate makes it easier to wire the Raspberry Pi and breadboard together as it means the wires are less likely to fall out. You could even make your own using an appropriately sized piece of plastic or thin wood.

Figure 1-5. *Raspberry Pi and a breadboard mounted together*

You will also need a way to connect between the Raspberry Pi and the breadboard. The Raspberry Pi has a male connector for the GPIO connector (explained in the next chapter), so a female connector is required. These are available as individual jumper wires which go from male to female. A selection is shown in Figure 1-6.

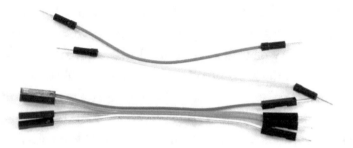

Figure 1-6. *Jumper wires. Male to male and male to female*

One disadvantage of using a breadboard is that wires or parts can be accidentally pulled out, so they are rarely used for a permanent circuit. Later, we will look at making more permanent circuits that can last much longer.

A First Breadboard Circuit

Our first circuit is a stand-alone circuit to get used to reinforce the explanation of needing a complete circuit and for a first practice in using a breadboard. The breadboard layout is shown in Figure 1-7. This diagram is created using Fritzing, which is covered in Chapter 13.

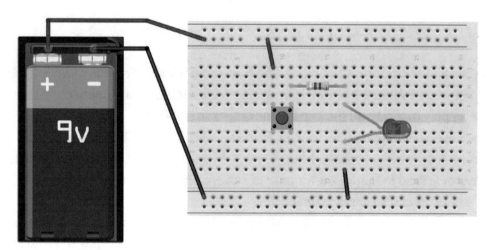

Figure 1-7. *Simple LED circuit*

Starting from the left, there is a 9V PP3 battery. These can be connected using a push-on battery connector with leads. These normally have stranded wire which as I said earlier don't work so well with a breadboard. Some have the ends of the wire coated which should connect to the breadboard, or if you are not able to connect it to the breadboard directly, then wires with crocodile clips can be used instead.

The next component is a miniature push-button switch. This should be a single-pole, single-throw type often known by its initials SPST. This means that there is a single switch inside, and that switch can change between two states (in this case, on and off). This is a push-to-make switch, which means that when the button is pressed, the switch contacts are connected.

Only two connections are needed for an SPST switch, but typically, they have four as shown in Figure 1-8. Each pair is interconnected on the left and right of the switch, respectively.

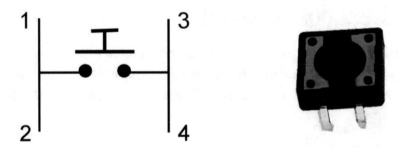

Figure 1-8. *SPST push-to-make switch*

As you can see in Figure 1-8, pins 1 and 2 are connected as are pins 3 and 4. Each side is connected when the button is pressed. In this circuit, we are connecting the positive supply to pin 1 and then taking the output from pin 3.

The next component is a resistor, in this case, a 470Ω, which is indicated by the different colored strips around the body, which are yellow, violet, brown, and then gold. The resistor is used to reduce the amount of current that can flow through the LED which would otherwise damage the LED.

The final component is a light-emitting diode known by the initials LED. This must be connected a specific way around. The anode connects toward the positive end of the supply (connecting to the resistor) and the cathode to the ground connection and on to the negative end of the battery.

You can tell which end is the anode (the positive terminal) as it normally has a longer lead. Failing that, there is normally a flat area on the plastic casing, which indicates the cathode (negative terminal). If all else fails, then this is a simple circuit where it would be safe to temporarily connect it either way around, and if it doesn't work, then try the other way around. This is one of the advantages of using the breadboard.

Once you have connected the components and the wires, pressing the button should cause the LED to light and releasing the button will turn it off again.

Calculating the Resistor Value

Earlier, I said that the resistor value was 470 Ω, but I did not explain how that value is worked out.

To calculate the resistor, you first need to know the current you want through the LED. This information is usually available from the supplier or from a datasheet. In this case, we are looking at a current of around 15mA to light the LED. We also need to know the voltage dropped across the LED which is typically around 2V for a red LED.

Once we know these, we know that there will be 7V across the resistor (9V from the battery minus 2V across the LED) and that we want to limit the current to around 15mA.

Using Ohm's law, the resistance = V ÷ I, which works out at 7 ÷ 0.015 = 467 Ω.

The nearest value of resistor is 470 Ω.

Static Sensitive Devices

You may already know that you can create static electricity by rubbing a balloon through your hair or using a comb to pick up bits of paper. You can also create static electricity by walking on a carpeted floor. While harmless to us, that same static electricity can cause permanent damage to some electronic components. Often static sensitive components will be supplied in special bags like the one shown in Figure 1-9, but that is not always the case.

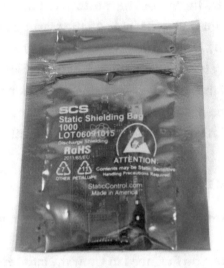

Figure 1-9. *Warning symbol for a static sensitive component*

It is worth getting an anti-static wrist strap and connecting to a suitable grounding plug. A wrist strap and grounding plug is shown in Figure 1-10. If you don't have a wrist strip, then you can discharge static electricity by touching a metal object that is connected to an electrical ground connection (also known as earth); this could be a grounded radiator or the outside case of mains electrical equipment. You should only touch the outside of electrical equipment and never open mains electrical equipment in search for an earth connection.

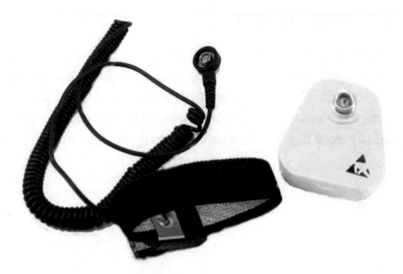

Figure 1-10. *Anti-static wrist strap*

More Circuits

In this chapter, we have looked at what makes a circuit and the importance of connecting a complete circuit which goes from the positive end of the power supply all the way back to the negative side.

We have briefly looked at Ohm's law which will come in useful later and then built our first stand-alone circuit using a breadboard and a few basic components.

To experiment further, you could try increasing the size of the resistor and watch the effect it has on the brightness of the LED or try swapping the LED and resistor with a buzzer (use the same voltage buzzer as the battery) for a noisy circuit instead.

In the next chapter, we will explore the Raspberry Pi and the GPIO ports that allow us to add electronic circuits to the Raspberry PI.

CHAPTER 2

All About Raspberry Pi

It's time to pull out the Raspberry Pi and get started. This chapter looks at the Raspberry Pi from both the hardware and software points of view. This chapter concentrates on the GPIO ports and the programming tools that will be useful for later chapters. It goes beyond the essentials, as a wider understanding of Linux will help with future projects involving the Raspberry Pi.

Introduction to the Raspberry Pi

The Raspberry Pi is a low-cost computer initially designed as a tool for learning computer programming. It also makes a great platform for hobbyists looking for a computer to use with electronic projects. Although the price is obviously appealing, arguably more important are the two rows of pins that can be used to connect electronics to the Raspberry Pi. These pins are collectively known as the GPIO pins and provide a way to interface the computer to homemade electronic circuits that wasn't available before. As a result, there are just as many adult makers who want a computer that can be used to create hardware projects.

There are now several different versions of the Raspberry Pi. The original Raspberry Pi (often referred to as Raspberry Pi 1) included 26 GPIO pins (17 of which can be used for inputs and outputs), but the newer increased the number of pins to 40 (28 of which can be used for inputs and outputs). The extra pins allow for more complex circuits and additional add-on boards known as HATs (Hardware Attached on Top). There is another option, which is the Raspberry Pi compute module. The compute module is designed to be incorporated directly into commercial circuits and is beyond the scope of this book.

The photo in Figure 2-1 shows two of the main versions of the Raspberry Pi on sale at the time of writing. These are the Raspberry Pi Zero W and the Raspberry Pi 4.

© Stewart Watkiss 2020
S. Watkiss, *Learn Electronics with Raspberry Pi*, https://doi.org/10.1007/978-1-4842-6348-8_2

Figure 2-1. *A Raspberry Pi 4 and a Raspberry Pi Zero W*

In Figure 2-1, the GPIO connector starts in the top left of each of the computers. As you can see, the default Pi Zero (left) does not include the GPIO header pins, which are factory soldered on the other versions. There is a version with these soldered on (Raspberry Pi Zero WH). Alternatively, you can solder on your own headers or wires directly to the board. More details on learning to solder are in Chapter 12.

Which Raspberry Pi to Use?

The original Raspberry Pi 1 is now very old and has less GPIO pins. It can still be used for interfacing with electronics; however, many of the projects in this book are based on a 40-pin Raspberry Pi. So, I suggest looking at either a Raspberry Pi 2 or Pi Zero as a minimum. The Raspberry Pi 3 and later and the Raspberry Pi Zero W include wireless networking which is easier than having to add an external adapter.

If you want a powerful Raspberry Pi that can run a full desktop, then I suggest a Raspberry Pi 4 with at least 2GB of memory, which is the standard model at the time of writing.

If you are working on a project that has limited space or that is battery powered, then you may want to consider the Pi Zero W instead. The Pi Zero W is particularly useful for low-power projects with an embedded computer, such as a simple robot. You will not get the same performance from the Pi Zero W (which is based on the same processor as the Raspberry Pi 1), but its size, low power consumption, and low cost are hard to beat.

Raspberry Pi GPIO Ports

As mentioned previously, the GPIO ports on the Raspberry Pi are a real game changer. They make it easier to connect simple electronic circuits to the Raspberry Pi providing a way to communicate with the physical world.

GPIO stands for general-purpose input/output. It is a common term used to refer to ports on a processor that can be used either as an input or an output. The GPIO pins on the Raspberry Pi are connected directly to the GPIO ports on the processor. The processor runs at 3.3V, and as such, the GPIO ports are designed for 3.3V. This is less than the 5V commonly used by some electronic circuits, and a 5V connected as an input to one of the GPIO pins could damage the Raspberry Pi. The output of the GPIO is only able to provide a current of up to 16mA for each pin and maximum of 50mA across multiple pins.

Caution   The GPIO ports do not include any built-in protection. Connecting a port to an input that is above 3.3V or drawing too much current from an output can permanently damage the Raspberry Pi.

The GPIO pins are on a two-row male header along one side of the Raspberry PI. Most of the GPIO pins can be used for normal input/output as well as some having alternative functions such as I²C and PWM. The recent versions of the Raspberry Pi have 40 pins. Of the 40 pins, 26 can be used for input/output ports, 2 provide a 5V power supply, 2 are connected to the 3.3V power supply, 8 are connected to ground, and 2 are for board ID recognition.

The Raspberry Pi 1 had only 26 pins, some of which changed during a revision. A summary of the main pin allocations for the 40-pin versions of the Raspberry Pi is shown in Figure 2-2; for the pin details of the other Raspberry Pi revisions, see Appendix D.

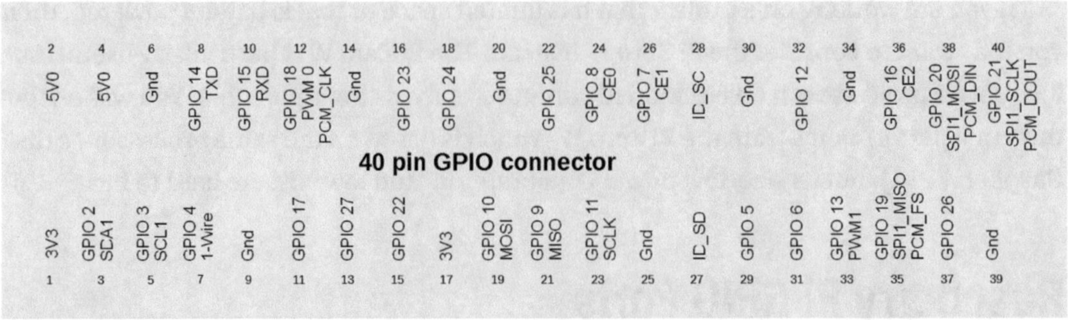

2	4	6	8	10	12	14	16	18	20	22	24	26	28	30	32	34	36	38	40
5V0	5V0	Gnd	GPIO 14 TXD	GPIO 15 RXD	GPIO 18 PWM 0 PCM_CLK	Gnd	GPIO 23	GPIO 24	Gnd	GPIO 25	GPIO 8 CE0	GPIO 7 CE1	IIC_SC	Gnd	GPIO 12	Gnd	GPIO 16 CE2	GPIO 20 SPI1_MOSI PCM_DIN	GPIO 21 SPI1_SCLK PCM_DOUT

40 pin GPIO connector

3V3	GPIO 2 SCA1	GPIO 3 SCL1	GPIO 4 1-Wire	Gnd	GPIO 17	GPIO 27	GPIO 22	3V3	GPIO 10 MOSI	GPIO 9 MISO	GPIO 11 SCLK	Gnd	IIC_SD	GPIO 5	GPIO 6	GPIO 13 PWM1	GPIO 19 SPI1_MISO PCM_FS	GPIO 26	Gnd
1	3	5	7	9	11	13	15	17	19	21	23	25	27	29	31	33	35	37	39

Figure 2-2. GPIO pin layouts for the 40-pin Raspberry Pi

The GPIO connector is in one corner of the Raspberry Pi. If you position the Raspberry Pi with the GPIO connector in the top left as shown in Figure 2-1, then the pins are numbered with 1 starting at the bottom left of the connector and then the odd numbers across the bottom and even numbers across the top. The last pin is pin 40 in the top right of the connector. This is shown in Figure 2-2, which shows the GPIO number and alternative function for many of the pins.

The GPIO ports can be referred to by different references. The most common is the GPIO number (which is the GPIO port number on the processor) or the pin number (based on physical position on the GPIO connector). Whenever GPIO is mentioned, this is the processor references, and whenever pin is mentioned, this is the pin number on the connector.

A summary of the ports and common alternative functions is provided in the table in Appendix D. Some of the alternative functions are listed as follows and covered in more details later in the book.

Serial Communications/UART

Serial communication is a way of sending information between two different devices. The data is sent one bit of data at time in sequence. You may be aware that older computers used to have a serial port based around RS-232 protocol. Before broadband communications were available, this was often used for modems to connect to the Internet. It has an even older history and is how terminals were connected to computers in the past when "the computer" was a big computer hidden away in the computer room, and it was accessed using terminals. Although few computers now come with an RS-232 serial port, the same protocols are still in use today.

The Raspberry Pi can communicate as a serial device in several ways. One is to use a device connected to the USB port using the Linux USB serial driver to connect to a microprocessor (such as an Arduino or micro:bit); another is to use Bluetooth (which can work as a wireless version of the RS-232 protocol), or serial communication can be provided through the GPIO ports. There are two GPIO ports which are connected to a UART (universal asynchronous receiver/transmitter) within the processor. The UART pins can be wired directly to another serial device which provides an alternative way to connect to an Arduino or similar device instead of using the USB port. The GPIO pins are physical pins 8 and 10, which connect to transmit (TXD) and receive (RXD). By default, these pins are used for the Linux console, so they may periodically send error messages from the operating system. This can be useful to identify problems when the Raspberry Pi is not connected to a screen, but the console may need to be disabled or redirected if those pins are used for another purpose.

As with all the GPIO ports, the serial ports work at 3.3V. This is less than the 5V used on RS-232 connector or some other processors such as the Arduino. If connecting to a 5V serial device, then you may need to use a level shifter to convert the signal voltage between the devices.

I²C: Inter-Integrated Circuit

Also known as I²C, this is another serial communication protocol that is used to communicate with peripherals. It works as a primary and secondary relationship. Typically, the Raspberry Pi will act as the primary and communicate with peripherals such as sensors or displays. The current Raspberry Pi models use I²C channel 1, which uses GPIO pins 3 and 5. These are the SDA1 and SCL1 ports, respectively.

SPI: Serial Peripheral Interface Bus

SPI is another form of serial communication for communicating with peripherals. It has a higher bandwidth than I²C and is commonly used for connecting to SD cards and other peripherals. A physical difference between SPI and I²C is that while I²C uses only two connections, SPI needs at least four and in some cases more.

SPI has one primary device which controls the bus (I will refer to this as the main device), and then the other devices are controlled by the primary device (I will refer to these as secondary). The connections are SCLK (serial clock), MOSI (main output, secondary input), MISO (main input, secondary output), and SS (secondary select).

These are pins 23, 19, 21, and 24. The secondary select is labeled as CE0 on the GPIO output, which means chip enable (and can be considered the same as SS). This is used to determine which of multiple secondary devices the master is communicating with. There is also another SS port on the GPIO, labeled as CE1 on port 26, which allows an additional secondary device to be connected. There is also a second SPI connection on the 40-pin GPIO ports using pins 40, 38, 35, and 36.

1-Wire

1-Wire is a form of serial communication for simple devices. Despite its name, there are actually two connections needed, one for the ground and one for the power and data. This is less than most other serial protocols which use either a separate send and receive wire or a connection to indicate which device is allowed to communicate. The ability to pass power over the same wire as signal can be useful for sensors which don't have their own power supply. 1-Wire has a low maximum bandwidth but is sometimes used for sensors such as temperature sensors.

Pin 7 (GPIO 4) can be configured for 1-Wire communications.

PCM: Pulse-Code Modulation

Pulse-code modulation provides a way to send analog values as an encoded digital signal. This is achieved by sampling the analog value and then sending the value as a digitally encoded signal. Four connections are available, which are data out (pin 40), data in (pin 38), frame sync (pin 35), and a clock signal (pin 12)

PWM: Pulse-Width Modulation

Pulse-width modulation is a technique used to provide an analog output from a digital pin. This works by turning the output on for a certain period of time and then off for a period of time. By varying the "width" of the on and off times, an equivalent average voltage can be calculated. This is useful for varying the brightness of an LED connected to a digital pin or varying the speed of an analog motor.

There are two physical PWM pins included on the GPIO connector which have hardware PWM support. PWM 0 is on pin 12, and PWM 1 is on pin 33. Other pins can be used for PWM by creating an equivalent signal from switching the appropriate pin on and off at the right time using software, but using the hardware ports is more accurate and less taxing on the processor. This will be useful in Chapter 4 where the hardware PWM output is used to control NeoPixels.

The hardware PWM pins conflict with the Raspberry Pi audio, so if you would like to use these ports for PWM, then you will need to disable the Raspberry Pi audio.

Getting Started with Raspberry Pi OS

The official operating system for the Raspberry Pi is known as Raspberry Pi OS, based on Debian Linux. Previously, this was known as Raspbian.

The Raspberry Pi OS is normally run from an SD card. The easiest way to install the operating system onto an SD card is to use the Raspberry Pi Imager available from the Raspberry Pi website at `www.raspberrypi.org/downloads/`. The default image includes a reasonable selection of software; however, if you have a fast network connection (for the initial download), I recommend choosing the Raspberry Pi OS other images and then the full Raspberry Pi OS image which includes additional software.

In the standard install for Raspberry Pi OS, the Raspberry Pi boots straight into the desktop, shown in Figure 2-3. The desktop looks a little different from other operating systems, but whatever operating system you normally use, it shouldn't be too difficult to get to grips with. The screenshot shows the Raspberry Pi logo background, which is no longer the default but makes it clearer to see for the purpose of this book.

Figure 2-3. *Screenshot of the Raspberry Pi OS desktop*

Here are some of the key pointers to navigating around the desktop:

- The application menu is in the top left indicated by the Raspberry Pi logo.

- There are lots of applications included. Here is a small selection:

    - The programming menu includes a selection of different programming languages including Scratch and Mu (a Python editor), which we will be using throughout this book.

    - There is no need to pay for a word processor or other office application because LibreOffice is included.

    - The Chromium web browser is a fully open source web browser closely related to the Chrome web browser.

    - There is a special version of Minecraft for the Raspberry Pi with an easy-to-use Python interface. This will be used in Chapter 10.

    - If any of these are not installed already, then you can add them through the Recommended Software program.

- You can adjust some of the desktop settings in the preferences menu.

    - The Raspberry Pi Configuration application provides a graphical way to adjust some of the key options for the Raspberry Pi.

- The terminal application provides a way to issue commands using a text interface. This provides a very efficient way to run commands and automate certain features of the Raspberry Pi.

- Using the icons on the top right of the screen, you can do the following:

    - Connect to Bluetooth devices (if supported by the Raspberry Pi).

    - Configure the network connection (including Wi-Fi).

    - Change the audio output and volume.

    - See the time.

If you need more information on any of these, hover your mouse pointer above them to see any hints, left-click for typical configuration changes, or right-click for further configuration options. For example, hovering over the audio icon tells you the volume setting, a left-click lets you change the volume, and a right-click lets you change whether the audio is sent to HDMI (to the TV) or as Analog (through the 3.5mm jack).

Connecting to the Raspberry Pi Using the Network

Although it's possible to follow the projects in this book using a screen, keyboard, and mouse connected to the Raspberry Pi, it is often useful to connect from a remote computer. This could be another Raspberry Pi or a desktop or laptop computer. You will use two methods of connecting here: SSH and VNC.

Before you can connect, you first need to know the IP address that has been allocated to the Raspberry Pi. In most cases, this will be a dynamic IP address provided by your home router, but it can be set manually instead. If you have connected the Raspberry Pi to the router using an Ethernet cable, then this should have been allocated already, but if you are using Wi-Fi, then you will need to enter your Wi-Fi network details through the network configuration tool (top right of the screen).

Once you have connected to a network, hovering over the network icon will display the IP address assigned. Figure 2-4 shows the IP address allocated to my Raspberry Pi which is 192.168.0.149.

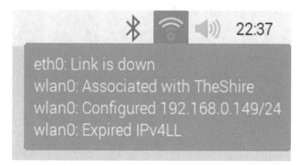

Figure 2-4. *Screenshot of Wi-Fi status message*

Alternatively, you can obtain the IP address on the command line by launching the terminal application and entering the command

```
ip addr
```

Secure Shell (SSH)

Secure Shell (often referred to as SSH) is a server that allows you to run instructions on the Raspberry Pi from a remote computer. It doesn't provide a graphical interface but allows you to type instructions using a keyboard and receive a response through a display terminal.

The SSH server is installed as standard on the Raspberry, but it is disabled by default. It can be enabled through the Raspberry Pi configuration program. Once enabled, it is simply a case of entering the IP address into an SSH client on the same network, and it is possible to log in using the normal username and password (by default, username *pi* and password *raspberry*).

For Linux and Mac OS X, an SSH client is available directly from the command line. For Windows, you need to download an SSH client, such as the open source PuTTY, available at `www.chiark.greenend.org.uk/~sgtatham/putty/`. Various SSH clients, including PuTTY, are also available for Linux and Mac OS X if preferred.

To connect using a terminal client on a Mac OS X or Linux, prefix the IP address with the username and the @ character:

```
ssh pi@192.168.0.149
```

From the graphical clients, such as PuTTY, enter the IP address and username in the appropriate fields, as shown in Figure 2-5.

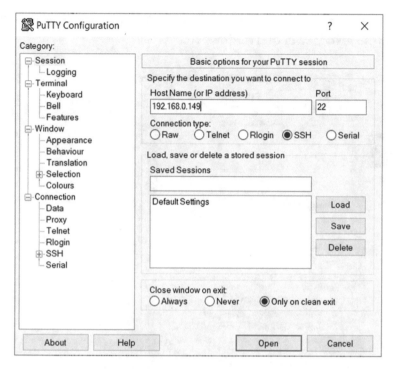

Figure 2-5. *PuTTY application, an SSH client*

Remote Desktop Using VNC (Virtual Network Computing)

Having access to a remote shell through SSH is a good way of running command-line programs, but a graphical interface can be useful at times. In fact, most of the screenshots in this book have been taken by connecting using VNC from my laptop.

There are different VNC servers which can be used. There is one pre-installed on the Raspberry Pi, which is from RealVNC. This is commercial software, but it can be used free of charge for non-commercial use. The VNC server allows the remote computer to see and control the screen on the primary display, whereas some other VNC servers create a separate virtual screen. Unless you want to simultaneously share a computer between users, it is usually better to control the primary screen.

You can enable the VNC server through the Raspberry Pi configuration, on the same screen as previously used to enable the SSH server. When running, you will see a VNC icon near the top right of the screen.

You may also need to install the VNC viewer (or one of the alternative VNC clients) on your local computer. If you don't already have a client installed, then you can download one from `www.realvnc.com/en/raspberrypi/`. Figure 2-6 shows how to connect using the VNC viewer on Windows 10.

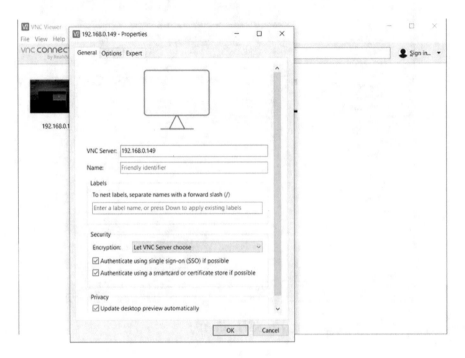

Figure 2-6. *Connect remotely using VNC viewer*

Once connected, you can run most software through the client as though using a mouse and keyboard on the Raspberry Pi. There are some limitations to what VNC can be used for, but for most applications, VNC provides a useful way to run programs remotely.

More Raspberry Pi

This chapter has looked at the different versions of the Raspberry Pi. We then looked at the GPIO interface pins and an introduction to Raspberry Pi OS, the Linux-based operating system that runs on the Raspberry Pi.

You may also want to spend some time exploring the installed software and games such as Minecraft.

This is the end of the initial theory. The next chapters involve hands-on electronics connecting to the Raspberry Pi. In Chapter 3, you connect your first circuit to the Raspberry Pi and learn to access the GPIO pins through the Scratch programming language.

## CHAPTER 3

Starting with the Basics: Programming with Scratch

Scratch is a visual-based programming language. It was designed at MIT for teaching programming to children but has become popular with young and old programmers. Some universities even use it as an introductory language for new students.

The latest version of Scratch is version 3, which is available through a web browser or as a native program on the Raspberry Pi. Unfortunately, Scratch 3 uses a lot of memory and so the native client may not work on older versions of the Raspberry Pi or those with limited memory. To run the native Scratch 3 program on a Raspberry Pi, it is recommended that you have a Raspberry Pi 4 with at least 2GB of memory. For other models, you should use Scratch 2 instead. The Raspberry Pi OS image includes Scratch, Scratch 2, and Scratch 3.

This chapter describes using Scratch 3, which is preferred as it has a similar interface to using a web browser, which is how most people first learn Scratch. If your Raspberry Pi is not up to running Scratch 3, then Scratch 2 is very similar, and the main differences are explained as required.

Introduction to Scratch

If you are not already familiar with Scratch, then here is a quick introduction. Scratch is available from the programming menu in Raspbian and when running looks like the screenshot in Figure 3-1. This looks almost identical to the web browser version but without the login options at the top right.

© Stewart Watkiss 2020
S. Watkiss, *Learn Electronics with Raspberry Pi*, https://doi.org/10.1007/978-1-4842-6348-8_3

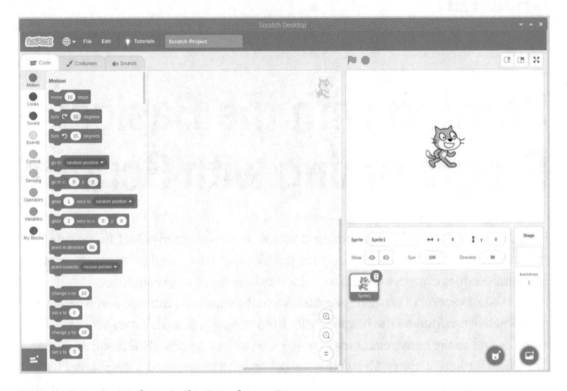

Figure 3-1. *Scratch 3 on the Raspberry Pi*

The application is split into four main sections. In Figure 3-2, I have shaded the main areas and labeled them as A, B, C, and D.

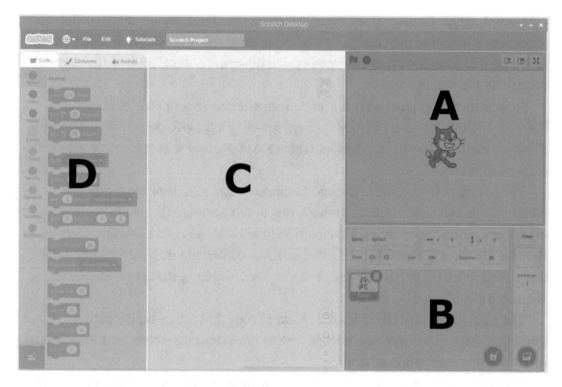

Figure 3-2. *The four main areas of Scratch*

The most significant difference from Scratch 2 is that these are positioned differently. On Scratch 2, areas A and B are at the left of the screen.

The most important part of the Scratch application is the stage area (section A); this is a representation of the screen when the program is running. The look of the game will be designed on the stage area, and it's also where you can see the program run. There is also a green flag, which is used to start the program running, and a red stop sign, used to stop the program.

If the screen is a stage, then the sprites are the actors, props, and lights used to create the show. These are stored in the sprite list area (section B). At the bottom of this section, there is a button for adding a new sprite (which is on the top right of that section in Scratch 2). There are different options for drawing your own sprite: choose an existing file (many are included with Scratch), upload your own file, or get a random sprite. In Scratch, a sprite can have its own costumes, scripts, and sounds associated with it. The stage is considered a special type of sprite and is shown next to the sprites list area with the same options for choosing a new backdrop.

If you want to change a sprite, then you load it into the sprite edit area (section C). Sprites are loaded into this section by clicking them in the sprite list, where they will then be shown with a border. There are three tabs in the sprite area called Code (or Scripts), Costumes, and Sounds.

In Scratch, the program code is grouped together into a script which is edited on the code or scripts tab. It is common to have several scripts associated with each sprite. The stage can also have its own scripts, which are often used to control the sprites or the stage background.

The costumes tab is used to change the look of a sprite. It does not need to be a different form of clothing (although that is one use of a costume); it could be used to represent a different object or completely different look, such as a firework rocket which changes to a burst of light when it explodes. When editing the stage, the costumes tab is replaced with a backdrops tab which can be used to change the scene. There's also a sound tab to add sound to the sprite.

The code blocks area (D) holds the blocks of code that can be built together to make the scripts. Each block of code is shaped with interlocking tabs which can be connected with other appropriate blocks of code.

The blocks of code are grouped into nine different group blocks which are labeled and color-coded the same as the code block color. The code for the sprite is created by dragging the appropriate code block from this area to the code area for the sprite. If you position the block close to another block, then they will snap into place.

Scratch with GPIO Support

The Scratch client includes special code blocks to support access to the GPIO pins. This is added by clicking the icon in the bottom left corner. Clicking that gives several different modules, including Raspberry Pi GPIO and Raspberry Pi Simple Electronics. Either of these modules can be used for this project as they provide very similar options. I recommend the Raspberry Pi GPIO module as it does provide additional options regarding the way inputs work.

The different code blocks available are shown in Figure 3-3.

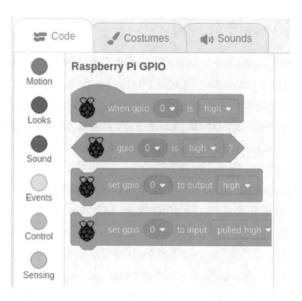

Figure 3-3. *Scratch code block extensions for the Raspberry Pi*

Scratch 2 has a similar extension which is chosen using the *Add an Extension* button. In Scratch 2, there is just one set gpio code block which handles both inputs and outputs, whereas it is split across two different blocks in Scratch 3. Scratch 2 doesn't have the code start event (the first option in Figure 3-3), but that is not required for the project in this book.

Controlling an LED Using Scratch

Before we create our program in Scratch, you need to create your first Raspberry Pi electronic circuit. You will start off with a very simple LED circuit which allows you to turn a light on and off depending upon events in a Scratch program. This will then be expanded to make our first game.

To understand the circuit, you first need to understand two components, the LED and the resistor. You have already seen these in the previous chapter, but I've included a more detailed explanation here.

Light-Emitting Diode (LED)

An LED is a component that gives out a light when an electric current passes through it. The LED is very efficient and so you will often see them used in battery-operated light-up toys. The fact that it doesn't use much energy is important as the amount of current we can supply from the GPIO pins is very small. If we instead used a light bulb such as those you may have in an older torch, then we would need a more complex circuit or risk damage to the Raspberry Pi.

An important thing about an LED is that it needs to be inserted the correct way around in the circuit. This is due to the diode part of its name. A diode is a component that acts like a one-way valve only allowing current to flow in one direction. As its name suggests, the light-emitting diode emits light when the current is flowing. Depending upon the materials used in the LED, it will light up a particular color.

The diode has an anode which should be connected to the more positive end of the connection and a cathode which goes to the other side. You can tell which end is the anode (the positive terminal) as it normally has a longer lead. If that's not obvious (such as if the lead has been cut short), then there is normally a flat area on the plastic casing which indicates the cathode (negative terminal). This is shown in Figure 3-4.

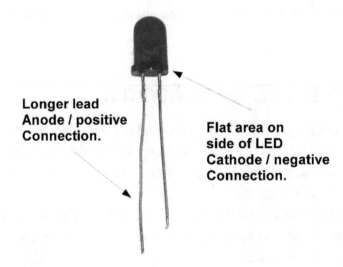

**Longer lead
Anode / positive
Connection.**

**Flat area on
side of LED
Cathode / negative
Connection.**

Figure 3-4. *A typical LED*

Resistor

A resistor acts to reduce the current flowing through a circuit. This is particularly important to protect a component from being damaged due to too much current flowing through.

The size of the resistor is measured in ohms (Ω), which is marked on the side of the resistor using a color code. You can see a photo of a typical resistor in Figure 3-5, and details of the color code markings are provided in Appendix C.

Figure 3-5. *A 220Ω resistor*

In this circuit, the resistor is required both to protect the GPIO port from too high an output current and to protect the LED from excessive current. To calculate the value of the resistor, we first need to know the voltage across the resistor and the current we want to limit it to.

The voltage of the GPIO output is 3.3V. Approximately, 2V of this is across the LED, so we have approximately 1.3V across the resistor.

While the maximum current that the GPIO can provide is 16mA, around 8mA is enough to light the LED to show whether something is on or off. To calculate the resistor, we divide the voltage by the current (see Chapter 1). The resistor size should therefore be 1.3 ÷ 0.008 which is 162Ω. Resistors come in standard values. In this case, I've selected the next highest in the E6 series of resistors which is 220Ω. If you have a set of E12 series resistors, then you could use a 180Ω resistor, but either will do. The color of the resistor is

1. Red (2)

2. Red (2)

3. Brown (x 10)

4. Gold

Due to differences in manufacturing, the resistor is not necessarily going to be the same as the specified value. The fourth entry is shown as gold which gives us the tolerance rating (how close the resistor must be to the specified value), in this case, 5%. Taking the tolerance into consideration, the actual resistor will be between 209Ω and 231Ω.

Note   This book is about teaching electronics, so the full calculation has been shown. The calculations are not particularly difficult, but there are also online resistor calculators which could be used if you would rather concentrate on the creativity rather than the math.

Connecting the LED to the Raspberry Pi

For this circuit, you can use GPIO port 22, which is physically pin 15 on the GPIO connector (see the GPIO diagram in Appendix D for more details). The breadboard layout diagram is shown in Figure 3-6.

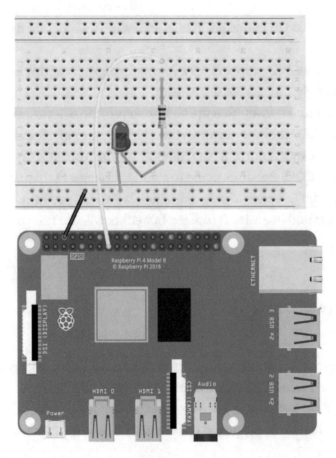

Figure 3-6. *LED circuit for Scratch GPIO*

Remember to make sure that the LED is the correct way. Looking at the diagram in Figure 3-6, the longer wire should be the one nearest the top, which is in the same block as the resistor. I have deliberately bent the leg on the diagram to make the anode (positive side) look longer. Do not worry if your wiring does not follow the exact same layout as shown in the diagram; the length of the legs on the components may make it easier to position slightly differently. The important thing is to connect to the correct ports on the Raspberry Pi and for the components to connect to the same row on the breadboard where required.

You can now move on to having Scratch turn the LED on and off. First, add the Raspberry Pi extensions as explained previously. Using a new Scratch program, add the code blocks to the Scripts tab of the default sprite (Sprite1 which is the Scratch cat). The code blocks are shown in Figure 3-7.

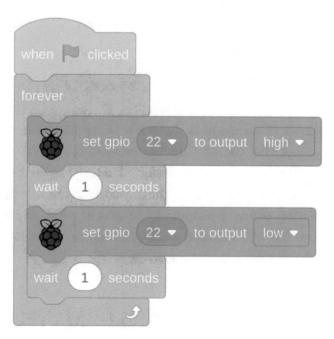

***Figure 3-7.** Initial LED script*

With Scratch 2, the code will look similar, although the Raspberry Pi blocks will be a dark gray color instead of green. If you click the green flag, then the program should run which will turn the LED on for 1 second and then off for 1 second. The code will continue to run turning the LED on and off one second at a time. Here's an explanation for how it works.

The block containing the green flag at the top of the script is from the *event blocks*. It has a curved top which indicates that this will start this script running. It is used to start the script whenever the green flag is clicked to start the program. All scripts should start with a start block, most of which are event blocks.

The forever block is from the control blocks and creates a loop which will run "forever". It runs any code between the forever at the top and the white arrow at the bottom of the loop. When you drag the block over, you will see it has a blank section in the middle, which is where you drag the code blocks that need to be run inside the loop. Although it is called forever, it will likely not actually run forever but will continue to loop while the program is running, until you click the red stop sign to stop the program.

The wait blocks are also from the control blocks and pause the script for running for a set length of time, in this case, 1 second. You can change the value in the wait, try changing it to a decimal fraction (say, 0.5), and see what happens.

The main thing we are interested is the Raspberry Pi extension block.

As the wording on the block suggests, this will set the gpio output value. You can choose the GPIO number from the pull-down list where it shows 22. As explained in Chapter 2, GPIO port 22 is the port that is connected to GPIO 22 on the processor, which is not the same as the physical pin number. The physical pin number that we have connected to is 15. Saying to turn an output high will set its output voltage to 3.3V which is the high or on value. This will turn on the LED. Turning an output low is the same as turning the output off and setting the voltage to 0V.

Adding an Input to the Scratch GPIO Program

Using the LED circuit (Figure 3-6) as a starting point, we will now add an input to the Raspberry Pi. Inputs can take many different forms; in this case, we will be using a simple switch.

Switch

A switch is used to create a break in a circuit or join two parts of a circuit together depending upon the position. There are different types of switches depending upon what the switch is being used for. The one we will use here is known as a push-to-make push-button switch. When the button is pressed, then it pushes the conductors together inside the switch completing the circuit. This is like a doorbell push switch which completes the circuit causing the doorbell to sound. When the switch is not pressed, then that is known as being open as the contacts inside open apart creating a break in the circuit. When the switch is pressed, it closes the contacts together completing the circuit, so it's known as being closed.

I recommend using a miniature push-button switch of the type shown in Figure 3-8, which is the same as shown previously in Chapter 1. This switch has four pins, although the pins on each side are connected together with just a single switch in the package. The ones I have used include clip-on button caps which make them stand out a bit more. The caps are not necessary and only fit on certain switches.

A photo of the switch along with its circuit symbol is shown in Figure 3-8.

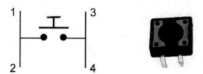

Figure 3-8. *Push-button switch and circuit diagram showing connections*

Using a Switch As a Digital Input

The GPIO port needs to be sent a digital on or off signal, which should be +3.3V for on and 0V for off; this is the same as the high- and low-output states. At first thought, you may consider using the switch to connect to the positive supply and rely on the pin being disconnected for a low 0V signal. Unfortunately, that is unlikely to work as when the power is disconnected, the input will be considered floating. When an input is floating, then the state is unpredictable and can often change between high and low.

Instead, we need to connect the input to the positive voltage so that the supply is high when the switch is not pressed. The switch then connects the pin to the 0V supply to bring it low when pressed. A high-value resistor (usually in the tens of kΩ) is required for the connection to the positive rail to prevent a short circuit. The Raspberry Pi has internal pull-up resistors that can be used rather than needing to add an external resistor. The pull-up resistors can be enabled using the input block from the Raspberry Pi extension with the state "pulled high". The Raspberry Pi also supports "pulled low" where you connect the switch between the GPIO port and the 3.3V supply, but it is more common to have the Raspberry Pi pin pulled high and then use the switch to pull it low.

Adding the Switch to the Circuit

The diagram in Figure 3-9 shows the LED circuit we used previously with the switch added. The switch is connected to GPIO port 10 (physical pin 19) and to the 0V ground pin on the Raspberry Pi.

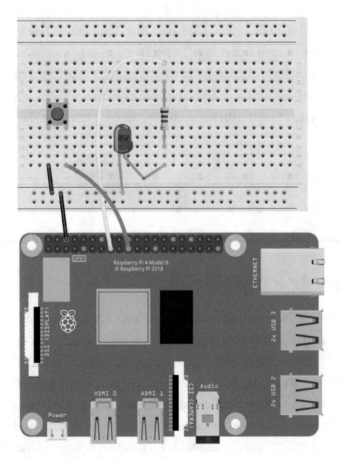

Figure 3-9. *Switch and LED circuit*

Now that you've connected the switch to the Raspberry Pi, it's time to add the code. You will need to add the code to detect the switch press to the existing script on Sprite1 to configure the GPIO port and detect when the button is pressed. The updated code is shown in Figure 3-10.

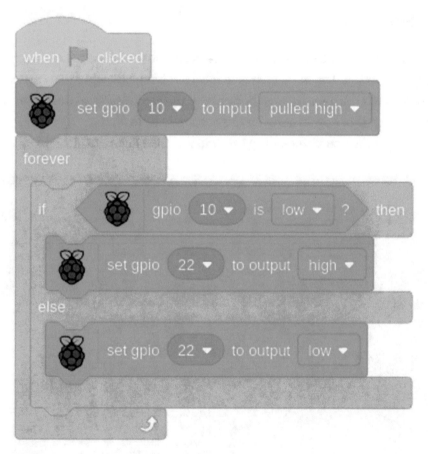

Figure 3-10. *Switch and LED Scratch code*

I have added a new block at the start sets GPIO port 10 as an input with a pull-up resistor.

In the forever loop, the GPIO block is used to check on the status of the switch. If the switch is not pressed, then the internal pull-up resistor sets the value to high. When the switch is pressed, then the input is pulled low by the switch and the sensor value will be low.

When the code has been entered and the program run, then the LED will be initially off, turning on when the switch is pressed and off when it's released. This is effectively performing the same as the LED circuit in Chapter 1, but now using an entire computer where the switch was able to handle this on its own. We have done this to introduce the way that inputs and outputs are handled in Scratch. We will now be adding a few more components and creating a game in scratch based on this circuit.

Robot Soccer

The reason for creating the circuit so far is that it can now be used to create a game, in this case, Robot Soccer. The basic idea is to have a robot goalkeeper that can move from side to side to catch the ball. This is a book about the electronics, so the programming is kept simple with lots of opportunity for improvement or to change to your favorite sport or other activity. When complete, the game will look like Figure 3-11.

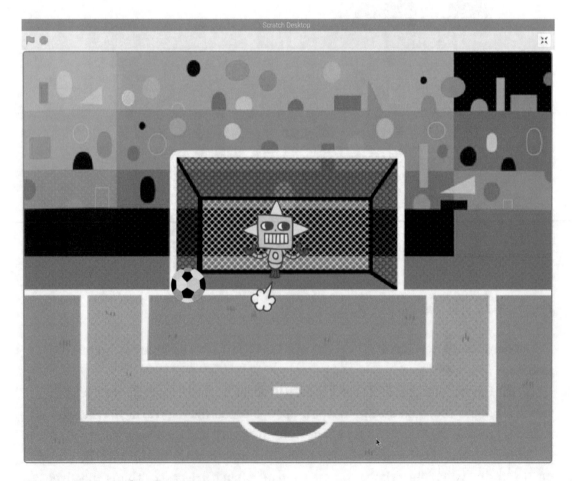

Figure 3-11. *Robot Soccer game*

To be able to move left and right, you need to add a few more components. This will involve duplicating the circuit so that instead of one switch and one LED, you have two switches and two LEDs. The existing LED is red to signify that the robot missed the ball; the new one we will add is green to signify that the robot reached the ball. The green LED needs to be connected through an appropriate resistor to GPIO port 23 (physical pin 16) and the second switch connected to GPIO port 9 (physical pin 21). This is shown in Figure 3-12.

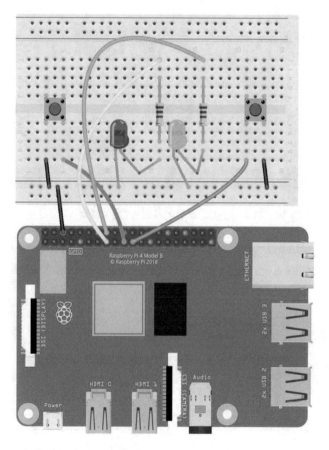

Figure 3-12. *Circuit for Robot Soccer*

Rather than editing the previous Scratch project, start a new one. Click File ➤ New which will create a new project with the Scratch cat sprite. Delete the cat sprite as that is not required. Click Choose a Backdrop and choose the Soccer backdrop image. This is shown in Figure 3-13.

Figure 3-13. *Adding the background for Robot Soccer*

Add the setup code in Figure 3-14 to the stage code tab. This is similar to the setup code used in the previous example, but this time it is on the backdrop.

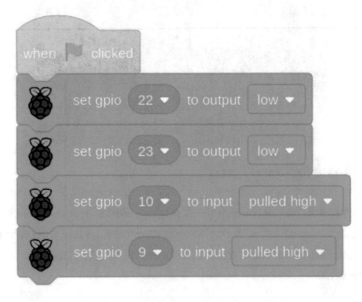

Figure 3-14. *Setup code for Robot Soccer game added to the stage scripts tab*

You now need to create the robot sprite. From the sprite section, click Choose a Sprite. Click Robot. This is shown in Figure 3-15.

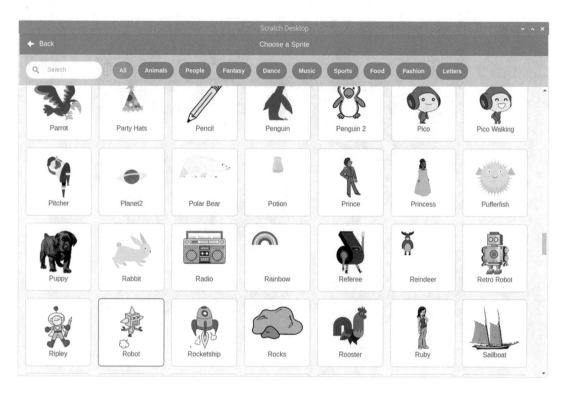

Figure 3-15. *Adding a new sprite using the Robot sprite*

There are lots of alternative sprites you could choose instead – whether you prefer the giant hand called Goalie, a dinosaur, or one of the people sprites. Change the size of the sprite to 50 and move the sprite so that it is centered in the goal posts.

There are three code blocks that need to be added to the code tab of the robot sprite. These are shown in Figure 3-16.

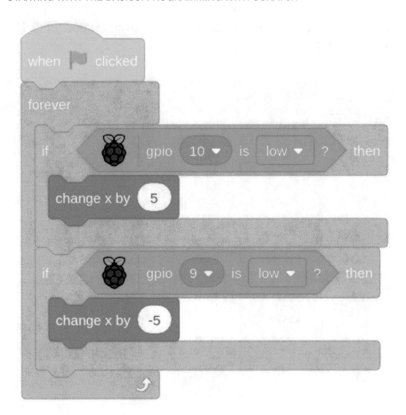

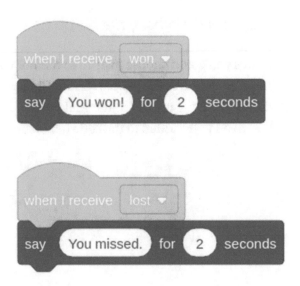

Figure 3-16. *Code to add to the scripts tab of the robot sprite*

The main part of the code on the robot sprite is a forever loop, checking for the status of the two GPIO pins 9 and 10. This is similar to the forever loop in the previous Scratch project, but using two switches to move the sprite across the screen. If a button is pressed, then it increases or decreases the x position of the sprite, which makes the robot move left and right as appropriate. One thing that you may notice is that based upon Figure 3-12 the switches are the wrong way around. It is easier to turn the circuit upside down when it comes to play the game so that you don't need to reach over the Raspberry Pi when playing.

The other two code blocks receive a broadcast message and use the say command to show a message. The broadcast messages are a way of sending messages between different scripts. When you add these, you will need to choose new message to define the broadcast messages. The broadcast message is sent by our final sprite which handles the rest of the logic.

The final sprite that needs to be added is the ball. A suitable ball is shown in Figure 3-17.

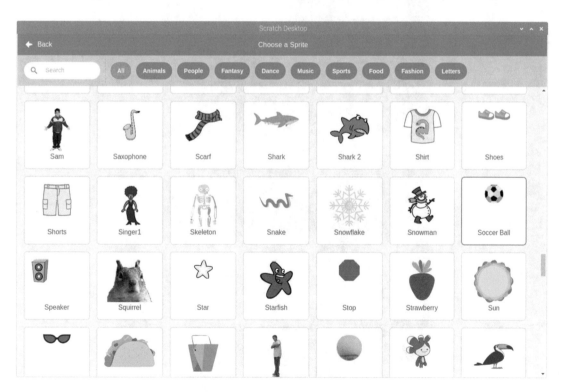

Figure 3-17. *Adding the ball sprite*

The code to add to the ball sprite is listed in Figure 3-18.

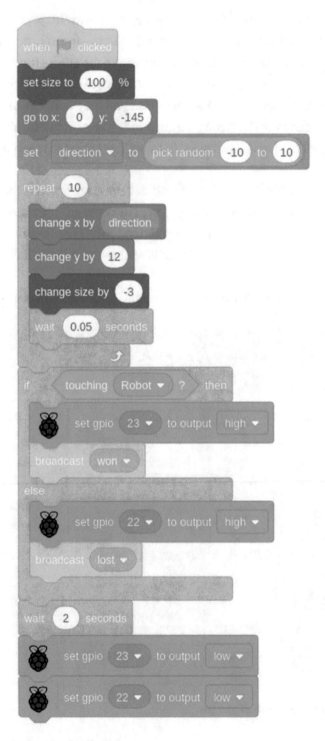

Figure 3-18. *Code for the ball sprite*

This code is a little more complicated than the previous code snippets, so this will be explained in more detail.

The first thing the code does is to set the size of the sprite to 100% and position it to the center front. During gameplay, the ball size will reduce to make it appear to go into the screen toward the goal. Setting the size back to 100% will reset the ball if it is still at a reduced size from a previous game. The set size block comes from the looks blocks, and the go to block is from the motion blocks.

You will now need to create a new variable called direction. The variable will hold a number that determines how far to the left (negative number) or right (positive number) the ball will move. To add the variable, select the Variables code blocks and then *Make a Variable* (see Figure 3-19).

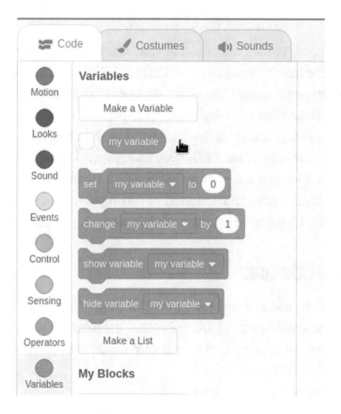

Figure 3-19. *Creating a variable in Scratch*

Next, you can set the variable to a random number by using the pick random from the Operators code blocks. The random number should be between −10 and 10.

The following block is a repeat block which will run the code to move and change the size of the ball ten times. The x direction changes based upon the direction variable. If the random number happened to be a large number (up to the maximum of 10), then the ball will go all the way over to the right; if it's a small number, then it will be near the center of the screen; if it's a large negative number, then it will go to the left. The y position has been changed slightly to make it appear as though the ball is rolling up the field. We also make the ball decrease in size as though it is getting closer to the robot. There is also a wait code block from the control blocks which slows the game down slightly.

Once that has repeated ten times, the repeat loop will finish, and it progresses to the *if* block. This tests to see if the ball sprite is touching the Robot sprite. If you chose a different sprite, then the name of your sprite should appear on the pull-down list instead.

The code then sends two broadcasts. If the ball was touching, then the robot managed to get to the ball; it turns the green LED pin high and sends a broadcast "won" which will trigger the robot to say "You won!" If the robot did not get to the ball, then it will turn the red LED pin high and trigger the "You missed!" message.

The code then waits for 2 seconds before switching the LEDs off again by setting them low. Note that it turns off both LEDs even though one is already off. Obviously, turning something off when it's already off will not do anything. We could have instead had a variable and an additional if statement, so we only sent the message to the LED that was switched on; it's a matter of personal choice which you prefer.

Playing Robot Soccer

Now that it is complete, you can play the game. The game has been designed to be mounted on a board which is turned around so that the breadboard and button are on the bottom. I have used a Raspberry Pi breadboard mount, but you could use a thin piece of wood or thick card.

The finished project is shown in Figure 3-20.

Figure 3-20. *Finished controller for Scratch Robot Soccer*

Click the green flag in the top right of the scratch stage to start. Press the left and right buttons to move the robot from side to side to stop the ball. The green LED will light up if you win and the red LED if you lose. Click the green flag to start again.

More Games

This chapter has looked at using a simple circuit based around the Raspberry Pi with LED outputs and switches as inputs. This has formed the basis of a simple controller for controlling a computer game.

The game can be changed to create your own personal game. If you don't like soccer, then change it into a tennis game or use the controller for a more complicated game.

The next chapter will look at using Python instead of Scratch and controlling some bigger and brighter outputs.

CHAPTER 4

Using Python for Input and Output: GPIO Zero

This chapter is going to look at lights – in particular, how lights can be controlled from the Raspberry Pi. This will control some fun disco lights and projects using multi-color LEDs; these are also known as RGB LEDs or a brand you may have heard of as NeoPixels from Adafruit. In the process, you will get to learn about the most important electronic component, the transistor. You will get to use some different types of transistors to switch lights on that would need more current than the Raspberry Pi can provide.

In Chapter 3, the projects used the graphical programming environment Scratch, but from here on in, we are going to be using Python, which is a text-based programming language. There are some rules about writing programs that need to be followed, but once you get the hang of that, it's not much more difficult than the code blocks from Scratch. Later in the book, we will create a graphical program for one of the projects.

For this chapter, we will be using the Python GPIO Zero module. This is a module which greatly simplifies controlling the GPIO ports using Python. This is included as standard with the Raspbian operating system.

Power Supplies

First, we need to look at the power supply needed for this. The circuits so far have relied on the output from the Raspberry Pi to drive the electronic circuits. This is OK for the simple low-power circuits but is not sufficient for some of the brighter lights that are used in this chapter.

Next, I will explain about a few different options that can be used to provide power for more powerful LED lights and for other circuits that may be connected to the Raspberry Pi, starting with DC circuits at first but will be discussing AC power

© Stewart Watkiss 2020
S. Watkiss, *Learn Electronics with Raspberry Pi*, https://doi.org/10.1007/978-1-4842-6348-8_4

supplies later in the chapter. If you are not already familiar with these terms, then DC is direct current which has a positive and negative terminal, where we consider the current to always flow in one direction from the positive to the negative terminal (using conventional current). AC power is alternating current where the direction of the current changes, so that for half of the cycle, it flows in one direction and the other half the other direction. In most AC supplies, the current changes direction around 50–60 times per second. Almost all the electronic circuits in this book are based around DC, but the mains electricity coming into your home will be AC. The following power supplies assume that we want a DC current to power the circuit.

+5V from the Raspberry Pi GPIO

If you look at the pin layout for the GPIO pins of the Raspberry Pi, you will see that some of the pins are labeled as 5V. As I have already said, the outputs from the GPIO pins are 3.3V, so why is there 5V as well? It is a fixed 5V power supply that can be taken off from the Raspberry Pi. In fact, you could even connect a 5V supply to one of those pins and use that to power the Raspberry Pi, although that would bypass the protection that the USB power supply includes. I won't be using this 5V supply in this chapter as the amount of current that can be taken from this supply is limited, especially on the older versions of the Raspberry Pi, but it could be used to power low-power electronic circuits, which will be covered later in the book.

Another USB Power Supply

A good form of power is through another USB power supply/charger separate to the one used to power the Raspberry Pi. These are readily available and inexpensive. You can buy a USB power breakout connector, which allows you to connect power to a breadboard. The one shown in Figure 4-1 is suitable for connecting to a micro-USB power supply; there are other breakout connectors for different USB connectors.

Figure 4-1. *A micro-USB power breakout connector*

You will need to check that the power supply provides sufficient current for the circuit. A good quality supply provides at least 1.5A at 5V. I recommend buying a good quality power supply from a reputable supplier. The official Raspberry Pi power supply is a good quality power supply. The official power supply is now available as a USB-C version for the Raspberry Pi 4 and a micro-USB version for other variants. These can provide 5V up to a maximum of 2A (3A for the USB-C version). A photo of the micro-USB power supply is shown in Figure 4-2.

Figure 4-2. *Micro-USB power supply*

Other External Power Supplies

The USB power supplies are good if you have a 5V circuit with modest power requirements, but if you have a circuit that runs at a different voltage or needs more power than the USB power supply can provide, then you may need to look at a different power supply.

These are available built in to plugs (sometimes called wall warts) or as a power brick, which connects to the plug through a lead. Most of these have a fixed voltage output, although it is possible to get ones that have a selector for different output voltages. I have a variety of different power supplies for different purposes and will be mainly using a 5V and a 12V power brick for projects in this book. A 5V power brick that will be useful for some of the projects in this book is shown in Figure 4-3.

Figure 4-3. *5V DC power adapter*

Power bricks normally come with barrel jack at the end for plugging into equipment. A common connector is known as 2.1mm barrel jack, which has a 2.1mm pin and a 5.5mm sleeve. The center of the jack (sometimes known as the pin or tip) is often connected to the positive supply and the outside of the barrel (sometimes called the sleeve) to the negative. This is not the case for all supplies though, so check the manufacturer's datasheet before connecting. The image in Figure 4-4 is of a DC power supply showing that it is a positive center supply.

Figure 4-4. *DC power adapter center positive indicator*

You will also need to check that it is a DC supply, as they are also available as AC power supplies. When choosing a power supply, you will need to ensure that the voltage matches the required voltage and that it is capable of supplying at least as much current as is required. There is no harm in connecting a power supply with a higher current rating than is required as the power supply will only provide the current that the circuit requires, but you should not use a power supply with a higher voltage unless you know that is within the tolerance of circuit power supply requirements.

You can get a female connector for mounting into an equipment enclosure or to connect to a trailing lead. These normally require soldering, but you can also buy a female connector to screw terminal, which is particularly useful for connecting to a breadboard when testing a circuit. An example of a DC power adapter to screw terminal is shown in Figure 4-5.

Figure 4-5. *DC power adapter to screw terminal*

As with the USB power supply, I recommend only using a power brick from a reputable supplier which meets the appropriate safety requirements. The output power supply from a power brick is normally low voltage and safe from electrocution (typically, 5–12V). A good quality power supply should also include short circuit overload protection, but you should not rely on this protection. Ensure that any circuits connected to these supplies do not draw more than the specified maximum current. As an extra precaution, you may want to include a fuse in your circuit, which I will explain later with the disco lights.

Mains Power Supply

It is possible to create your own low-voltage power supply by building a power supply circuit which connects directly to the main supply. I do not recommend doing so.

The mains power supply in your home is dangerous. If you come into contact with a live connection, then it can kill through electrocution, or overloading a supply, or wire could cause a fire. Unless you know what you are doing, you should only connect equipment to the mains power supply that already includes the appropriate insulation and protection (such as a wall wart or power brick).

Caution   Do not attempt to connect a homemade circuit direct to the mains electricity supply unless you know what you are doing – it is not worth the risk!

Batteries

Batteries can be used to power external circuits as well as the Raspberry Pi. Using a battery to power the Raspberry Pi itself will be covered in more details in Chapter 9. If it is just an external circuit that is being used and the power requirements are quite low, then batteries can be a good way of powering the circuit. An obvious advantage of batteries is that they are portable and so make it easier to move your project around but do make sure that the batteries have enough charge. If the circuit isn't working or behaves differently to how you expect, then it could be because the batteries need replacing or recharging.

Brighter LEDs with a Transistor

In Chapter 3, there were some simple circuits which had LEDs and a resistor connected direct to the Raspberry Pi GPIO ports. This worked well with a standard LED which uses only a small current, but when swapping for larger or brighter LEDs, the current needed to light the LED is going to be higher. The maximum current that can be drawn from an individual Raspberry Pi GPIO ports is around 16mA. It will be even less if you have lots of devices connected.

The LED used here is a 10mm white LED. This is a bright LED that needs around 20mA to give off a good amount of light. This is more than the GPIO port can supply, so now it's time to look at adding an electronic component that can increase the amount of current flowing (amplify the output). The component we will use is a transistor.

Transistor

The transistor is a semiconductor device, which means that under some conditions it allows current to flow (acts as though it's a conductor) and in other conditions restricts the flow of current. It is this property that is so important in electronics and is the basis of most electronic circuits including computer processors.

The first transistor most people learn about is known as a bipolar transistor. Specifically, this will be an NPN bipolar transistor (the NPN relates to how the transistor is made and as a result how it operates). The transistor has three connections, known as the collector, base, and emitter (represented by the letters C, B, and E on diagram which you can see in Figure 4-6). When a small amount of current flows between the base and emitter, it allows a much larger current to flow between the collector and the emitter. The transistor is an analog component; varying the base current changes the corresponding collector current. By providing an appropriate signal, the transistor can act as a digital switch. This is achieved by working at the two extremes of the transistor. The first condition is where it is switched off, not allowing any current to flow through the collector. The other extreme is where it is switched fully on, allowing a large current to flow through the collector. We refer to this as using it as a "transistor switch," and we refer to the full-on condition of the transistor as the saturation region. A circuit diagram of the transistor switch is shown in Figure 4-6.

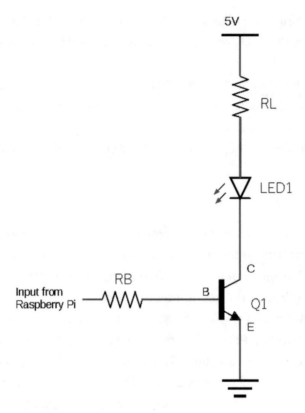

Figure 4-6. *Circuit diagram for a transistor switch*

You will notice that Figure 4-6 looks very different from the earlier circuits. Previously, we had a breadboard layout that showed the physical appearance of the components and wiring. This diagram shows the components as symbols rather than showing their physical appearance and shows the connecting wires as straight lines. This is known as a circuit diagram, or schematic. We will look at circuit diagrams in more details later in this chapter; for now, we will use the diagram to show how the components are connected.

The circuit shows two resistors labeled RB and RL, an LED labeled LED1, and a transistor labeled Q1. The connection from the Raspberry Pi GPIO port goes through a resistor RB and connects to the base of the transistor. When the GPIO port is switched on, the current flows from the GPIO port, through that resistor, and between the base and emitter of the transistor. The current flowing between the base and emitter switches the transistor on. This allows a larger current to flow through resistor RL, the LED, and then from the collector to the emitter of the transistor. The power supply used for the LED is from a 5V supply independent of the Raspberry Pi power supply, although the ground (0V) connections need to be connected together.

When using a transistor as a switch, the main characteristics of the transistor that need to be considered are the maximum current that it can switch which is referred to as the collector current (usually provided as I_C) and the current gain of the transistor (referred to as h_{FE}). We will also need to know about the voltage between the base and emitter to work out appropriate resistors, although that is not necessarily a characteristic that is used to decide on which transistor to use.

There are several different transistors that could be used for this circuit, but this covers two different types 2N2222 (in particular, P2N2222A[1]) and the BC548. These are both common transistors used for hobby projects. Only one of these is for calculating the appropriate resistors, but it will be possible to use either in the circuit depending upon which component you are able to buy. It will also provide a useful comparison of different transistors, which can be useful when designing your own circuits in future.

First, we need to check the suitability of these transistors. The maximum collector current for the 2N2222 is 600mA and the BC548 is 100mA. So, both are easily able to support the 20mA that is needed to control the bright LED.

The gain gives us details of how much more current can flow through the collector compared to the current through the base of the transistor. The actual value depends upon several factors and depends upon conditions at the time of manufacture; in the case of the 2N2222, it is about 75 and for the BC548 about 110. If we take the lowest of these, then it means that either transistor can switch at least 75 times the current through the collector compared to the base current. We shall use the 2N2222A for the rest of these calculations, but due to the similarity between these two transistors, it means that either transistor can be used in this circuit.

Calculating the Resistor Sizes

There are two resistors that you need to calculate the size of. The first is RL which protects both the LED and the transistor from having too much current through them. If too much current flowed through the LED, then not only would it be a waste of energy but could result in permanent damage.

---

[1] I will refer to this as 2N2222, but there are differences between different versions of this transistor. The specifications of P2N2222A have been used.

To work out the resistor size, you need to know the voltage across the resistor. This will be the supply voltage minus the voltage dropped across both the LED and the transistor. The voltage drop across the LED is quoted as 3.3V. The voltage drop across the transistor varies depending upon the manufacture and the current flowing through it. It may be shown as a graph on the specification, but the value needed for this is when the transistor is in the saturation region, which can normally be taken from the general information. The voltage between the collector and the emitter is referred to as $V_{CE(sat)}$ on the transistor specification. The value is approximately 250mV.

To summarize, here is a list of the values:

- Supply voltage 5V.

- Voltage across the LED 3.3V.

- Voltage across transistor 250mV.

- Desired current through the LED is 20mA (0.02A).

The voltage across resistor RL is therefore 5V – 3.55V = 1.45V.

To calculate the resistor value, we use Ohm's law, which is V / I:

1.45V / 0.02A = 72.5 ohms

There isn't a resistor value of 72.5 ohms, so the nearest available resistor should be used. Using the next value up in the E12 series of resistors is 82 ohms (82Ω).

You can now work out the actual current using the selected resistor to check that the current is appropriate. Using Ohm's law, the current is V / R. This works out as 1.45 / 82 = 18mA.

Alternatively, we could have used a 68Ω resistor, which would have worked out at 21mA. Again, this would have been OK as it would still have been within the 30mA maximum that the LED could use. This is a common occurrence within digital circuits where it is possible to use components whose values are near to the desired value.

To calculate the size for RB, you need to work out the current we want to flow into the base of the transistor and then choose an appropriate resistor. The current needed at the base is worked out using the collector current divided by the gain (h_{FE}). We will use the h_{FE} from the 2N2222A as this has the lowest gain.

This gives 20mA / 75 = 0.3mA.

You should then multiply the figure by 10 to ensure that we are well above the required base current. This isn't a fixed rule but is something that is normally done to ensure that the transistor is fully in the saturation region where the power lost within the transistor will be at its minimum.

Multiplying by a factor of 10 gives us 3mA, which is the current needed at the base of the transistor.

The following is now needed to calculate the value for the base resistor:

- Voltage from the GPIO pin 3.3V

- Voltage drop across the transistor (V_{BE}) 0.7V

- Required current calculated above 3mA

The voltage across the resistor will be the GPIO high voltage less the voltage dropped in the transistor. 3.3V – 0.7V = 2.6V.

The transistor needs 3mA entering the base, so using Ohm's law to calculate the resistor gives 2.6V / 0.003A = 866Ω. The nearest value is 1kΩ using the next higher value or 820Ω for the next lowest.

I have used 1kohm which gives around 2.6mA to the base of the transistor. Although our desired value is 3mA, this included a factor of 10, so we will still be well within the saturation region.

So, the values used are

- RL = 82kΩ

- RB = 1kΩ

The resulting circuit layout on a breadboard is shown in Figure 4-7.

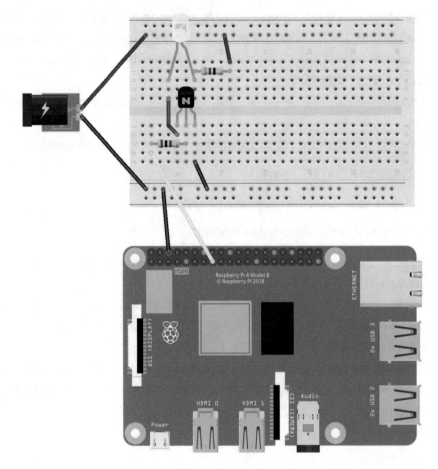

Figure 4-7. *Breadboard layout for the bright LED circuit*

You will see that I have used an external power connector in this circuit. You could use any of the other power supplies discussed earlier. This needs to be connected the correct way around with the red wire going to the top of the breadboard being from the positive supply of the power connector. Also note the orientation of the transistor which is placed with the flat part of the transistor facing forward in Figure 4-7. The pin layout for both the 2N2222 and the BC548 is the same, although that is not the case for all transistors. You will also need to ensure that the LED is the correct way around with the long lead connecting to the resistor (this was explained in Chapter 3 and shown in Figure 3-4).

This circuit uses the same GPIO port that we used in our first Scratch LED circuit, which is GPIO port 22 (physical pin 15). If you would like to try this as a brighter version of the LED circuit, then you can run the code from Chapter 3, Figure 3-7. The next step is to develop some code in Python, which is a more powerful programming language.

Introduction to Python

Python is a popular programming language that is used throughout education and industry. Python is a text-based language which involves writing the code that is run by the Python interpreter. The examples we use here will be run from the command line, but you will see how a simple GUI (graphical user interface) application can be used in Chapter 7.

I won't be providing a full guide to Python in this book, but we will look at some of the basics to get you started. If you haven't done any programming in Python before, then there are many books dedicated to teaching Python programming.

There are two versions of Python installed on the Raspberry Pi. The first is version 2.7 which is the last version of the *old Python* and Python 3 upward which is a newer version, but which is not fully compatible with the earlier version. I encourage using the new version as that is the future of Python and that's what is used in this book.

The first thing to notice about Python is that it is a text-based programming language. If you have been used to a block-based programming language like Scratch, then this can be a big jump at first, but it shouldn't take you long to get used to it. Once you've learned the basic rules, the additional flexibility will increase the scope of what you can achieve.

To get started with Python, I recommend using the Mu editor. You can then go on to develop using other editors in future, but Mu includes some features that allow us to run our code directly. Mu is included in the full version of the Raspberry Pi OS. If it's not already installed, then you can install it from the recommended software application. Mu can be launched from the start menu under programming as shown in Figure 4-8.

Figure 4-8. *Launching Python Mu editor*

When you launch the Mu editor for the first time, it will prompt you to select which mode to run in. For most of the code in this book, you should choose Python 3. You can change the mode using the Mode icon on the editor. The editor will then load an empty document which is untitled. It has a line starting with a "#" character which indicates that this is a comment. The comments are ignored when you run the program but can be very useful for other people to understand how the code works and can be useful as a reminder for yourself when revisiting the code at a future date. I strongly suggest you get into the habit of putting comments in your code.

The editor window can be used to write your code. You can then test the code by clicking the Run button. There's also a useful button titled REPL. This stands for read-eval-print loop; it provides a way to run commands through the Python interpreter without having to save it into a program. This can be useful to test a short snippet of code or to understand what a certain function does, but for most programs, you will want to save your code in the text editor so that you can run it again without having to re-enter it.

Figure 4-9 shows the Mu editor with the classic Hello World program running with the output from the program shown at the bottom of the editor.

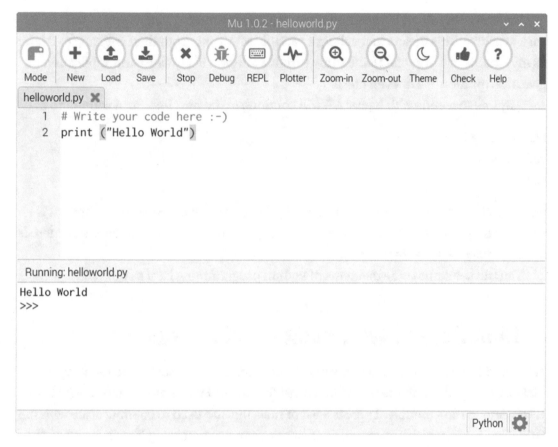

Figure 4-9. *Mu editor running Hello World*

If you haven't saved the program first, then you will be prompted for a filename. Subsequently, the editor will auto-save whenever you press Run.

Commands are written in the text editor using a similar language to what you have already seen in Scratch. There are a few syntax rules that need to be followed.

The first is that indentation and white spaces are important. This is one of the most noticeable things in Python as very few other languages are as strict in enforcing rules about spaces. In most other languages, such as C and Java, any spaces or tabs at the beginning of a line are ignored. In Python, they are used to determine whether you are inside an if statement, loop, or function. Not only that, but in Python 3, it is fussy about whether they are tabs or spaces as well. By default, Mu will replace all tabs with four spaces which is a good way to deal with the spaces. Python will ignore any completely blank lines (that have only white space characters).

Another thing about Python and most other programming languages is that it is case-sensitive. This means that calling a variable MyVariable but then referring to it later as myvariable will not refer to the same variable and will likely cause the application to give an error message or even crash.

Any line that ends with backslash will continue to the next line. So, a command like

```
sum = value1 + \
value2 + \
value3
```

will add all three entries together even though they are split across multiple lines. It is very rare that I use this feature in the code I write, but it is useful in a book where there is a limited page width to fit the code in.

You will see some more elements of Python programming later in this book.

Getting Started with Python GPIO Zero

To control the GPIO ports involves some complex code that is specific to the Raspberry Pi. Fortunately, this has already been written for you and made easy to use thanks to the GPIO Zero Python module. There is a list of rules that are used to communicate with the GPIO Zero code, which are known as an application programming interface or API. We won't go into the full details, but a summary of the API is included in the following.

The module needs to be loaded from within the Python program using from gpiozero import <name>, where <name> should be replaced with the name of the feature you would like to import (e.g., LED) or * to mean import everything in that module. You can then refer to the various interfaces by their name such as LED or Button. There is a list of supported devices given at https://gpiozero.readthedocs.io/en/stable/.

Here is a simple program using GPIO Zero, which will flash an LED on and off. Note that while the name is LED, this will just turn a GPIO pin high and low. The LED function can therefore also be used to control some other circuit that needs a simple high and low output. In our case, the LED turns the input to the transistor high and low rather than the LED directly. There is also a generic OutputDevice or GenericOutputDevice, but the code looks simpler if you use the LED object. This is shown in Listing 4-1.

Listing 4-1. Simple program to flash an LED

```python
from gpiozero import LED
from time import sleep

LED_PIN = 22

led = LED(LED_PIN)

print ("on")
led.on()
sleep(1)
print ("off")
led.off()
sleep(1)
print ("on")
led.on()
sleep(1)
print ("off")
led.off()
sleep(1)
```

In Mu, create a new file and enter in the code. Save it as a file called flashled.py and then click Run from the menu. This is shown in Figure 4-10.

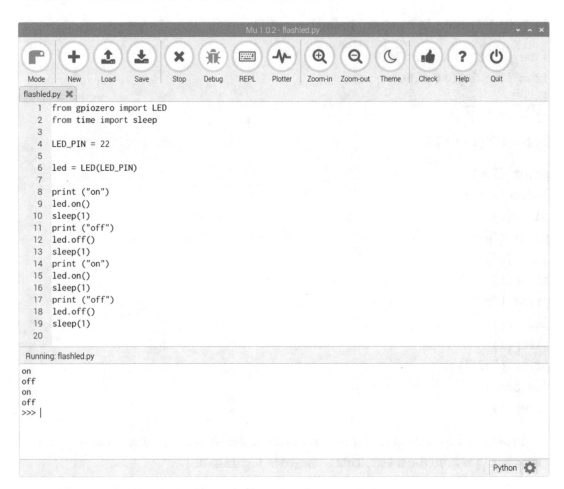

Figure 4-10. *Running the GPIO Zero LED code*

The source code is also available in the book source code available to download. The file is in the Chapter 4 folder called flashled.py.

In Figure 4-10, the code is shown in the editor with the output from running the program at the bottom of the editor. Obviously, the main output is in the form of the LED flashing on and off, but I have also included some print statements so that it shows the expected status on the screen. The LED should flash twice, coming on for one second and then off for one second each time. If the LED does not flash as expected, then check the wiring matches Figure 4-7 and check that the transistor and LED are correct the right way around.

The code starts by importing two modules. The first is gpiozero, and the second is the time module, which is used to add a delay between the instructions. When gpiozero is imported using "from" format whenever you want to refer to LED, then you can just call it LED.

The next entry creates a variable called LED_PIN and stores the value 22. This is to store the GPIO port we are using, so that instead of having to remember it is gpio 22, you can instead type LED_PIN. This is a constant as it will never change during the program; Python doesn't support constants, but using uppercase for a variable name indicates to the programmer that it shouldn't change. It's usually a good idea to list any constants at the beginning of a program, so that if in future you change which port the circuit is connected to, then you only need to change the value in one place. Whenever you see LED_PIN through the code, it will be replaced by the value 22 when the program runs.

It then creates an instance of the LED object using LED from the gpiozero module. I have called it led (in lowercase), which is how it will be referred to when turning its output on and off. This will set the port, entered within the brackets, as an output port and allow us to change the state of the output.

The next block of code changes the status of the LED. First, there is a `print` statement which sends a message to the shell where the program is running. This is not necessary but can be helpful when testing as it tells you whether the LED should be on or off.

The lines `led.on()` and `led.off()` turn the output pin on and off as appropriate and `sleep(1)` tells the computer to sleep (do nothing with this particular program) for one second.

Using a While Loop

The previous code relied on individual entries to turn the LED on and off each time, so if you wanted the LED to keep flashing for a reasonable length of time, then this would need a lot of repeated code. So instead, you can change it to a while loop that will keep running. This next program will use a "while True" loop, which will run the loop forever. This is like the forever loop in Scratch. The updated code is shown in Listing 4-2.

Listing 4-2. Program to flash an LED using a while loop

```
from gpiozero import LED
from time import sleep

LED_PIN = 22

led = LED(LED_PIN)

while True:
    print ("on")
    led.on()
    sleep(1)
    print ("off")
    led.off()
    sleep(1)
```

The text within the while loop is indented. This tells Python that those instructions are within the while loop. If they were not indented, then they would not be within the loop and so would not run as Python will never exit the loop. To stop the program from running, you need to be in the command shell and press Ctrl and c at the same time.

The source code is also in the source code for the book, with filename flashled2.py.

Circuit Diagram and Schematics

For most of the circuits so far, the diagram has shown the breadboard layout. This is a good way to see how to wire up the circuit but can be quite difficult to see how the circuit works. For example, in Figure 4-7, there is a transistor on the breadboard but without knowing which pin of the transistor is the base, collector, and emitter, it's difficult to visualize how the transistor works within the circuit. It is also very difficult to show larger circuits using a breadboard layout as the wires crossing each other could end up looking like a bowl of spaghetti. Instead, the circuit needs to be shown on a diagram which shows how the components fit together without showing the actual physical positioning. The diagram that can provide that is called a circuit diagram or a schematic. In a circuit diagram, the components in the circuit will not look like the physical components, but instead be replaced with circuit symbols.

The circuit diagram shows the components as symbols connected with straight lines. These lines are generally replaced with wires or copper tracks on a PCB.

The best way to understand circuit diagrams is to see some. The first shown in Figure 4-11 shows the first LED circuit from Chapter 1 both as a circuit diagram and as the breadboard layout used previously.

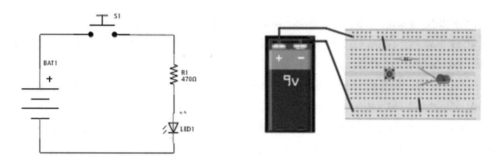

Figure 4-11. *Simple LED circuit as circuit diagram and breadboard layout*

As you can see, these look very different, although if you follow the lines around the circuits, you will see that the same components are used and that they are connected in the same order on both circuits.

Unfortunately, different people may use different symbols when creating their diagrams. There are some different standards that provide recommended symbols. The two most common standards are an international standard IEC 60617, which is commonly used in Europe, and ANSI standard Y32.2, which is commonly used in the United States. One of the most obvious differences between symbols is the resistor. Figure 4-12 shows two different symbols for resistors – the one on the left is the US ANSI symbol and the one on the right is from the international standard IEC 60617.

Figure 4-12. *The resistor circuit symbol using the US and international standards*

A selection of different symbols for the LED is shown in Figure 4-13. Unlike the different resistors which are very different, the differences between these are much more subtle.

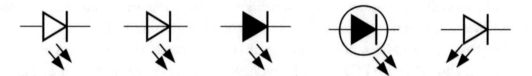

Figure 4-13. *Different symbols for the LED*

The variations shown in the LEDs are common differences that also appear with some other components. This includes shapes that may or may not be filled, or there may be a circle around the symbol.

For this book, most of the symbols are the ones used by the Fritzing application. Creating diagrams with Fritzing will be covered in more detail in Chapter 13. The components in Fritzing are based on the US circuit symbols, so this book primarily shows the US resistor symbol. I have made a few deviations for some components such as using a specific symbol for a push-button switch, which differs from the generic switch symbol used by Fritzing. Some of the most common symbols that are used in this book are shown in Figure 4-14.

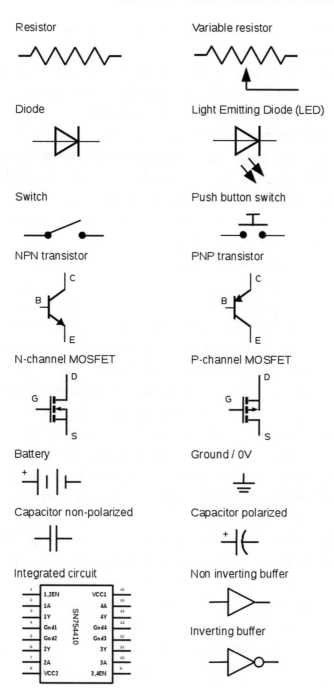

Figure 4-14. *Common circuit symbols*

Each of the symbols is briefly explained as follows with more details of the actual component provided in Appendix B.

The **resistor** has already been used several times in the book to reduce the amount of current. The **variable resistor** adds a third connector which can be moved along the length of the resistor providing a different resistance value.

A **diode** only allows current to flow in one direction. The symbol shows the direction of current going from the positive end of the component (anode) on the left to the negative end (cathode), which is on the right. The **LED** (light-emitting diode) is a specific version of the diode that gives out light when current flows.

The **switch** symbol can be used for any type of switch, although sometimes different symbols are used for different types of switches. The **push-button switch symbol** is sometimes used for switches which are only closed when the button is being pressed and then open when released.

The **NPN transistor** is a semiconductor device already shown in Figure 4-6. There is another variation called the **PNP transistor** which relies on the current flowing out of the base rather than into the base. The base (B), collector (C), and emitter (E) are shown on the symbol but are not normally shown in a circuit diagram.

The **MOSFET** will be explained later in this chapter. The drain (D), gate (G), and source (S) are shown on the symbol, although these are not normally shown on a circuit diagram.

A **battery** symbol is shown. Many diagrams will just show this as a power supply by indicating the voltage rather than specifically showing it as a battery. There is a longer line for the positive terminal on the battery. The + symbol for the positive terminal is sometimes included and sometimes not. The positive terminal will normally be at the top of the diagram.

The **ground** symbol is used to indicate the ground 0V connection of a power supply. There may be multiple ground connections on a diagram. All the ground connections are connected which can reduce the number of lines on the diagram.

A **capacitor** is used to store electrical charge. They are available as non-polarized capacitors, which can be connected either way around, or polarized capacitors, which need to be connected the correct way around. It is important that polarized capacitors are connected the correct way around, as otherwise they can explode.

Finally, two different ways of showing an **integrated circuit** are shown. The first shows the integrated circuit as a rectangle with each of the pins as connection into the symbol; the model of the integrated circuit is shown in the center. Usually the pins are shown in numerical order, although sometimes they are rearranged to fit in with the circuit. The pin numbers are often shown, especially when they are not in numerical order. The pins' function is shown inside the symbol using abbreviations. A common abbreviation shown in the diagram is EN, which indicates an enable pin which turns on the appropriate part of the circuit. For other abbreviations, you may need to look in the specification to find the meaning of the pins.

The other way for an integrated circuit to be shown is by its function. The **non-inverting buffer** and **inverting buffer** are shown by their function. In this case, the power supply connections to the integrated circuit are not shown but will still need to be physically connected. The circle at the end of the buffer indicates that it is inverting, which means that it will give a low output for a high input and a high output for a low input.

Other circuits and boards, including the Raspberry Pi, are shown in a similar way to the integrated circuits.

One more to be aware of is about how lines cross each other. In the past, it was common to have a small bridge symbol indicating where a wire crossed another rather than joining. This was not so easy for early CAD systems and so the convention changed, and now two lines crossing are most commonly shown as two lines crossing at 90 degrees to each other. Where wires are connected, they are shown with a filled circle over the join; this is often referred to as a dot. The different types of crossing and connecting wires are shown in Figure 4-15. I have marked the first as my preferred style and the other as an alternative.

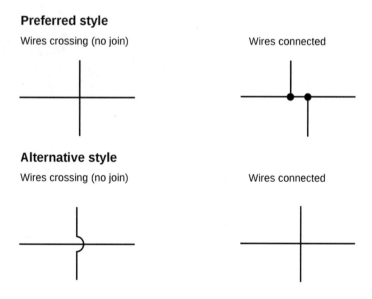

Figure 4-15. *Circuit diagram representation of crossing and connecting wires*

Note that the two different styles using the same straight crossed line mean the opposite. It is the presence of either the dots or the bridge that indicates which style is being used.

The circuit diagram for the Robot Soccer game is shown in Figure 4-16. The Raspberry Pi is shown in the center of the diagram with the components around it. The switches have been placed on the same side as the GPIO ports that they connect to. The LEDs are both on the right even though the GPIO port that one of them is connected to is on the left. This makes it easier to see that the inputs are on the left and the outputs are on the right. The lines crossing at the top do not have a dot at the join indicating that they cross and do not join. The positive power supply is shown at the top and the ground connection at the bottom.

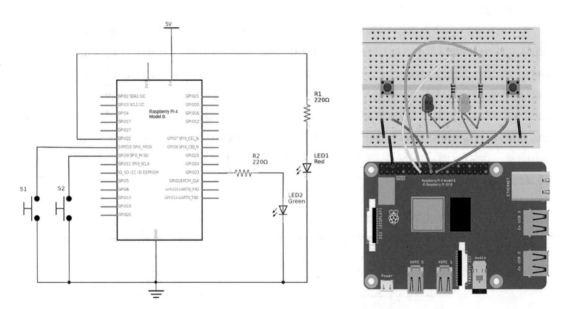

Figure 4-16. *Circuit diagram for the Robot Soccer game*

Brighter LEDs with Darlington Transistors

The transistor switch is useful to switch loads that need more current than the Raspberry Pi GPIO ports can provide, but it still has its limitations. For the next circuit, I have used a USB-powered light, which is much brighter than the single LED. Looking inside the light, I can see that there are actually ten LEDs and their associated resistors as shown in Figure 4-17.

Figure 4-17. *LED light with and without the top removed*

The USB light was bought from a discount retail shop rather than a specialist electronics supplier, and as such, there is no technical information provided. Connecting to a 5V USB power supply, the light draws around 500mA, although when it does, the supply voltage also drops to around 4V.

Looking at the BC548, that is not able to switch 500mA and so could not be used, but what about the 2N2222? The 2N2222 transistor can supply the 500mA current we need, but you also need to take into consideration the amount of base current needed to switch the transistor into saturation.

In the previous LED example, it needed around approximately 3mA to switch the 20mA required for the bright LED, so to switch 200mA, you will need approximately 25 times that value which at 75mA is much more than the 16mA that the GPIO port can provide.

If a transistor can increase the current, then how about adding a second transistor to increase the current a second time? The combination of two transistors to increase the gain is known as a Darlington pair. The collector for each transistor is connected, and the emitter from the first stage is used to provide the input to the second transistor's base. This is shown in Figure 4-18.

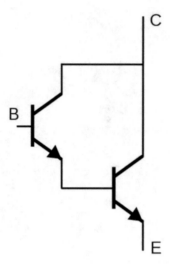

Figure 4-18. *Darlington pair*

We could make this up using two 2N2222 transistors, but a Darlington pair is also available in a single package, usually known as a Darlington transistor. The model used in this circuit is the BD681. The specification of the BD681 gives the following values:

- V_{BE} is 1.5V.

- $V_{CE(sat)}$ is 1.5V.

- h_{FE} (gain) is 750.

- I_C (maximum collector current) is 4A.

These values can be used in the same way as a single transistor. Note that the voltage required at the base and the voltage dropped across the collector and emitter are both noticeably higher than a single transistor, but so is the gain. The maximum collector current is also much higher.

The circuit diagram for the Darlington transistor light is shown in Figure 4-19.

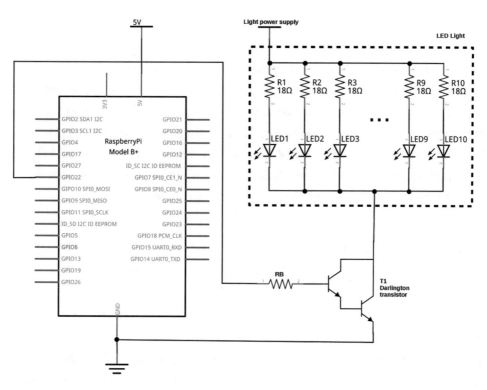

Figure 4-19. *Darlington light circuit*

For this circuit, I have shown the LEDs and resistors that are inside the light, using a dashed box. This is done to show which parts are within the USB light rather than in the circuit I created. Due to space, I have only shown five LEDs, but there are actually ten within the light.

There is a potential problem with this circuit. The resistors in the LED light will have calculated assuming a 5V power supply connected to the light. But assuming we stick with a 5V supply and then with 1.5V drop across the Darlington transistor, we will be running the light at 3.5V for the total light. You can perform some quick calculations to check this.

The resistors in the light are labeled 180, which indicates that these are 18Ω resistors (18 x 10⁰). Assuming a 50mA current through each LED and associated resistor, this works out as 0.9V (18 x 0.05) dropped across the resistor. There is also some resistance in the USB lead of a little over 3Ω. While 3Ω does not sound like it will make much difference, the lead carries the full 500mA total current, which works out at about 1.5V dropped within the lead. After rounding the figures, the forward voltage of the LEDs is around 3A, which I verified using a multimeter.

Based on the 1.5V voltage dropped across the Darlington transistor, will there still be sufficient power to light the LEDs? If not, then what can we do about it?

It turns out that in practice this does still work and there is only a small drop in the brightness. When switched using the Darlington transistor, due to the voltage dropped across the transistor, the current flowing through the LEDs is less than when it is connected direct to the power supply. This means that the voltage dropped within the lead and resistors will be lower and there is still enough current flowing to light the LEDs. It appears that we can use the Darlington transistor. There is a risk that due to the tolerance of the components used, it may not work for every LED light.

Caution   When designing circuits for your own pleasure, you can often "get away" with working outside of the specified range. This is something you should be much more cautious of if designing a circuit for commercial purposes.

So how do we ensure that it will work?

You could remove the resistors all together and replace them with a direct link or a zero ohms resistor, which would help bring it closer to the original current as there would just be the resistance within the lead. This is generally a bad idea unless you are going to permanently attach the lights to our circuit. If we leave the USB connector on the end, then there is a risk that someone could plug it into a computer or other power supply, and without the resistors, it could attempt to draw too much current damaging either the USB light or the source of the power.

The safe solution is to increase the power supply to accommodate for the voltage dropped in the Darlington transistor. If you replace the 5V power supply with a 6.5V power supply (if one was available), then this would allow the full 5V for the USB light. A more common power supply is 7.5V, but then you'd need to add a further resistor to reduce that by the extra 1V, which would again be a waste of energy. As this works in practice using a 5V, I've just worked all the calculations based on 5V. To calculate the appropriate resistors, you can use the same calculations as for standard transistor switch circuit but substituting in the equivalent values for the Darlington transistor. As you already have the resistance for the LEDs, it is just RB that we need to calculate.

To calculate the size for RB, you first need to work out the current you want to flow into the base of the transistor. The current we need at the base is the collector current divided by the gain (h_{FE}).

This gives 500mA / 750 = 0.7mA.

When a transistor is used as a switch (or in this case, the Darlington transistor), it is common to use a factor of 10 to ensure that the current is well above the required base current. This ensures that it is in the saturation region where the power lost within the transistor will be at its minimum.

Multiplying by a factor of 10 gives 7mA, which is the current needed at the base of the transistor. The voltage dropped across the base to emitter is 1.5V. This gives

3.3V – 1.5V = 1.8V dropped across the resistor.

Using Ohm's law to work out the resistance from the voltage and the current gives

$$R = V / I$$

$$0.8 / 0.007 = 257\Omega$$

A suitable resistor value (using the E6 series) is therefore 220Ω.

The BD681 Darlington transistor comes in a different package to the transistors used previously. The pins are also in a different order. Figure 4-20 shows the pin layout for the BD681, which is shown with the label to the front.

Figure 4-20. BD681 Darlington transistor pin-out

This circuit uses the same GPIO port as we have used in the previous examples, so it will work with our existing code. Remember that GPIO port 22 is physically pin 15 and that the ground needs to be connected to an appropriate pin such as pin 6.

Such a bright light is more useful as a time delay light, which with an appropriate delay can be used as a time delay night-light, or a really bright egg timer. The light will turn on when a switch is pressed and then off again after a set delay, for that we need an input which we will add next.

Reading a Switch Input with Python GPIO Zero

I've added a push button to our circuit using the same switch configuration that was used in Chapter 3. This gives the updated circuit diagram as shown in Figure 4-21.

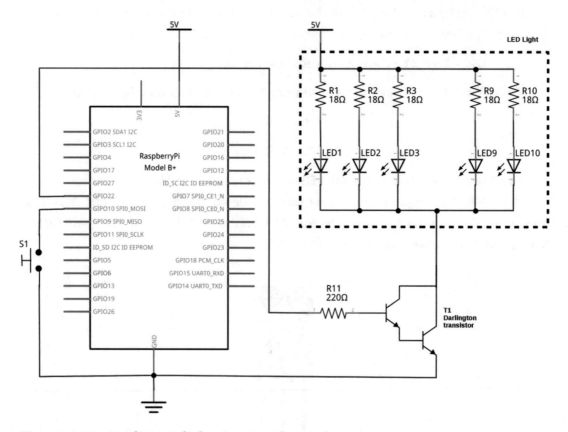

Figure 4-21. *Darlington light circuit with switch*

Detecting and handling the button is made easy in the same way that Python GPIO Zero makes it easy to turn an LED on and off. The first thing is to import Button from the gpiozero library. This can be done in the same way as we previously did with an additional line:

```
from gpiozero import Button
```

To save on typing and make the code a little shorter, these can be combined into a single line as

```
from gpiozero import LED, Button
```

Then create a button as button = Button(GPIO_Number). By default, GPIO Zero assumes that a Button should have the pull-up resistors enabled which is exactly what we want. If you don't want the pull-up resistor, then pull_up=False should be added as a second parameter to the Button function.

There are a few different ways to detect whether the button is pressed or not. The first checks for the is_pressed state of the button. If the button is pressed down, then this gives a True value; if not, then it gives a value of False. This is useful if you have other things that you need to test for.

An alternative, which is the way I've coded the next program, is to use the wait_for_press() method. This pauses the execution of the code until the button has been pressed. It then turns on the LED and uses sleep() to wait for a set delay period. The LED is turned off again, and the while loop starts again. I've also added some comments (prefixed with a #) to explain what the constants are used for.

The complete code is shown in Listing 4-3.

Listing 4-3. Simple program for an LED timer

```python
from gpiozero import LED, Button
from time import sleep

# GPIO port numbers for the LED and Button
LED_PIN = 22
BUTTON_PIN = 10
# Time to keep the light on in seconds
DELAY = 30

led = LED(LED_PIN)
button = Button(BUTTON_PIN)

while True:
    button.wait_for_press()
    led.on()
    sleep(DELAY)
    led.off()
```

This code is also available in the source code to accompany the book. The file is called ledtimer.py.

When run, this will wait until the button is pressed and then turn the LED on for the set period of time (30 seconds) and then turn it back off again. If the button is held down or pressed again, then it will turn the LED back on again for a further period. Press Ctrl-c to cancel if you would like to stop the program from running.

One of the disadvantages of the Darlington transistor is the voltage drop between the collector and emitter is high. This results in quite a bit of wasted energy in the transistor. The next example will cover an alternative that can be a more efficient way of switching bright lights.

Disco Lights with MOSFETs

Now to get even brighter! The LED light that was used in the last project was around 2.5 watts, this one uses 5W LEDs. Not only that, there are four of them with a total of 20 watts of power being controlled from the Raspberry Pi.

Firstly, an explanation about power, which is a measure of the rate of energy being used. Chapter 1 explained about the voltage which indicates the amount of potential energy that is available and current which is the flow of electrical charge around the circuit. If you combine these, then you can work out how much power is being used. The measure of power is a watt and denoted by the letter W. The formula for working out the amount of energy used in a DC circuit is

$$P = V \times I$$

where P is the amount of power in watts, V is the voltage in volts, and I is the current in amps.

The LED light used previously was designed for a 5V supply and used 500mA (0.5A), so this gives 5 x 0.5 = 2.5W. This is the total power used by the light, which includes the power that is wasted in the resistors and the cable.

The lights used here are PAR 16 theater spotlights, which I use as disco lights for a mobile DJ setup. The lights are shown in Figure 4-22, which include different colored gels at the front of the lights so that each light is a different color.

Figure 4-22. *PAR 16 spotlights used as multi-colored disco lights*

The PAR 16 spotlights are available as two different types. Some are designed for mains electrical voltage using GU10 light bulbs, and others are designed for low 12V operation using MR16 light bulbs. The following circuit is intended for the 12V light bulbs only.

Caution   The circuit used here is only suitable for low-voltage (12V) bulbs. Do not attempt to use this circuit to control bulbs that are designed to be connected directly to the mains electricity.

As well as choosing the correct spotlights, you will also need to ensure that you have appropriate bulbs. The bulbs need to be MR16 LED bulbs that can be powered using 12V DC. These spotlights are normally intended to be connected to a 12V AC (alternating current) supply rather than DC (direct current), but most MR16 LED bulbs will work with either AC or DC. You may want to check with the technical information for the LEDs that they are suitable for use with DC before purchasing them. The photo in Figure 4-23 shows one of the bulbs I have tried, which clearly say 12V AC/DC on the packaging, indicating it can work wither either. It will not be possible to power halogen bulbs using this circuit as they need a lot more power, typically between 25W and 50W.

Figure 4-23.   *MR16 LED bulbs which work with 12V AC/DC*

Another thing that is needed is a powerful 12V DC power supply. The one that I use is a power supply designed for an LCD monitor. It is a 12V DC power brick which can provide up to 10A current, which is 120W. This is more than enough power for our requirement. The power brick is shown in Figure 4-24.

Figure 4-24. *Power brick for the disco lights*

One risk with using such a powerful power supply is what happens if there is a problem with the circuit. Most good quality power supplies should have overcurrent or short circuit protection, but it does still mean that you are able to provide 120W of power into a circuit before that kicks in. I therefore recommend adding your own fuse or protection into the circuit. This should be rated above the maximum current that you expect to draw, but less than the total power output of the power supply. I have used a polyfuse in my own setup, which is a self-resetting fuse. Effectively, the fuse will break the circuit when the current is exceeded but when left to cool will then reset and work again.

That has covered the lights, the bulbs, and a power supply, so the next thing is an electronic circuit. The first thing to look at is the amount of power that it needs to control. The LED packaging states 5W, but looking at the technical specification (which varies between manufacturers), the current draw is actually 625mA, which is 7.5W. This looks like the rating on the packaging is based on the amount of energy that is used to create the light, and the rest is lost as heat energy. This is much less energy wasted than an incandescent or halogen bulb, but it's important to make sure that you look at the actual current rather than the marketing information on the front of the box.

You could use the same Darlington transistor circuit used previously. At 625mA, this is only a little more than the previous example which had a current of 500mA; however, as already explained, the Darlington transistor does have a relatively high voltage drop which results in a lot of wasted energy in the transistor. Not only is this wasting energy, but it may mean needing to add a heat sink to the transistor to dissipate the heat. Instead of using the Darlington transistor, a better option is to use a MOSFET which is a type of field-effect transistor (FET).

A field-effect transistor is a type of transistor which is switched using electrical charge instead of the base current that is used in a bipolar transistor. A MOSFET is named based on its construction, which stands for a metal-oxide-semiconductor field-effect transistor. An advantage of the MOSFET over the bipolar transistor is that it uses a much lower current to switch it on, which is more efficient, particularly when used in integrated circuits. In our case, the voltage drop across the MOSFET is the most important factor. It has a much lower voltage drop across the device resulting in less power wasted. For the chosen MOSFET, the drop across the transistor is around 0.2V, which for a 12V supply is negligible and much less than the 1.5V from the Darlington transistor.

The MOSFET switch circuit is shown in Figure 4-25. This uses an IRL520 MOSFET transistor.

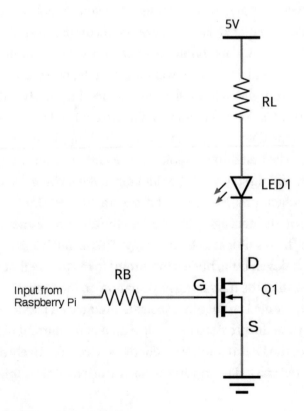

Figure 4-25. *MOSFET switch circuit*

You will see from the circuit diagram in Figure 4-25 that the terminals of the MOSFET are labeled G, D, and S. This refers to the Gate (like the base), Drain (like the collector), and Source (like the emitter). Whereas the bipolar transistor was turned on by a current flowing into the base, the MOSFET instead needs a positive voltage at the gate to turn it on and a low voltage at the gate to turn it off. The resistance between the Gate and Source is very high and so only a tiny current will flow. We do not need to worry about any gain within the MOSFET as setting the output high is enough to turn the MOSFET on.

In theory, the high internal resistance within the MOSFET would mean that you don't need the resistor RB at all; however, the MOSFET behaves differently when it is first switched on, allowing a larger initial current to flow. You should therefore provide a suitable resistor to reduce this in-rush current.

This resistor just needs to be enough to protect the Raspberry Pi GPIO port, so assuming 3.3V output and 16mA maximum current, we have the resistance as 3.3 / 0.016 = 206Ω. So, I have used a 220Ω resistor.

As the LED unit is designed to be connected direct to a 12V supply, you don't need to add a resistor for RL as that is already included within the LED. So, there are only two components needed for each LED, the switch and the resistor, which go between the GPIO port and the gate of the MOSFET.

This completes the circuit for a single LED, so you just need to choose the GPIO ports to use as outputs. You can use any suitable GPIO ports, but I used these:

- GPIO 4 (pin 7)
- GPIO 17 (pin 11)
- GPIO 23 (pin 16)
- GPIO 24 (pin 18)
- Ground (pin 9)

The reason for using these ports is because I had an LED board that already used those ports, so I could use that board to test the code without needing to connect all my disco lights.

The completed circuit is shown in Figure 4-26.

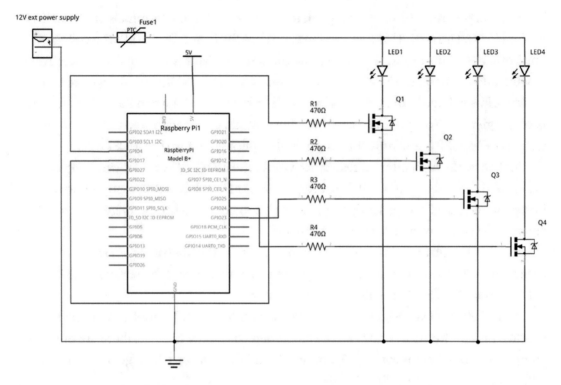

Figure 4-26. *Disco light circuit*

There are a few things to note about this diagram. Firstly, the device shown as Fuse1 is a self-resetting polyfuse used to protect against someone connecting an inappropriate bulb such as a halogen bulb. For simplicity, I have only shown the LEDs as a single LED and ignored their internal resistance. **This is designed for use with 12V LEDs only,** and connecting a standard LED in this configuration would most likely result in damage to the LED and possibly other components.

You may also note that the circuit symbol of the MOSFET is slightly different to the one used previously. This circuit symbol is the one used on some of the MOSFETs in Fritzing, which shows that there is an internal reverse biased diode within the MOSFET; this is still the same component, as that is an internal characteristic of the MOSFET. This is another example of how circuit symbols can vary slightly.

Light Sequence Using a Python List (Array)

Now that the circuit is complete, it's time to create the code to make the lights flash in sequence. This code will create a light sequence that goes from left to right. To achieve this, we shall control the GPIO ports using a Python list. This is like an array used in other programming languages. Python does include support for arrays (which can be more efficient in certain circumstances), but a list is easier to use and more versatile.

A list is a data structure that can hold the value of multiple variables. So instead of having individual variables called light1, light2, light3, and light4, we can have a single list called lights which has four entries, one for each of the lights.

One thing to consider is that computers start counting from 0, and therefore, the index of the first element in the list will be at address 0. Scratch does things a little differently as it is aimed at a younger audience, so if you have used a list in Scratch, then you may have started at 1, but in Python and just about all other programming languages, you start at 0.

A list holding the GPIO port numbers for each of the LEDs is shown as follows:

```
LIGHTGPIO = [4, 17, 23, 24]
```

The square brackets are used to denote this as a list. This creates a list called LIGHTGPIO (in uppercase to signify that these won't change later in the code). Inside this are four values, one for each of the lights. These can be referred to in the code later by the address position. So, to access the GPIO number for the first entry which has value for, use

```
LIGHTGPIO[0]
```

To access the second entry (counting from 0), we use LIGHTGPIO[1]. Python can store much more than just numbers in a list. In fact, we can use a list to store all the instances of the GPIO Zero LEDs. So, this gives us

```
lights = [LED(LIGHTGPIO[0]), LED(LIGHTGPIO[1]), LED(LIGHTGPIO[2]),
LED(LIGHTGPIO[3])]
```

This creates a list of instances of the LED object using the appropriate entry from the LIGHTGPIO list for the port number.

This now allows you to add code that will flash each light in turn as a light chaser. This is shown in Listing 4-4.

Copy the following code and save it in a file called disco-chaser.py. The file is also included in the source code for the book.

Listing 4-4. Programming for light sequence

```
from gpiozero import LED
from time import sleep

# GPIO port numbers for the light
# Physical pin numbers:
# 9 = gnd, 7 = GPIO 4, 11 = GPIO 17, 16 = GPIO 23, 18 = GPIO 24
LIGHTGPIO = [4, 17, 23, 24]
# Time between each step in the sequence in seconds
DELAY = 1

lights = [LED(LIGHTGPIO[0]), LED(LIGHTGPIO[1]), LED(LIGHTGPIO[2]),
LED(LIGHTGPIO[3])]

# Track our position in the sequence
seq_number = 0

while True :
    if (seq_number > 3):
        seq_number = 0
    for x in range (4):
        lights[x].off()
    lights[seq_number].on()
    seq_number = seq_number + 1
    sleep(DELAY)
```

Based on the previous description, you should be able to follow the code up to the while loop. The while loop is another forever loop. The first step within the loop is to check to see if it has reached the end of the sequence. There are four lights, so 3 is the last entry in the list. If it is greater than 3, then it resets the sequence number to 0.

Next, there is a for loop which runs the next line four times. This works by using range (4) which expands to four entries 0, 1, 2, and 3. So it runs the loop the first time with x set to 0, and then with x set to 1, until it reaches the end of the fourth loop (number 3) when it exits from the for loop.

The line lights[x].off() turns the light off for each light. It then turns just the one light on using lights[x].on(). So if this is on sequence number 1, this would turn on the second light.

Finally, it increments the sequence number and waits for the set delay (1 second) before turning on the next light.

If you run the code, you should now see each light turn one in turn.

Switching AC Lights Using a Thyristor and a TRIAC

So far, all the lights we have been switching have been LEDs, which used a DC power supply. The bulbs used in the disco lights would normally be powered using an AC power supply, although I used a DC power supply as it's easier to get a DC power brick suitable for a portable disco light controller.

The mains electricity coming into your home will be AC. One of the biggest advantages of AC is that it's fairly easy to step the voltage up and down using a transformer. An example of a transformer designed for running 12V AC halogen lights is shown in Figure 4-27.

Figure 4-27. *AC mains to 12V AC transformer*

The first device that can be used for switching AC power supplies is the thyristor. This is a device that acts as a switch, which allows a current to pass in one direction only when it receives a positive signal to its gate terminal. Once triggered, it will normally continue to conduct as long as there is a forward current passing through it, even if the gate is subsequently taken low again. This has limited use in a DC circuit as it's difficult to turn off, but in an AC circuit, the current will change direction each cycle and so will turn off whenever the current changes direction. By controlling when a thyristor switches on, they can be used as dimmers in lighting circuits.

The disadvantage of a regular thyristor is that it only works in one direction, so a better solution is the TRIAC which is a bidirectional thyristor. Effectively, this is like two thyristors connected back to back, but which can be turned on with either a positive or negative voltage to the gate and (assuming AC) turned off with 0V at the gate.

The circuit symbol for a thyristor and a TRIAC is shown in Figure 4-28. The symbol on the left is a thyristor which has an anode and cathode appropriate to the direction of current flow, the one on the right as a TRIAC showing the terminals as A1 and A2 as it can be connected either way around.

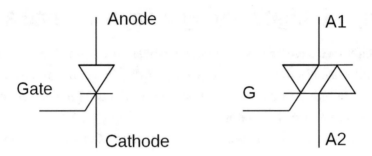

Figure 4-28. *Thyristor and TRIAC circuit symbols*

You could connect the TRIAC direct to the GPIO of the Raspberry Pi (with a suitable resistor); however, this would involve connecting the DC circuit to a common connection on the AC circuit. Instead, it is better to use an optoisolator which provides a way of controlling one circuit from another without any form of electrical connection between the two. This is particularly important if using mains voltage on the AC side (although that is not recommended unless you really know what you are doing). The physical separation is achieved by using an infrared or similar light that is emitted from the sending circuit to a receiver on the other circuit. This is all contained within a single package, so there is no risk of external interference. This is best understood by looking at the circuit symbol in Figure 4-29 which shows an optoisolator with a phototriac output. The optoisolator is controlled by providing a DC voltage to the (infrared) LED on the left, which switches on the phototriac on the right. The receiving device can also be a photo transistor or provide a MOSFET output for DC circuits.

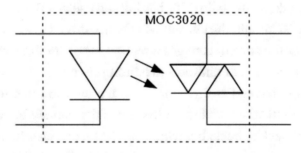

Figure 4-29. *Circuit symbol for a TRIAC optoisolator*

The complete circuit with the TRIAC and optoisolator is shown in Figure 4-30.

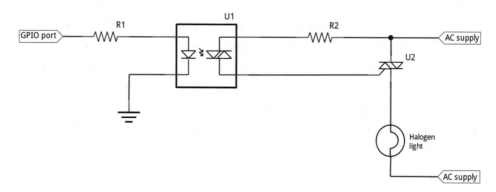

Figure 4-30. *Circuit diagram of an AC TRIAC circuit*

This circuit is intended for use with low-voltage 12V circuits. With appropriate components, this circuit could be used to switch mains electricity, but as with the warning earlier, this can be very dangerous, and you should only consider that if you really know what you are doing. In particular, if using mains voltage, then the circuit needs to be fully enclosed. The TRIAC itself can have live mains electricity connected to its outer body and if appropriate the heat sink.

More GPIO Zero

This chapter has looked at different external power supplies and how you can increase the small signal from the GPIO output to switch a much bigger load. This also provided a first introduction to the Python GPIO Zero module and how lists can be used to track multiple variables. From an electronics perspective, it covered the transistor, a two-stage transistor known as a Darlington transistor, and a MOSFET, which has been used to switch increasingly large loads. It also covered the TRIAC which would be used to control AC rather than DC circuits.

This chapter has also introduced the concept of circuit diagrams, which we will be using going forward instead of the breadboard layouts from the previous projects. You should now be able to decide on an appropriate position on the breadboard and wire up the circuit based on the diagram.

If you've followed along with the practical circuits, then the first LED should have been easy enough to buy, and the second one can use any suitable USB-powered light. The final project does use a more specialist light and power supply, but this can be replaced with the LED from one of the previous two projects (and resistor RL in the case of the first project). Alternatively, you could look at substituting the LEDs for other outputs such as a buzzer. You should avoid motors for the moment as anything using electrical motors needs some extra protection that will be covered in Chapter 6.

The disco lights will be left for a while but revisited in Chapter 7 which looks at creating more advanced software and Chapter 13 when I explain about the disco light printed circuit board that I created.

In the meantime, I suggest you look at creating code to create different light sequences. Can you make two of the lights come on during each cycle instead of just one? Think up some other sequences and write code that makes them light up the appropriate lights.

## CHAPTER 5

PIR, Light, and Infrared Remote Control

The previous chapter covered some inputs and outputs using Python GPIO Zero. This chapter will look at some more sensors and outputs relating to infrared and light. Some of these can be used with the GPIO Zero module and others using other Python libraries. This will include detecting people entering a room, detecting light, and sending and receiving infrared signals.

PIR Sensor

This project will look at using a PIR (passive infrared) sensor to detect someone entering a room and turning on a bright light. This will introduce two new components, one being the PIR sensor and the other a light-dependent resistor used to detect brightness level.

Using a PIR Sensor As a Motion Sensor

To detect someone in the room, you can use a passive infrared sensor, usually known as a PIR motion sensor. The PIR sensor detects infrared radiation, which is given off in the form of body heat. As the sensor detects body heat move across its view, then that can be used to detect the presence of a person or animal. There are a few different sensors that can be used with the Raspberry Pi. The sensor I used is the HC-SR501 sensor, which is commonly available. On the sensor board is a small circuit which detects the body heat and triggers a high signal. A photo of the sensor is shown in Figure 5-1.

© Stewart Watkiss 2020
S. Watkiss, *Learn Electronics with Raspberry Pi*, https://doi.org/10.1007/978-1-4842-6348-8_5

Figure 5-1. *PIR motion sensor*

The motion sensor is powered by 5V but gives a 3.3V output signal, which is just what you need for connecting to the GPIO port. The sensor needs to be connected to the power supply pins and then the output to any GPIO port. In this case, I used GPIO port 4 (physical pin 7).

The circuit to connect a PIR is very simple and consists of only three wires, which can be connected directly to the Raspberry Pi. The 5V power supply is connected to pin 2, the ground to pin 6, and the sensor to physical pin 7. The PIR sensor includes male pins, which can be connected to the Raspberry Pi using female-to-female jumper leads (sometimes known by the brand Dupont connectors). This is shown in Figure 5-2.

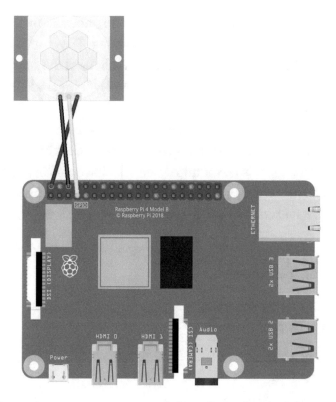

Figure 5-2. *PIR motion sensor connected directly to the Raspberry Pi*

The wire connections to the PIR sensor are based upon the terminals being positioned at the bottom of the sensor. You can check what each pin does by removing the Fresnel lens (white plastic lens) to see the pin labels on the circuit board.

This PIR sensor is supported directly by GPIO Zero, known as a MotionSensor. The GPIO Zero module also includes two functions specifically for this sensor, which can cause the program to wait until the sensor is triggered or alternatively cause the program to wait when the sensor is triggered and then continue running after no motion has been detected for a set period of time.

Again, you can make this easier by using the from import function:

```
from gpiozero import MotionSensor
```

The MotionSensor object can then be created by using MotionSensor and the GPIO port as the parameter:

```
pir = MotionSensor(4)
```

The methods are wait_for_motion and wait_for_no_motion. An alternative is for your own code to check for the value of motion_detected. The method needed for this is wait_for_motion which will cause the program to wait until the sensor is triggered. With the default settings, the wait_for_motion method will wait indefinitely if there is no motion, but you could instead add a timeout, which means that the program will continue to execute after that timeout period has been exceeded. I have not included a timeout, but that could be useful if you wanted to periodically check that the Raspberry Pi is still running even if there is no motion detected. I have also included a delay to prevent the sensor from constantly triggering if there is someone present in the room.

A simple program that can be used to test the motion sensor is provided in Listing 5-1, called pir-test.py.

Listing 5-1. Testing the PIR sensor

```
from gpiozero import MotionSensor
from time import sleep

# PIR sensor on GPIO pin 4
PIR_SENSOR_PIN = 4
# Minimum time between captures
DELAY = 5

pir = MotionSensor(PIR_SENSOR_PIN)

while True:
    pir.wait_for_motion()
    print ("Motion detected")
    sleep(DELAY)
```

Enter this code and run it to test that the PIR sensor is working. You should try running the code and leaving the room and then re-enter the room to ensure it is working correctly. You may need to adjust the sensitivity variable resistor if the sensor is not triggering properly.

Using the PIR Motion Sensor to Trigger a GPIO Port

The next thing to do is to have the motion sensor set a GPIO port to high, which can then be used to turn an LED or light on. This is straightforward using GPIO Zero module as used previously. If you are just using this for testing purposes, then you can connect this to a standard LED and a 220Ω as previously used in Chapter 3, Figure 3-6. You could also use the high-power LED circuits in Chapter 4.

The complete source code for this is in Listing 5-2.

Listing 5-2. PIR triggered LED

```
from gpiozero import MotionSensor, LED
from time import sleep

# PIR sensor on GPIO pin 4
PIR_SENSOR_PIN = 4
# Pin for output signal
LED_PIN = 22
# How long to activate the light for
ON_TIME = 5

# Create pir and LED objects
pir = MotionSensor(PIR_SENSOR_PIN)
led = LED(LED_PIN)

while True:
    if (pir.motion_detected == True):
        led.on()
        time.sleep(ON_TIME)
    else:
        led.off()
```

This code is an extension of the pir-test.py code, but using the `pir.motion_detected` variable instead of the `wait_for_motion` method. This means that the code can be used to turn off the light after the set time has passed if there is no further motion.

The code is saved as pir-light.py.

Sensing Light

The next circuit is designed to detect the level of light which could be used to automatically trigger an action when it gets dark. It can be useful when used in conjunction with the PIR sensor to turn a light on when it is dark *and* there is someone in the room.

This is going to need a bit of an explanation on how to detect an analog signal using a digital input pin. First, you will need to know what the different components are to understand how it will work.

Light-Dependent Resistor

A type of light sensor commonly used is known as a light-dependent resistor (LDR). The LDR is a resistor whose resistance changes depending upon the light levels received on its sensor. You can find the expected values on the datasheet, or more simply, you can connect a multimeter set on the resistance scale and measure the actual values. When I tested the LDR I have, it gave a value of around 500Ω in bright light, 7kΩ in indoor daylight, and over 20kΩ when in a dark room. A photo of an LDR on a mini breadboard is shown in Figure 5-3.

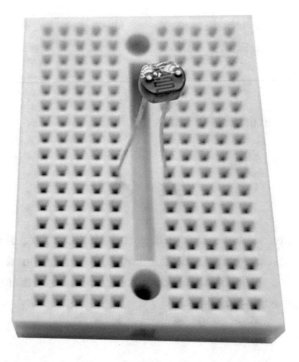

Figure 5-3. *Light-dependent resistor (LDR)*

Capacitor

This circuit is also going to need a capacitor. A capacitor is a device that can hold an electronic charge. It is like having a very small rechargeable battery, storing the energy as electrical charge. A capacitor can react very quickly to a change in voltage, going from the charging state to supplying power to the circuit almost instantly.

While capacitors can switch between charging and discharging very quickly, the speed at which they charge and discharge is based upon the power they are supplied with and what they are powering. This is a useful property, allowing capacitors to be used for timing circuits or as filters to block certain frequency signals often used in an analog circuit.

A capacitor is created using two conductive plates separated by a non-conductive material. The plates can be flat but may also be rolled around internally within the capacitor to create a cylinder. The insulator between the plates is known as the dielectric. There are different types of capacitors depending upon the material used for the dielectric. Some capacitors are polarized and need to be connected a certain way around. These are known as electrolytic capacitors, with markings on the case indicating the negative terminal. The negative terminal is usually represented by a 0 or – symbol, perhaps with an arrow pointing to that pin. Other capacitors (such as ceramic and polyester film capacitors) are not polarized and can be connected either way around.

The symbol for a capacitor is two lines representing the two plates of the capacitor. If the capacitor is polarized, then the negative end may be curved and/or the positive end may have a + sign next to the terminal. This is shown in Chapter 4 as Figure 4-14. There are also photos of some common types of capacitor in Appendix C.

The capacitance is measured in farads (F). However, one farad is a huge value, so it is more common to see these measured using International System of Units (SI) notation. While you are likely familiar with some SI values such as kilo (used to indicate thousands such as a kg or a kΩ), those for very small numbers are less well known. Typically, capacitors are measured in microfarads (µF) where 1 microfarad equals 0.000001F, nanofarads (nF) where 1 nanofarad equals 0.001µF, or picofarads (pF) where 1 picofarad equals 0.001nF. This is shown in the table in Figure 5-4.

Picofarads (pF)	Nanofarads (nF)	Microfarads (µF)
1	0.001	0.000001
10	0.01	0.00001
100	0.1	0.0001
1,000	1	0.001
10,000	10	0.01
100,000	100	0.1
1,000,000	1,000	1
10,000,000	10,000	10
100,000,000	100,000	100

Figure 5-4. *Capacitor value translation table*

Capacitors will be referred to using the most convenient value to reduce the number of zeros in the value. Note that although using scientific notation millifarads is a valid measurement, it is rarely used. For example, a common capacitor value is 2200µF, which using scientific notation would be 2.2mF but is normally written in microfarads. The capacitor used in this circuit is 0.1µF or sometimes known as 100n.

Measuring an Analog Value with a Digital Input

The sensors covered previously have all provided a digital signal that the Raspberry Pi can use directly. The LDR is different, in that it is an analog component. The Raspberry Pi GPIO port does not have an analog input, so there needs to be a way of determining the value of an analog sensor using a digital input pin. The standard solution is to use an analog-to-digital converter which converts an analog signal into a digital value. While an analog-to-digital converter (ADC) can be used for this, it is more complicated than is needed for this simple sensor. An analog-to-digital converter will be discussed in Chapter 6. Instead of an ADC, there is a simpler way which can be used to measure resistive values such as the LDR. This example uses a technique which works by detecting the resistance of an object using an RC (resistor-capacitor) timing technique.

To determine the resistance using only digital inputs, you need a resistor (in our case, the LDR) and a capacitor. The circuit first discharges the capacitor, so it is empty and then charges the capacitor through the resistor measuring how long it takes to charge. As the capacitor charges, the input to the GPIO pin will change from a low value to a high value. The higher the resistor, the longer it takes to charge the capacitor. When it is dark, the resistance is higher and so the time to charge the capacitor to switch from a low to a high input is longer. This is not the most accurate way of measuring the resistance (see analog-to-digital converter later in this chapter), but it is adequate for a simple light sensor.

The circuit diagram showing these parts is shown in Figure 5-5.

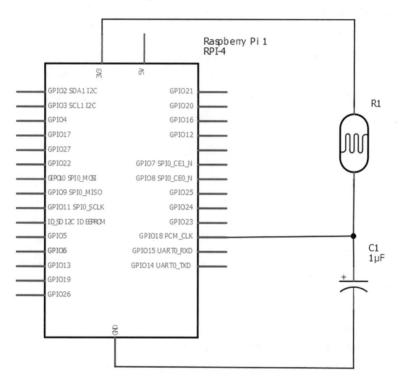

Figure 5-5. *Light sensor circuit with LDR*

The value of capacitor is 1μF. The higher-value capacitors (1μF and higher) are normally electrolytic and so need to be connected the right way round. Alternatively, there are polyester film capacitors which go up to 1μF; either option works in this circuit.

To work out the light level, the Raspberry Pi must switch the GPIO pin between an input and an output. This is done in the following steps:

- Set the pin as an output and set it as low.

- The capacitor (C1) will discharge through the input.

- Set the pin as an input. It will be low initially.

The capacitor will charge through the LDR (R1).

The lower the resistance of the LDR, the quicker the capacitor will charge.

- Detect when the input changes from low to high based on the voltage on the capacitor.

Fortunately, the GPIO Zero library already includes the code to handle this and makes it simple to use. If you only want to detect a light level for on and off, then there are methods wait_for_dark and wait_for_light which will stop the main program until the light level is at the appropriate level. If you want a more accurate measurement, then I have created the test code in Listing 5-3. I've called this ldr-test.py which will show the light level as a value between 1 (very dark) and 10 (very bright).

Listing 5-3. LDR test program to show light level

```python
from gpiozero import LightSensor
from time import sleep

LDR_PIN = 18

sensor = LightSensor(LDR_PIN)

while True:
    light_value = int(sensor.value*10)+1
    print ("Value is "+str(light_value))
    sleep(1)
```

This can be combined with the light circuits from Chapter 4 to switch a light on when a certain brightness threshold is reached. It can also be used in conjunction with the PIR sensor to turn a light on when it is dark *and* the PIR sensor is triggered.

The code in Listing 5-4 gives an example of how the LDR and PIR sensors can be used to trigger a bright LED. This is saved as ldr-pir-light.py.

Listing 5-4. Program using both LDR and PIR sensors

```python
from gpiozero import LightSensor, LED, MotionSensor
from time import sleep
```

```
LDR_PIN = 18
LED_PIN = 22
PIR_SENSOR_PIN = 4
DELAY = 5

light_threshold = 5

sensor = LightSensor(LDR_PIN)
led = LED(LED_PIN)
pir = MotionSensor(PIR_SENSOR_PIN)

while True:
    light_value = int(sensor.value*10)+1
    if light_value < light_threshold and pir.motion_detected:
        led.on()
    else:
        led.off()
    print ("Light value is "+str(light_value) + " Motion " +
    str(pir.motion_detected) )
    sleep(DELAY)
```

This combines three circuits and associated code to create a motion sensor that only activates when it is dark. The darkness threshold can be adjusted using the variable light_threshold. Note that the light sensor needs to be positioned so that it doesn't detect the light coming from the bright light; otherwise, it will flash on and off as it detects the light levels change.

Infrared Transmitter and Receiver

The next pair of sensors is an infrared transmitter and receiver pair. This is using the same technology as used in most television and entertainment remote controls. The circuit in this chapter will be able to receive signals from a remote control which are passed to the Raspberry Pi; these can be used to find the codes needed to control the device. Those codes can then be used to control a light from the Raspberry Pi.

In the earlier version of this book, this was controlled using LIRC (Linux Infrared Remote Control), which is used by Linux media centers. Using LIRC is complicated to set up and has some issues with current version of the Raspberry Pi OS, so instead this book uses pigpio which provides an easier way to record and reply infrared messages. The electronics has remained the same and the same circuit which can be used with LIRC if you prefer.

Infrared Receiver

The infrared receiver that I have used is the TSOP2438. This is an infrared receiver with built-in pre-amplifier. The sensor has three pins connected to the supply, ground, and a sensor output, which can be connected to a GPIO port on the Raspberry Pi. The sensor can take a supply voltage of between 2.5V and 5.5V. Its output signal is dependent upon the supply voltage; as the sensor needs to work with the 3.3V GPIO ports, it needs to be connected to the Raspberry Pi 3.3V supply. It is recommended that a 100Ω resistor is used between the 3.3V on the Raspberry Pi and the supply for the sensor and that a 0.1 μF capacitor is used across the supply voltage, although it should still work without these. Adding a capacitor across the supply will reduce the amount of electrical noise on the power supply. Ideally, it should be as close as possible to the receiver.

There are similar receivers that could be used instead. The same series of sensors has several different versions which are similar, and different suppliers may only stock a subset of the range. The TSOP2238 is an older version that can be used as a direct replacement, and the TSOP2436 and TSOP2440 are designed for a slightly different infrared frequency but should still work for most remote controls. There are however some other sensors such as TSOP4438 and TSOP4838 which while very similar in operation do have a different pin-out, so you will need to adjust the circuit accordingly if using one of those. The pin-out for the TSOP22xxxx and TSOP24xxxx infrared modules is shown in Figure 5-6.

The output from the sensor is connected to GPIO 18 (physical pin number 12).

Out V$_s$ Gnd

Figure 5-6. *Pin-out for the TSOP2438 and similar infrared receivers*

Infrared Transmitter

The infrared transmitter is essentially the same as an LED that we have used before but designed to give out infrared rather than visible light. Infrared is part of the light spectrum; it travels in waves like visible light but has a slightly longer wavelength so is outside of the range of human vision. The emitter used here is the TSAL6400 Infrared Emitting Diode, which has a wavelength of 940nm. This one is designed for high-power requirements and can give a range of over 5 meters (15 feet) when it has a clear light of sight from the top of the emitter. The circuit to drive the infrared emitting diode is the same as we used for the brighter LED in Chapter 4, Figure 4-6.

This will be powered from the 5V supply connection on the GPIO connector. The infrared emitter diode can operate with up to 100mA of current, but for this circuit, I have based the current flow on around 60mA, which provides a good compromise between output strength and power requirement. I have used a 68Ω resistor for RL and 220Ω for RB. When tested, this worked as long as the emitter was within about 2 meters (6 feet) of the device being controlled.

As with an LED, the infrared emitter diode needs to be connected to the correct pins. The longer lead is the anode which needs to be connected to the positive end (toward the resistor).

The signal for the transmitter circuit is connected to GPIO 17 (physical pin number 11).

Infrared Transmitter and Receiver Circuit

The complete circuit of the infrared transmitter and receiver is shown in Figure 5-7. As mentioned previously, you can see that the sensor is powered from the 3.3V power connection from the Raspberry Pi, but the emitter from the 5V power supply. They both use the same ground connection, although these are shown separately as a way of reducing the number of crossing lines.

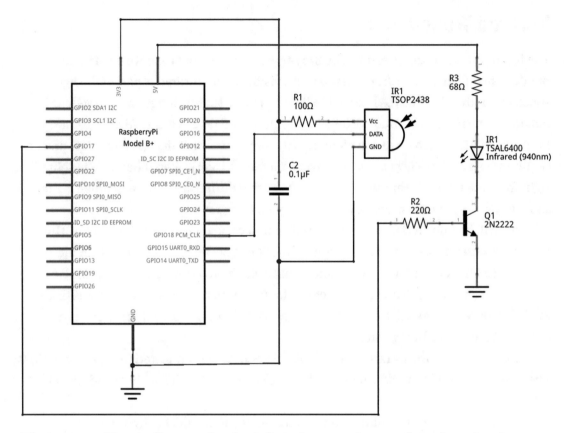

Figure 5-7. *Circuit diagram for the infrared transmitter and receiver circuit*

In this case, I have shown a single circuit for the transmitter and receiver. This can be very useful as a way of recording the remote signals and replaying them for the transmitter. For this project, you could create them separately as the receiver is only needed for detecting the signals from the remote control and then the transmitter for sending the signals to the device.

Configuring the Infrared Transmitter and Receiver Using pigpio

A simple way to capture and reply infrared signal is to use pigpio. This monitors for the infrared signal, creates a code for the signal it receives, and then allows this code to be retransmitted through the infrared transmitter part of the circuit. This isn't the same as other libraries (such as LIRC) which analyze the protocols, but pigpio makes it easier to set up.

You will need a suitable infrared remote-control device and corresponding remote control for this section. In my case, I used a Crystalite color-changing LED bulb which is designed to replace a standard spotlight bulb. A photo showing the light and the remote control is included in Figure 5-8.

Figure 5-8. *Infrared color-changing LED bulb and remote control*

To use pigpio involves a server daemon running on the Raspberry Pi, and then a client program can use the pigpio libraries to talk to the daemon to send and receive signals to the GPIO ports. The pigpio library can be used for other services as well, but it is only used for the infrared functionality in this book. The pigpio daemon and libraries are already included in the standard Raspberry Pi OS or are available from http://abyz.me.uk/rpi/pigpio/.

To start the daemon, run

```
sudo pigpiod
```

Alternatively, it can be set to run automatically at boot with the following command:

```
sudo systemctl enable pigpiod.service
```

The easiest way to capture the codes is using the irrp.py program, which can be downloaded from http://abyz.me.uk/rpi/pigpio/code/irrp_py.zip.

To capture the codes for a light remote control, you can use the following command:

```
./irrp.py -r -g18 -f light_codes on off brighter dimmer red green blue
white flash strobe fade smooth
```

The arguments from "on" onward are the labels for the buttons. I have only mapped the most common 12 buttons from the remote. You can map the rest of the buttons or use different names for the buttons as appropriate. For each button, it will prompt you to press the button at least twice, which is to ensure that the code is the same both times it is detected. Once complete, you will have a file called light_codes, which contains a hash code for each of the buttons.

You can replay a command using the following format:

```
./irrp.py -p -g17 -f light_codes on blue
```

Note that this will send the "on" infrared code, followed by the "blue" infrared code. You will need to ensure that the infrared emitter has a clear line of sight to the light and that it is close enough for the signal (long jumper leads can be used to extend the reach of the emitter if required).

Sending an Infrared Code Using Python

You can use the irrp command to send an infrared signal from the command line.

There isn't an official library for sending these codes from Python, but the instructions that are needed are included in the irrp command. I have extracted those details and put them into my own Class file which can be used instead. The Class file is included in the book source code in the file irsender.py. An example program that uses that file is included in Listing 5-5 which I have saved as sendcodes.py.

Listing 5-5. Example code using IRSender to send infrared codes

```
from irsender import IRSender

# Test program to send some simple commands using an infrared emitter
# Requires irsender.py in the same directory
# and a codes file in the constructor call to IRSender.

codes = ["on", "flash"]

irs = IRSender("/home/pi/infrared/light_codes")

if not irs.connected:
    print ("Unable to setup infrared connection - is pigpiod running?")
    exit (0)
```

```
for this_code in codes:
    print ("Sending code "+this_code)
    irs.send_code (this_code)

irs.close()
```

You will need to save the light_codes into the appropriate file referenced in the source code.

The codes list contains a list of the commands to send. In this case, it sends the "on" command, followed by the "flash" command which sets the light flashing.

It then tests that the connection to pigpiod is connected; if not, then remember to start the server as mentioned previously. There is then a for loop which goes over each of the commands, prints to the console what is sent, and then sends the signal to the emitter. It then closes the connection to the gpiod program to clear the connection.

The irsender.py file is basic with only simple error handling but is sufficient to demonstrate how you can send infrared signals.

Other Infrared Receivers and Transmitters

Infrared remote control has been popular for many years. While there are competing technologies including the use of radio remote control and Bluetooth, it is likely that infrared will continue to be useful for some time to come. As such, this can be a useful circuit to have as a permanent install. Instructions on making a more permanent circuit are explained in Chapter 12. An alternative is to buy a pre-made add-on board for the Raspberry Pi; one such device is the Energenie Pi-Mote IR control board (ENER314-IR) which uses a similar circuit to the one we made earlier.

More Light and Infrared Ideas

This chapter has looked at different inputs including a PIR motion sensor, a way to communicate with infrared devices using an infrared transmitter. This has also shown how different sensors can be used together to add more functionality. This can be used to unlock opportunities for other inventions. For the PIR motion sensor, you could look at having the Raspberry Pi place a recorded message through its audio output port whenever someone walks near, or it could take a photo when the sensor is triggered.

For the infrared remote control, look at what other devices you have that could be controlled using infrared. The obvious devices are TVs and media centers, but infrared is also used in other devices including toys.

The next chapter will look at some other devices that use specific protocols or that may need some form of conversion before they can be used.

CHAPTER 6

Interfacing with Other Devices

This chapter will look at how to interface with other devices using serial protocols such as I²C and SPI. It will also cover ways to connect devices that need different voltages and converting between analog and digital signals. This will include projects that display an output on an LCD display and how to change the brightness of an LED output using a digital output.

You will then learn how you can control DC motors using a H-bridge motor driver circuit and how the PWM signal can be used to control the speed of the motor.

Changing Voltage with a Level Shifter

Sometimes it is necessary to convert signals between different voltages to be able to communicate with a device designed for a different supply. Recall that the Raspberry Pi GPIO ports are designed for 3.3V inputs and outputs. There are however many devices that work at different voltages. Another popular voltage is 5V, which was the standard voltage for many electronic circuits in the past and continues to be a popular voltage for components. In some cases, you can just select sensors and other components that are also designed for 3.3V, but some other components are designed to operate at 5V. This includes certain protocols such as I²C, which is commonly used for sensors and output devices. Here, we will consider conversion between 3.3V of the Raspberry Pi GPIO and 5V for other devices, but the same techniques can be used for different voltages.

There are three different approaches that can be used to change the voltage depending upon whether you need to reduce a higher voltage so it can be used as an input to the Raspberry Pi, if you need to increase the output of the Raspberry Pi so that it is sufficient for connecting to a 5V output device, or if you need to be able to communicate in both directions.

115

© Stewart Watkiss 2020
S. Watkiss, *Learn Electronics with Raspberry Pi*, https://doi.org/10.1007/978-1-4842-6348-8_6

Voltage Divider Circuit to Reduce Input Voltage

The first example is the most basic, but it is very useful. This is used if you have a sensor that has a 5V output that you then want to use as an input to the Raspberry Pi. What is needed is a way of dropping the signal voltage from 5V to 3.3V. This can be used by using a voltage divider (also known as a potential divider) circuit, which consists of two resistors as shown in Figure 6-1.

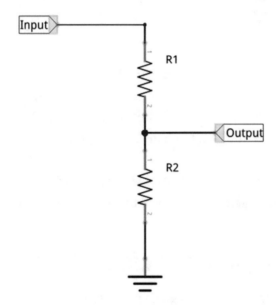

Figure 6-1. *Voltage divider circuit*

The input signal is connected across both the resistors in series. When a voltage is present from the sensor, a current flows through the two resistors. The voltage will then be shared across the two resistors based upon the ratio of their resistance. The output voltage is taken at the top of R2, which is the just voltage dropped across R2. This is the same as saying the output voltage is equal to the input voltage less the voltage across R1. As the current is the same through both resistors, the voltage of the outputs is a ratio based on the value of both resistors. If the values of the resistor are equal, then the output will be half the input as 2.5V will be dropped across R1 and 2.5V dropped across R2. As we need an output of 3.3V from a 5V input, that means we need 3.3V across R2 and 1.7V across R1. This is approximately two-thirds. So, the value of R2 should approximately twice as large as R1.

Now we know the ratio, but what actual value of resistors do you need? To determine that you need to consider both the input signal to the potential divider and what will be connected to the output of the voltage divider.

For the sensor, we need to ensure that the current we are going to put through the potential divider is not going to exceed the amount that the sensor is able to provide. For the output, you need to ensure that there is enough current to turn on the device connected and to ensure that the load does not significantly alter the output voltage.

In the preceding example, it is assumed that all the current flows through the two resistors, but the moment we add a device to the output, some current will flow through that instead of going through R2 which can change the output. If we are using a MOSFET (and in the case of the Raspberry Pi GPIO, it will be similar), then that is triggered by voltage and very little current will flow into the load so the effect on the signal will be minimal. If the output is connected directly to a load or even to a transistor that was switching a large load, then the current flowing through the load could change the signal. If the current through the resistors is very small, then it may also see false signals due to electrical noise. Choosing a low value for the resistors will help avoid the signal degradation, although in that case you need to ensure that the current through the load and the resistors does not exceed the current that the sensor can provide. Having a low value for the resistors will also use more energy. If the maximum current from the sensor is too low, then you could add a MOSFET switch or a buffer to increase the signal prior to the voltage divider.

In the case that you are using the signal as the input to the GPIO of the Raspberry Pi which has a high input impedance, we don't need to worry about the amount of current, and so you can just choose resistors that add up to a fairly high value such as 10kΩ. This results in a current of around 0.5mA (or 500nA). If you have a device which needs a higher current, then choose lower-value resistors.

Using the standard sizes, these are suitable resistors

R1 = 3.9kΩ

R2 = 6.8kΩ

which give around 3.2V, which is an ideal input for the GPIO port.

Unidirectional Level Shift Buffer

Sometimes you may want to increase the 3.3V output from the Raspberry Pi so that it can drive another circuit that expects a 5V input. This is something that will be required later for driving RGB LED strips.

The first thing to check is whether this is needed. While a circuit may be designed to operate at a certain voltage, there is usually a range of inputs that it will accept. Also, there is a range of voltages that the Raspberry Pi can provide as an output. In the case of the Raspberry Pi output, then for a low (off) signal, it will be less than or equal 0.8V, and if it's a high (on) signal, then it will try and set the output to 3.3V, but depending upon the current of that and other GPIO ports, it may be as low as 1.3V. Obviously, 1.3V is very low, but in reality unless there is a high load across the GPIO ports, it is likely to be close to the 3.3V output.

In Chapter 7, there is a project using WS2812 RGB LEDs. These are addressable LEDs which need a signal voltage within 0.5V of its supply voltage. Assuming they are connected to a 5V supply for maximum brightness, then even a full 3.3V output from the GPIO is well below the 4.5V required. It is possible that the circuit will still work, but the problem is that when you are operating outside of the designed range for the components, the components can become unpredictable. Having a circuit that is unreliable can be worse than having one that doesn't work at all; with a system that doesn't work, you can track down the problem, but with one that works sometimes, it can be very difficult to troubleshoot.

There are integrated circuits designed specifically as buffers that are often used in these circumstances. In particular, the 74HCT125 will accept input voltages as low as 1.6V–2V and provide a high output close to the supply voltage of 5V. Note that this is specifically for the TTL version of the chip denoted by the letter T, the 74HC125 is designed for a higher voltage input, and while it's likely to work with the Raspberry Pi GPIO, it may not under certain conditions.

As this book is about learning electronics, I think it is useful to look at a simpler version that we can create using a MOSFET. The circuit shown in Figure 6-2 shows a simple MOSFET voltage buffer.

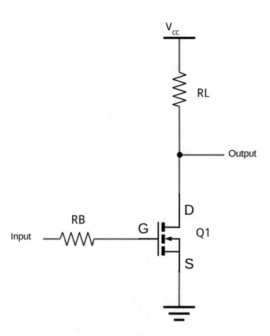

Figure 6-2. *MOSFET-based voltage shift buffer*

The circuit shown is an inverting buffer that will produce a high output when the input from the GPIO port is low and vice versa. It's normally possible to change the software to send and inverted signal to counteract this, or a second stage could be added to invert the signal back to its original form, although if you need non-inverting, it may be better to use a non-inverting buffer such as the 74HCT125 instead.

The circuit is essentially the same as the MOSFET switch used in Chapter 4 but replacing the load (LED) with a pull-up resistor. When the input to the MOSFET is low, the MOSFET is open circuit (switched off) and the pull-up resistor RL will result in the output being high. When the input to the MOSFET goes high, the MOSFET will switch on pulling the output down toward 0V (there will still be the voltage across the MOSFET V_{DS} which depends upon the MOSFET and current but for this circuit will typically be less than 0.5V).

The value of RB has already been discussed in the earlier MOSFET switch circuit in Chapter 4 (220Ω), but again the value of the RL depends upon the load and what current that needs to operate. Typically, the resistors will be between 1kΩ and 100kΩ, although I have used a lower value when creating an LED RGB circuit to allow for loses in a long cable between the circuit and the LED strip.

Bidirectional Level Shifter

Sometimes you need to have a voltage shift in both directions. This is required when two devices can communicate in both directions across the same wire. An example of this is using the I²C protocol, where the signal goes in both directions from a *low voltage* (3.3V) Raspberry Pi to a *higher voltage* I²C device. This is slightly different from the circuit used for some other communication protocols as I²C uses pull-up resistors, which we can take advantage of. The circuit we will look at is based on one used by Adafruit and SparkFun in their bidirectional level shifters. These are based around surface mount MOSFETs on a small breakout board. A photo of the board is shown in Figure 6-3.

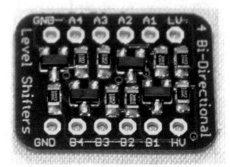

Figure 6-3. *Adafruit bidirectional level shifter*

This board has four channels, each of which has the same circuit. The circuits use the BSS138 MOSFET. As these use surface mount devices (SMDs) which are fiddly to use and the level shifters are inexpensive, I would recommend just buying a level shifter board. It is useful to understand how the level shift works. The circuit diagram of one of the channels is shown in Figure 6-4.

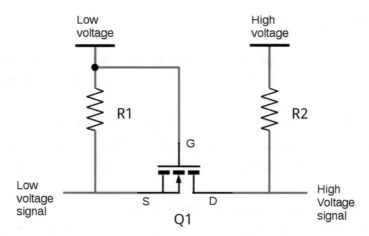

Figure 6-4. *Circuit diagram for one channel of the bidirectional level shifter*

The circuit uses an MOSFET in an unusual configuration with the Drain and Source used to connect between the left and right sides of the circuit. If both sides are high, then the MOSFET is switched off and the two pull-up resistors ensure that both sides are high using their own supply voltages. If the low-voltage signal (left) drops low, then the MOSFET will be in the forward configuration, and thanks to the input to the gate, the MOSFET turns on bringing pulling the high-voltage end down as well. If the high-voltage end (right) goes low, then due to an internal characteristic of the MOSFET it allows a small current to flow in the reverse direction. As this happens, the voltage of the source connection dips causing the MOSFET to turn on and hence pull the source down further based on the low signal connected through the MOSFET.

An alternative is to use an appropriate IC such as the 74LVC245. The 74LVC245 is not compatible with I²C due to the requirement for pull-up resistors but can be used with SPI and other sensors that do not required a pull-up resistor.

I²C LCD Display – True or False Game

The next project will make use of I²C. It will use this to connect an LCD display to the Raspberry Pi and create a True or False game.

LCD Character Display

The display for this project is an LCD character display. These are commonly used where a simple text display is required. These are perhaps most familiar as the display used for drink and snack vending machines.

For this, I have used a display, which has 4 rows and 20 characters per row (known as a 4x20 display). Another popular configuration has 2 rows and 16 characters per row, one of these can be used instead but will need some changes to the code and will only allow short questions.

The LCD character displays can normally operate between 3.3V and 5V, so if an appropriate voltage is chosen, then it can be connected direct to the GPIO port of the Raspberry Pi. The disadvantage of this is that it needs to use at least six ports from the Raspberry Pi GPIO ports (plus two power supply connections) and quite a bit of wiring. An alternative is to use I²C which reduces the number of pins to only two I²C connections (plus two power supply connections), and even then, the I²C connections can still be shared with other devices.

I²C

Also known as I2C is a serial communication protocol that is used to communicate with peripherals. It works in a primary secondary relationship. Typically, the Raspberry Pi will act as a primary and communicate with peripherals such as sensors or displays.

I²C is popular for connecting to low-speed devices. It is bidirectional so can be used for both input and output devices. You may also see references to SMBus (System Management Bus), particularly in reference to the device drivers. SMBus is a subset of I²C and uses a stricter set of criteria, including a restriction that it only works with lower-speed devices. I will refer to I²C, but if you see SMBus in the software references, then it essentially talks about the same thing.

The main feature of I²C is that it uses only two ports for communication, which can be shared across multiple devices. There are two connections a data connection referred to as SDA and a clock signal known as SCL. There is a downside to this in that as multiple devices share the same connections, they also have to share the bandwidth; this is not an issue for devices with low-bandwidth requirements, but some I²C devices such as cameras do have high-bandwidth requirements. This is the reason for the Raspberry Pi changing which I²C bus is connected to the GPIO connector. In earlier versions of the Raspberry Pi, channel 0 was connected to GPIO pins 3 and 5, but that is also used by the Raspberry Pi camera, which uses a lot of the available bandwidth. The more recent Raspberry Pi versions, including the Raspberry Pi 2 and later, use I²C channel 1 for the GPIO connector. Pins 3 and 5 are connected to SDA1 and SCL1, respectively.

I²C uses a primary secondary relationship, which is shown in Figure 6-5. The Raspberry Pi will normally be the primary acting as a controller, which will communicate with other devices on the bus telling the secondary devices when they should send and receive data.

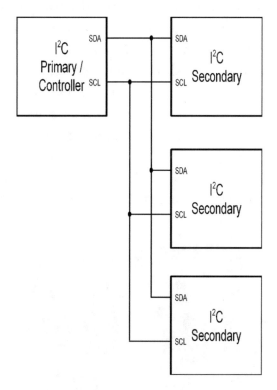

Figure 6-5. *Example of I²C secondary devices connected to a single I²C controller*

The I²C connections are open drain. This means that an external pull-up resistor is required. There are pull-up resistors on the Raspberry Pi which are enabled through the software, but the level shifters and some I²C devices also include pull-up resistors on board.

Although I²C can support a range of different voltages, it is recommended that the bidirectional level shifter is used when connecting a Raspberry Pi to devices that are designed for 5V.

Each I²C device has an address which needs to be unique to all the devices connected to that bus. To allow multiple devices of the same type to be connected, there are often three pins or dip switches on secondary devices which can be connected in different configurations to provide a unique address.

I²C Backpack for the LCD Character Display

For an LCD character display, they are available with I²C backpack connected to the ports on the display. This allows you to send messages to the I²C backpack which it then converts to the signals that the display needs. This is a small circuit board module that can be mounted on to the back of the display, hence the name backpack. The use of I²C greatly reduces the number of connections needed, leaving more ports free on the GPIO for other components and circuitry. These backpacks are available as stand-alone modules or pre-soldered onto a suitable LCD display. The backpack that I used is based around a PCF8574 8-bit I/O expander for I²C bus, which is common. This uses the I²C connection to control up to eight ports, which is perfect for the LCD display. A photo of the LCD display (front) and the I²C backpack (rear) is shown in Figure 6-6.

Figure 6-6. *Photo of the LCD character display and backpack mounted on the rear*

The links that can be used to change the I²C address are visible in Figure 6-6 as small solder pads below the variable resistor. For some devices, the address is selected using jumpers or DIP switches, but in this case, they would need to have a link soldered across them to enable that pin. There is no need to add any links as long as there are no further devices on this bus that use the same address.

True or False Game Circuit

In addition to the LCD display connected through a level shifter, I have also used three of the other GPIO ports for push-button switches. These buttons are for "Start," "True," and "False" which we will use to turn this into a simple quiz game. The ports for the switches are GPIO 23 for the start button, GPIO 22 for the true button, and GPIO 4 for the false button.

The complete circuit diagram is shown in Figure 6-7.

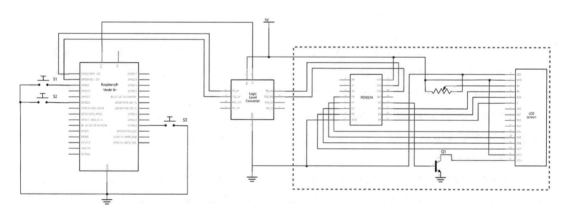

Figure 6-7. *True or false game circuit diagram*

This circuit diagram shows the internal wiring of the backpack (shown in the hashed box) which makes the diagram quite large. As a result, it is difficult to see. I have therefore split the circuit diagram in half. Figure 6-8 shows the backpack and LCD display, and Figure 6-9 shows the Raspberry Pi, level shifter, and the switches.

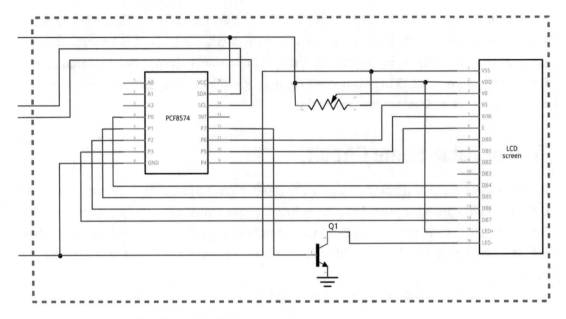

Figure 6-8. *LCD display with I²C backpack*

As you can see in Figure 6-8, the PCF8574 IC is used to send the appropriate signal to the LCD display. The variable resistor is used to adjust the contrast which may need to be adjusted to ensure that the characters are clearly visible.

There are only four connections shown on the left, two of which are for the I²C channel as well as a connection to the ground and 5V power supply (which can be taken from the Raspberry Pi).

The ports A0–A3 are the address selection connections. By changing which of these is set to high and low will change the address. We will leave these to their defaults and will perform a search of I²C devices to identify which you need to use.

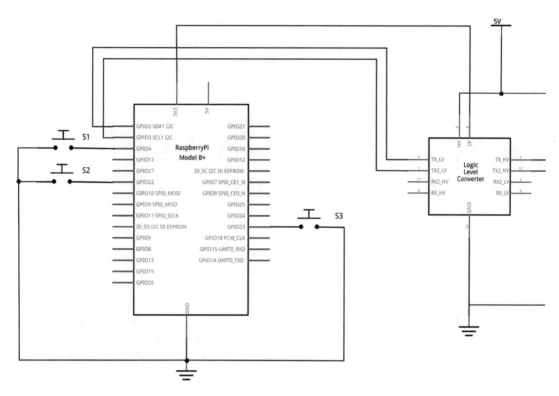

Figure 6-9. *Raspberry Pi with I²C level shifter and button switches*

In the diagram in Figure 6-9, you can see the level shifter and the position of the buttons. The switches all connect to ground so you can use the pull-up resistors within the Raspberry Pi to provide the high level when not pressed. The part name for the level shifter in Fritzing is logic level converter, which means the same but refers to changing between different types of logic. The level shifter is available as a small PCB with headers that need to be soldered on. With these soldered on (as shown in Figure 6-3), the level shifter can be inserted into a breadboard.

Setting Up the I²C Connection and Adding the Code

With the circuit in place, there needs to be some configuration changes as well as the program to turn this into a game. First, you need to enable I²C on the Raspberry Pi and then identify the port that we need to communicate with. It then needs the code to put it all together.

The first thing that is required is to enable I²C on the Raspberry Pi. This is needed as the drivers are disabled by default. This can be enabled using the Raspberry Pi configuration tool, choosing the Interfaces tab, and then enabling the I²C entry. This is shown in Figure 6-10.

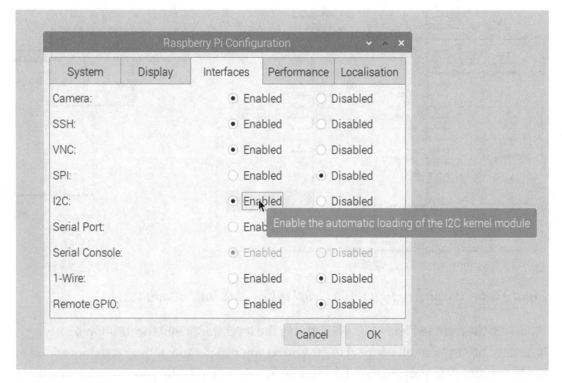

Figure 6-10. *Enabling I²C through the Raspberry Pi configuration tool*

A reboot is then required to cause the appropriate kernel module to be loaded.

Identify which address is being used by running sudo i2cdetect 1. The option 1 is to scan for bus 1. This comes with a scary warning message, but that is fine if you are setting up the connection rather than using it for real data.

```
sudo i2cdetect 1
WARNING! This program can confuse your I2C bus, cause data loss and worse!
I will probe file /dev/i2c-1.
I will probe address range 0x03-0x77.
```

```
Continue? [Y/n] y
       0  1  2  3  4  5  6  7  8  9  a  b  c  d  e  f
00:            -- -- -- -- -- -- -- -- -- -- -- -- --
10: -- -- -- -- -- -- -- -- -- -- -- -- -- -- -- --
20: -- -- -- -- -- -- -- -- -- -- -- -- -- -- -- --
30: -- -- -- -- -- -- -- -- -- -- -- -- -- -- -- 3f
40: -- -- -- -- -- -- -- -- -- -- -- -- -- -- -- --
50: -- -- -- -- -- -- -- -- -- -- -- -- -- -- -- --
60: -- -- -- -- -- -- -- -- -- -- -- -- -- -- -- --
70: -- -- -- -- -- -- -- --
```

As you can see from the preceding output, a single I²C device has been found at address 3f.

There are several different libraries around for communicating with I²C devices and for the LCD character display. I did not find one that met my requirements and was simple enough to use, so I've created a slightly modified version based on an existing project (more details are included in the source file). The code for the Python module is called I2CDisplay.py. This is included in the source code for the book or can be downloaded directly from GitHub using the following address: https://raw.githubusercontent.com/penguintutor/learnelectronics/master/quiz/I2CDisplay.py.

The module has already been updated with the address of the backpack using I2C_ADDR = 0x3f and the number of characters available on my LCD display using LCD_WIDTH = 20. These can be changed to reflect the LCD display if required. This file needs to be downloaded to the same directory as the code you will create.

It's useful to first try some test code that just sends a message to the LCD display. This is called i2c-test.py shown in Listing 6-1.

Listing 6-1. Test code for I²C display

```
from I2CDisplay import *
import time

# Initialise display
lcd_init()

# Send some test
lcd_string("Learn Electronics",LCD_LINE_1)
lcd_string("with Raspberry Pi",LCD_LINE_2)
```

```
lcd_string("by",LCD_LINE_3)
lcd_string("Stewart Watkiss",LCD_LINE_4)

time.sleep(20)
lcd_clear()
```

The first line imports the I2CDisplay module. This is a local Python file so needs to be stored in the same directory as the file. As all the functions are imported, it's just a case of calling each function directly.

The first function that is called is lcd_init which sets up the LCD display and clears the screen.

The program will then send for lines to the screen, using LCD_LINE_1 to LCD_LINE_4 to determine which line to send the output to. It then sleeps for 20 seconds before issuing the lcd_clear command to clear the screen.

Enter this into the Mu editor and run, and you should see the message displayed on the LCD display. If it doesn't run, then ensure that you have the I2CDisplay.py file in the same directory as the test file. You may also need to adjust the brightness by adjusting the trimmer on the back of the display.

You can now add the rest of the code to turn this into a full program. This is shown in Listing 6-2, called truefalse.py. You will also need some questions in a file quiz.txt; an example file is included in Listing 6-3.

Listing 6-2. True or false game program

```
from I2CDisplay import *
from gpiozero import Button
import time

# File holding questions
# 4 lines are the question and then the
# 5th is T for true or F for false
# Repeat for Q 2 etc.
quiz_filename = "quiz.txt"

start_button = Button(23)
true_button = Button(22)
false_button = Button(4)
```

```python
# Initialise display
lcd_init()

# Send some test
lcd_string("Raspberry Pi",LCD_LINE_1)
lcd_string("True or False quiz",LCD_LINE_2)
lcd_string("",LCD_LINE_3)
lcd_string("Press start",LCD_LINE_4)

start_button.wait_for_press()

# Note that there is no error handling of file not exist
# Consider using a try except block
# Open the file
file = open(quiz_filename)

questions = 0
score = 0
answer = ''

while True:
    # print 4 lines as the questions
    thisline = file.readline().rstrip("\n")
    # First line is mandatory - otherwise perhaps end of file
    if thisline == "" : break
    lcd_string(thisline,LCD_LINE_1)
    thisline = file.readline().rstrip("\n")
    lcd_string(thisline,LCD_LINE_2)
    thisline = file.readline().rstrip("\n")
    lcd_string(thisline,LCD_LINE_3)
    thisline = file.readline().rstrip("\n")
    lcd_string(thisline,LCD_LINE_4)
    # Next line should be T for answer = True or F for False
    thisline = file.readline().rstrip("\n")
    if thisline == "" : break
    if (thisline == "T"):
        answer = "T"
```

```python
    elif (thisline == "F"):
        answer = "F"
    # should not reach this unless the question file is invalid
    else : break

    # wait on True or False pressed
    while (true_button.is_pressed == False and \
        false_button.is_pressed == False):
        time.sleep (0.2)
    # Increment number of questions attempted
    questions = questions+1
    # Once one of the buttons is pressed
    # also check the other is not pressed to avoid cheating
    if (answer == "T" and true_button.is_pressed \
        and false_button.is_pressed == False):
        score = score+1
        lcd_string("Correct!",LCD_LINE_4)
    elif (answer == "F" and true_button.is_pressed == False \
        and false_button.is_pressed):
        score = score+1
        lcd_string("Correct!",LCD_LINE_4)
    else:
        lcd_string("Wrong.",LCD_LINE_4)
    # Wait 2 seconds before next questions
    time.sleep(2)
    # Finished this question return to the start
# Outside of the quiz loop - give the score
lcd_string("End",LCD_LINE_1)
lcd_string("Score",LCD_LINE_2)
lcd_string(str(score)+" out of "+str(questions),LCD_LINE_3)
lcd_string("",LCD_LINE_4)
time.sleep (5)
file.close()
```

Although this is quite long, most of this is a combination of the LCD display test code used previously and GPIO Zero used to test for when the buttons are pressed. Something that is new is that it is reading in the contents of a file to get the questions and expected answers. Details of the file format are explained later.

The first thing it does is to import the appropriate modules, add a variable with the filename for the quiz file, and then set up the buttons using GPIO Zero. A message is then sent to the LCD display, and we use `wait_for_press` to wait until the start button has been pressed.

The file is opened using `file = open(quiz_filename)`. There is no path included in the file; if you are running in the Mu editor, then it will look in the mu_code directory; running from the command line will use the current directory. You can change this to the full path if preferred. After setting the number of questions and score to zero, the code enters a loop to read in each question in turn and get a response from the user. This has been created as a `while True` loop, which is normally used when you don't expect to exit out of the loop. The code will instead be exiting at the appropriate point in the loop using a `break` command when the end of the file is reached or if it encounters a problem.

Once in the loop, the code uses readline to read the next line from the file. The readline command will keep the terminating character which is the newline character "\n". You don't want to send that to the LCD display, so rstrip is used to remove any new lines. The resulting value is the contents of the line without the newline character, which is stored in the variable thisline. The code then checks if this is an empty string, which will indicate that there are no more questions left. If the line is empty, then the break command is called which will cause the execution of the while loop to stop and the control to move to the next line outside of the loop.

The first four lines are the question, so these are sent direct to the lcd_string function. The next line contains a letter T if the answer should be True and the letter F if the answer should be false. This is stored in the variable answer so it can be compared with which button is pressed.

The next thing is a while loop waiting for either the true or false buttons to be pressed, which is as follows:

```
while (true_button.is_pressed == False and \
        false_button.is_pressed == False):
        time.sleep (0.2)
```

You cannot use the `wait_for_press` method used previously, as this time it needs to check for the state of two different buttons. Instead, the check is contained within a nested loop which will continue to run until one of the buttons is pressed. During the while loop, there is a sleep function to sleep for 0.2 of a second. This is just added to reduce the load on the Raspberry Pi. Without the sleep, the program will be constantly checking the status. The time is set to be small enough that the user wouldn't notice a delay of 0.2 seconds between them pressing the button and the computer responding, but that length of time would allow another program on the system to do some other work. It then checks the status of both buttons to see if the button pressed matches the one that is expected. Even if the correct button is pressed, it still needs to check if the other button is not pressed otherwise the user could cheat by pressing both buttons at the same time.

If appropriate, the score is then updated, and it tells the player whether the answer was correct or not. The program will display the status for 2 seconds before moving on to the next question.

When the end of the file is reached, the program will exit from the while loop, display the score, and wait for 5 seconds. It then calls close on the file to ensure that the file is closed correctly. Note that I didn't include an `lcd_clear` function. This means that the display will continue to display the score after it has finished running.

Finally, you need a file containing the questions. The file I used is shown in Listing 6-3, called quiz.txt.

Listing 6-3. Questions data file for True or False game

```
The Raspberry Pi 2
has 1GB of RAM.

True or False?
T
PiZero is the
name of a Python
electronics library.
True or False?
F
The Raspberry Pi
Zero has an
Ethernet port.
True or False?
```

```
F
The RPi 4 model B
has 4 x USB ports.

True or False?
T
The HDMI Connectors
on the RPi 4
are micro-HDMI.
True or False?
T
```

You will see that for each question, there are four lines for the questions, followed by the letter T or F as appropriate. Note that a blank line is included when that line does not need to display any text.

One problem with the program is that it doesn't include any error checking. So, for instance, if the quiz.txt file does not exist, then you will get a rather ugly error message like this one:

```
Traceback (most recent call last):
  File "quiz.py", line 29, in <module>
    file = open(quiz_filename)
FileNotFoundError: [Errno 2] No such file or directory: 'quiz.txt'
```

This is not a very user-friendly error message, so it is a good idea to add additional code to check for conditions that have a high probability, such as a missing file.

SPI Analog-to-Digital Input

Most of the sensors so far have provided a digital signal. This works well with the digital inputs on the Raspberry Pi, but not all sensors are digital. An analog-to-digital converter (A-to-D converter also known as ADC) can be used to convert an analog signal into a digital signal, which can be used by the Raspberry Pi. This example uses an integrated circuit that uses the SPI (Serial Peripheral Interface Bus) to read the value from the analog-to-digital converter.

Creating an Analog Value Using a Potentiometer

The analog sensor used is going to be based around a potentiometer, also known as a variable resistor. This allows you to change the value of the sensor manually to get an understanding of how this works. This can be replaced by other analog sensors in future. Variable resistors are often used on speakers to set the volume.

A potentiometer (or pot for short) is usually a rotary device and is commonly used for setting inputs to a device, such as a volume control on a music player. They are also available as slide potentiometers or can be found as small devices, which are often not accessible to the end user, or one designed to be rarely changed; these are known as trimmers, or trimmer pots. You may have needed to adjust the trimmer on the LCD character display used previously to adjust the brightness.

To use a potentiometer to provide an analog signal, it can be connected across the supply voltage and use the variable pin as our analog value. This is like the potential divider circuit but is used across the supply, and the resistance can be varied. This can then be used as an input to the analog-to-digital converter. This is shown in Figure 6-11.

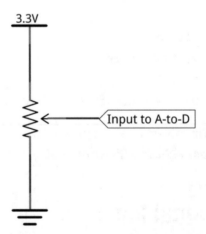

Figure 6-11. *Using a potentiometer to get an analog input*

There are a few different symbols for a potentiometer which show the arrow in a different way; this particular symbol is good at showing how this works. With the potentiometer set to the center position, there is effectively half the resistance above and below it resulting in half of the supply voltage as the output. If the potentiometer is moved toward the top of the resistor, then the voltage increases, and if it's moved down, then the voltage decreases.

Analog-to-Digital Conversion

The analog-to-digital converter integrated circuit that is used here is the MCP3008. This IC uses an SPI interface to pass the digital value to the Raspberry Pi. Other integrated circuits are available, including ones that we could connect to multiple pins of the Raspberry Pi GPIO connector (although that would use a lot of pins) or I²C. The main reason for choosing SPI is to show an alternative serial communication protocol, which is commonly used for various input and output devices.

The way that this IC works is known as successive approximation analog-to-digital conversion. This works by storing the input value and then comparing it against a varying signal until a match is reached. This is then the digital value provided as the output.

SPI (Serial Peripheral Interface Bus)

SPI is the main alternative to I²C as a serial communication protocol for communicating with electronic devices. It is a bidirectional communication protocol which allows full duplex communication where information can be passed in both directions at the same time. This compares with I²C which while still allowing bidirectional communication only allows communication to go in one direction at a time. The downside is that SPI needs more connections with four wires required for the first device (in addition to ground) and then one more connection for each subsequent device added. This is shown in Figure 6-12.

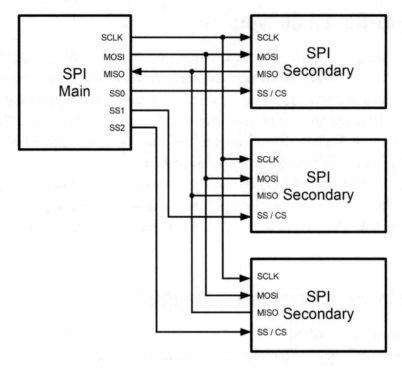

Figure 6-12. *SPI bus connections*

The common connections are

- SCLK – SPI Clock Signal

- MOSI – Main Out, Secondary In

- MISO – Main In, Secondary Out

Then for each secondary device, a secondary select (SS) connection is required. On the end device, this could be referred to as chip select (CS) or chip enable (CE). The secondary select is normally a low to enable and a high to disable, so it is often shown with a bar (line) above it.

Another advantage of the use of SPI is that it can be connected to a 3.3V power supply, so no voltage level shifting is required. This assumes that the sensor connected to the ADC is also able to operate at 3.3V as the reference voltage should not exceed the supply voltage.

Potentiometer SPI Circuit

The circuit is shown in Figure 6-13. This uses a 10kΩ variable resistor, which can be either mounted to the breadboard (if using a trimmer) or connected by wires to a panel mount style potentiometer. Other values of variable resistor can be used such as 1kΩ, which will increase the current through the potentiometer. The image of the MCP3008 shows each of the pins of the IC, although not all are connected. Pin number 1 is the pin nearest the small dimple or notch on the side of the chip with the numbers going anti-clockwise from there.

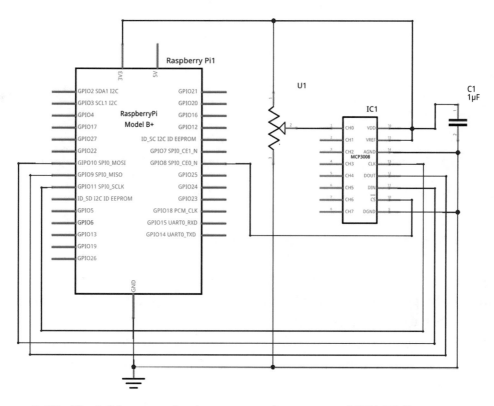

Figure 6-13. *Variable control using a potentiometer and SPI ADC*

This shows the potentiometer connected to channel 0 of the MCP3008 and then the appropriate data lines connection to the Raspberry Pi. Note also that there is a capacitor connected across the supply voltage. This is known as a bypass capacitor (to remove noise on the power line) and should be connected as close to the IC as possible. This is sometimes omitted but according to the datasheet should always be included for reliability.

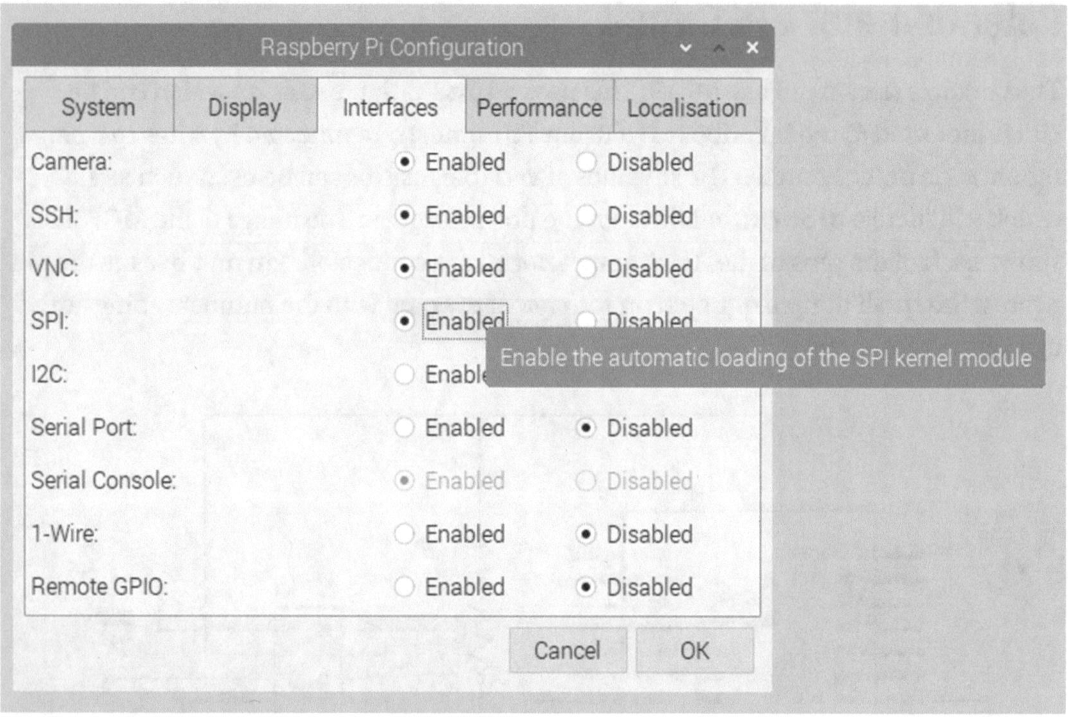

Figure 6-14. *Enable the SPI kernel module*

Accessing the ADC Using Python

The first thing that is required is to enable the SPI kernel module. This can be achieved through the Raspberry Pi configuration tool as shown in Figure 6-14. This will require a reboot before the changes take effect.

There are several SPI devices which are supported by GPIO Zero, which includes the MCP3008. The code for displaying the position of the potentiometer as a percentage is shown in Listing 6-4.

Listing 6-4. Test code for reading the value from an ADC using SPI

```
from gpiozero import MCP3008
from time import sleep

adc = MCP3008(channel=0, clock_pin=11, mosi_pin=10, miso_pin=9, select_pin=8)
```

```
while True:
    print ("{:.0%}".format(adc.value))
    sleep(1)
```

The MCP3008 is imported and then an instance of that created. The values shown are all the default values and so it could instead have been created without any parameters. The two parameters that you may wish to change in future are the channel number which allows different input pins on the IC to be used and the select_pin which may need to be changed if you have other SPI devices connected. This pin needs to be unique for each device.

The input value is then provided as a value between 0 and 1, which is retrieved using adc.value. The print function uses the percentage string formatting which shows it as a percentage value.

This example used a simple potentiometer, but other analog sensors can be used such as a light-dependent resistor, a temperature sensor, or an analog joystick. For resistive sensors (such as the light-dependent resistor), you will need to use a voltage divider circuit like that in Figure 6-1. The sensor can be used in place of either R1 or R2 depending upon whether you want the value to increase or decrease as the resistance changes.

The analog input can be used to control other circuits. This will be shown in the next circuit, which expands on the current circuit to change the brightness of an LED based on the input voltage.

Digital to Analog Using PWM

There are different ways in which you can create an analog output voltage from a digital circuit. If you need an accurate signal, such as if you are looking for a high-quality audio output, then you will need an accurate digital-to-analog converter (DAC). These work by taking a digital signal (essentially a binary number) with different resistor values and summing them together through an amplifier. If you need this for quality audio, then a pre-built board or an integrated circuit can be used.

Outside of audio applications, many times that you need an analog signal output, an approximate output is enough. The most common example is controlling the speed of a DC motor, which is normally controlled by changing the voltage going to the motor.

The technique commonly used is known as pulse-width modulation or PWM. Pulse-width modulation works by turning the supply on and off quickly. If that signal turns on and off at a high speed, then it will have the same effect as varying the voltage to the motor. Another way that this can be used is with an LED where the LED turns on and off very quickly, it appears to human eyes that it is on constantly but that the brightness has reduced.

Each of the on states is considered a pulse, and as its name suggests, we vary the width of the pulses to change the equivalent voltage output. This is shown in Figure 6-15, which shows the output from the GPIO pin on the top trace and the effective voltage output on the bottom trace.

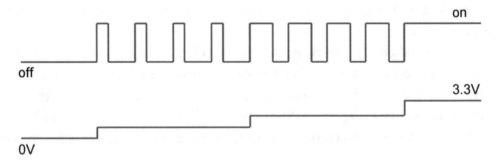

Figure 6-15. *Analog output voltage using PWM*

On this trace, the y axis represents the output voltage and the x axis time. The time is measured in milliseconds with all this happening very quickly. Starting on the left, it shows the GPIO output completely off which is effectively 0V output. The first four pulses shown have a ratio of 3:7, with the pulse lasting for three tenths of a cycle, followed by an off period of seven tenths of a second. Assuming 3.3V output, this will give us approximately 1V of equivalent output. The next four traces are twice as wide providing an output for six tenths of the cycle time, so an effective output of around 2V. Finally, the last part on the right is fully on which is 3.3V.

These voltages are based on the output voltage of the Raspberry Pi GPIO port. If required, these can then be used to switch a higher voltage device, either using the MOSFET switch circuit or by controlling a suitable integrated circuit.

If this is used to control a motor, then it will change the speed of the motor, but it does not necessarily mean that the relationship between the voltage and the speed of the motor is linear. There will be a range of low voltages which won't provide enough power to actually move the motor at all.

It is possible to provide PWM using both hardware and software. Hardware PWM has the advantage of having less load on the CPU. There are three hardware PWM ports on the modern versions of the Raspberry Pi, although one of those is normally used for the audio driver used for generating sound. In practice, using software PWM is normally acceptable.

LED Brightness Adjustment

To demonstrate how PWM can be used, you can add an LED and resistor to the previous ADC circuit using the variable resistor to change the brightness of the LED. This is shown in Figure 6-16.

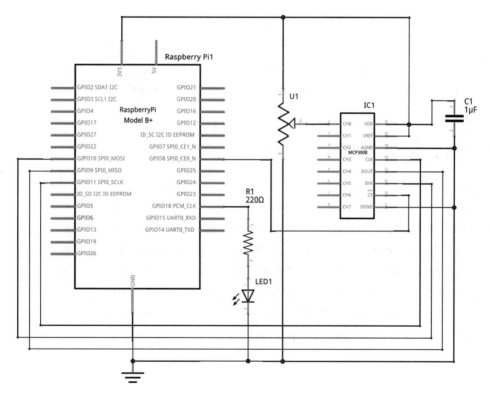

Figure 6-16. *ADC circuit with PWM-controlled LED*

The GPIO Zero module includes support for PWM through a PWMLED device. The PWMLED has an attribute called value, which takes a value between 0 and 1. This is the same as the value that is provided by the ADC so the value can be passed between the two. This results in the code shown in Listing 6-5, called adc-led.py.

Listing 6-5. Adjusting LED brightness based on variable resistor position

```
from gpiozero import MCP3008, PWMLED
from time import sleep

LED_PIN = 18

adc = MCP3008(channel=0)
pwm_led = PWMLED(LED_PIN)

pwm_led.on()

while True:
    print ("{:.0%}".format(adc.value))
    pwm_led.value = adc.value
    sleep(0.2)
```

This circuit is just controlling a standard LED; however, you could combine it with one of the bright LED circuits from Chapter 4 to control a brighter LED.

Controlling Motors

There are three types of motor that are commonly used in low-power situations, a DC motor, a servo motor, and a stepper motor. The DC motor is the most basic which takes a DC voltage and converts that to linear motion. The servo motor has a power supply and a control signal connection. The motor moves a set distance based upon the signal received on the control signal (using the on time from a PWM signal). The stepper motor has different magnetic regions so that the motor only moves a certain distance each time, known as a step. This is useful when the motor movement needs to be accurately controlled such as in a printer or 3D printer.

DC Motor

The low-power DC motor is the simplest type. Wire is wrapped around many times, creating a magnetic field when current flows through it. This magnetic field interacts with fixed magnets positioned around the motor. The direction of the electrical current determines the direction of the magnetic field, and so to reverse the direction of rotation, the motor needs to be connected in the opposite polarity. A DC electric motor will typically spin very fast, much too quickly to drive a wheel directly so many include an integrated gearbox. The motor in Figure 6-17 shows a DC motor mounted with a configurable gearbox. In this motor, it is possible to change the gears to provide a different gear ratio and alter the speed of the drive shaft.

Figure 6-17. *DC motor with adjustable gearbox*

Motors are often provided as a combined motor and gearbox. There are different ratios of gearbox which can be selected based upon the speed required. The speed of the motor can be adjusted using PWM. To change the direction of motion, the polarity of the power supply needs to be reversed which can be achieved using a H-bridge circuit.

H-Bridge Motor Control

The H-bridge configuration is a common way to change the direction of the power supply. The H-bridge is named as it is shaped a little like a letter H and uses two pairs of switches that need to be switched together. It is easiest explained using diagrams.

Figure 6-18 shows the H-bridge controller in the off position. There are four switches labeled S1–S4 and all are in the open position. There is no electrical connection to the motor.

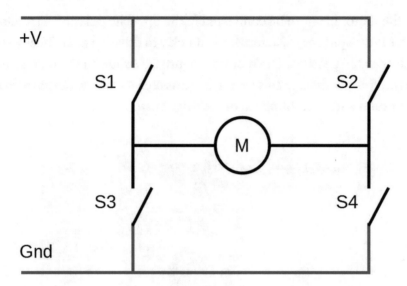

Figure 6-18. *H-bridge motor controller in the off position*

The next setting is shown in Figure 6-19. This shows switches S1 and S4 closed, which allows the current to flow through the motor in one direction.

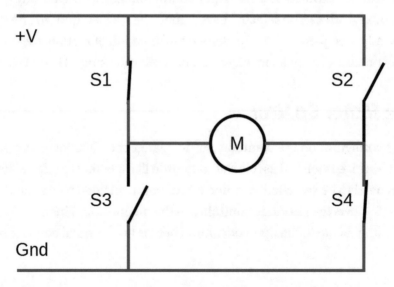

Figure 6-19. *H-bridge motor controller in one direction*

The other configuration is with S1 and S4 open and S2 and S3 closed. This causes the current to travel in the opposite direction across the motor and so the motor moves in the opposite direction. This is shown in Figure 6-20.

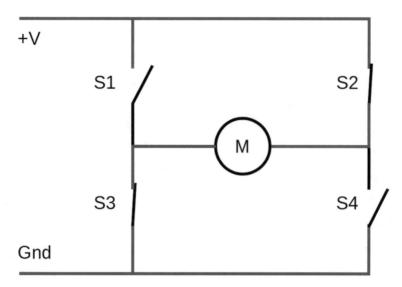

Figure 6-20. *H-bridge motor controller in the opposite direction*

These three are the only valid configuration options. It is important that the two switches on the same side are never turned on together, for example, if S1 and S3 were ever closed together (even for a short time), then this will cause a short circuit which could cause physical damage to the circuit or power supply.

Caution   Never allow the two switches on the same side to be closed together. If possible, this should be prevented using the physical control circuit.

You can make a H-bridge yourself using MOSFETs, using a similar circuit to the one used in Chapter 4. The one difference would be that we would need to use P-channel MOSFETs for those that are on the positive side of the power supply (switches S1 and S2). The P-channel MOSFET is like the N-channel MOSFET but works on the voltage at the gate being less than that at the drain to turn it on.

One problem with that approach is that there is risk of accidentally switching the wrong pairs of MOSFETs, which could create a short circuit. It is therefore often better to use an integrated circuit which takes care of all this for us. This example uses a SN754410 quad half H-bridge driver IC. As its name suggests, this has four half H-bridge circuits. These are normally grouped into two pairs which make two full H-bridge drivers able to drive two motors. This is shown in Figure 6-21.

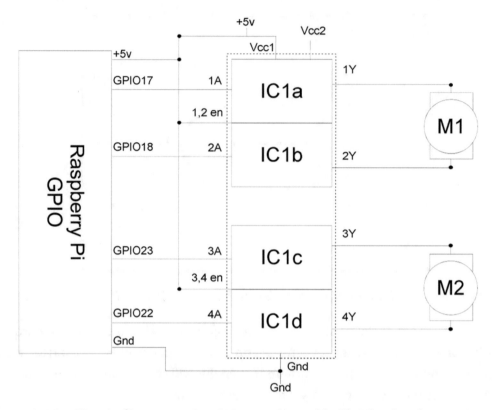

Figure 6-21. *Circuit diagram using SN754410 quad half H-bridge driver IC*

As you can see, there are four half H-bridges within the circuit. These have been grouped, such that half H-bridge circuits 1a and 1b form the first full H-bridge and 1c and 1d the second. In terms of the pin labeling, these are 1A and 2A for the first H-bridge and 3A and 4A for the second. The output is supplied as 1Y and 2Y for the first H-bridge and 3Y and 4Y for the second.

You will notice that the diagram in Figure 6-21 is different from others that I have provided in this book. That is because sometimes it is easier to show a diagram in terms of its functionality rather than the pin layout that Fritzing provides. The Fritzing diagram is shown in Figure 6-22.

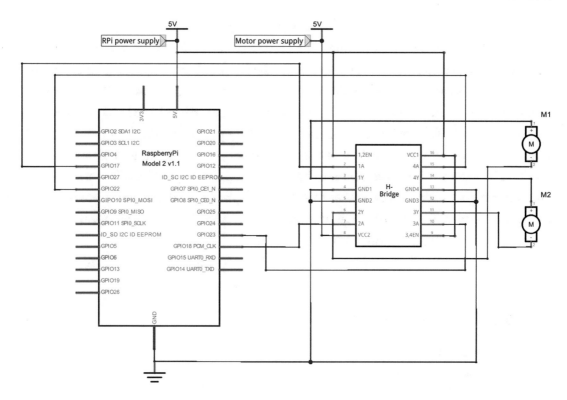

Figure 6-22. *Fritzing circuit diagram using SN754410 quad half H-bridge driver IC*

As you can see, the two diagrams provide the same circuit, but the earlier manual diagram is easier to understand than the later more formal style circuit diagram.

There are two distinct 5V power supplies shown. This shows that the motors do not have to be connected to the same power supply as that used for the Raspberry Pi and the H-bridge IC. These could be connected to the same supply or different supplies with either the same or different voltages. Even if they are the same voltage, it is sometimes useful to separate these due to the noise from driving an inductive load (motors) and the high initial current and potential current draw if the motors stall.

The enable pins (EN) are connected direct to the 5V power supply. This is one technique, and it means that the output of the motor will be enabled whenever the appropriate input is received. With the enable pin set high, the first motor output will be turned on whenever the appropriate inputs are set on 1A and 2A and likewise for the second motor. An alternative is to connect the enable as another connection to the Raspberry Pi, but that needs an additional two ports on the GPIO to be used.

There are no external protection diodes in this circuit. Normally, when a magnetic load is used, such as a motor or a relay, then as the power is disconnected, there can be a reverse voltage generated from the magnetic device (in effect, it becomes an electrical generator). This can be enough to damage some electrical components. It is therefore often advisable to include a flyback diode to allow any reverse voltage to be absorbed within the circuit. The SN754410 IC already includes a protection diode within each output, but older versions of the datasheet suggested connecting additional external diodes. The external diode requirement has been dropped on the Texas Instruments 2015 revision of the datasheet, and as this IC only supports small motors, there does not appear to be any problems when they are not included. It is something you should consider adding if creating your own H-bridge circuit.

The code to drive the motor is shown in Listing 6-6, called motor-test.py in the source code.

Listing 6-6. DC motor control

```python
from gpiozero import Motor
from time import sleep

m1 = Motor (17, 18)
m2 = Motor (23, 22)

m1.forward()
m2.forward()

sleep (1)

m1.stop()
m2.stop()

m1.backward(0.5)
m2.backward(0.5)

sleep (1)

m1.stop()
m2.stop()
```

This program moves both motors forward at full speed and then drives them backward at half speed. The speed is controlled using PWM, turning the output on and off appropriately.

Servo Motor

Another popular motor is the servo motor. This is a motor with built-in control circuitry, allowing it to be controlled using a PWM signal. The motor includes a built-in position sensor to provide accurate positioning. They are usually limited in the distance that they can move; the motor that I have is a SG92R which can move 90 degrees in each direction with a total distance of 180 degrees. Some motors can go further, and you can also get a continuous rotation servo motor which can turn continuously. A photo of the SG92R is shown in Figure 6-23.

The PWM signal sent to the servo motor determines the position to move to. A typical servo motor varies from 1ms to 2ms, where 1ms is fully to the left, 1.5ms is in the middle, and 2ms is fully to the right. The SG92R is slightly out of that range varying between 0.75ms and 2.25ms.

The SG92R has the benefit that it can run as low as 3V and so can be driven directly from the 3.3V of the Raspberry Pi. For other servos that need a higher voltage, you may need to use a voltage level shifter such as the examples earlier in this chapter.

Figure 6-23. *An SG92R servo motor*

The wiring on the motor is red for the positive terminal which is connected to 3.3V on the Raspberry Pi, brown for ground, and orange for the signal which I connected to GPIO 17 (physical pin 11).

The code in Listing 6-7 shows an example code which I've named servo-test.py.

Listing 6-7. DC motor control

```
from gpiozero import Servo
from time import sleep

servo = Servo(17)

while True:
    servo.min()
    sleep(1)
    servo.mid()
    sleep(1)
    servo.max()
    sleep(1)
    servo.value = 0
    sleep(1)
```

The code uses the min, mid, and max methods to move the servo to the appropriate position. The final entry sets the value to 0 which is the same as calling the mid method.

Stepper Motor

The final motor covered here is called a stepper motor. The stepper motor allows accurate positioning by moving the motor a step at a time. This still uses the same principle of creating a magnetic field using a DC current, but instead of the motor in a spin, the stepper motor just moves along a small amount. The magnetic field then needs to be applied to the next coil, which moves the motor along the next step. If the appropriate magnetic coils can be turned on in the correct order, then the motor will turn. The rotation distance is much more accurately controlled than the standard DC motor. Stepper motors are used in a variety of different applications, including moving the printhead on a printer or adjusting the focus on a digital camera.

An example stepper motor, known as the Mercury Motor, is shown in Figure 6-24.

Figure 6-24. *Stepper motor*

This stepper motor is a bipolar stepper motor, which means that it has single pair of windings per phase. In this motor, there are two fields which are connected to four wires. To drive the motor needs a dual H-bridge circuit. The circuit in Figure 6-22 can be used but instead of using two motors connecting the circuit to the two pairs of windings on the one stepper motor. For larger stepper motors, a more powerful IC may be needed such as the L298N. The pin rows for the L298N are offset which makes it difficult to connect to a breadboard. It is available pre-built as a small circuit board with pin connectors for connecting to the Raspberry Pi GPIO and screw terminals for the motor. The circuit board will normally include appropriate diode protection. Different stepper motors may use different color wires; the one I have is connected as follows: red (out1) and green (out2) for one pair and yellow (out3) and blue (out4) for the other pair.

The programming is more complicated for a stepper motor as it needs to apply power to the appropriate coils in order. There are different ways of activating the steps in Listing 6-8. I have used the half-step mode which provides the most accurate control. This is called stepper.py.

Listing 6-8. Program to drive a stepper motor in half-step mode

```python
from gpiozero import DigitalOutputDevice
from time import sleep

motor_pins = [DigitalOutputDevice (17), DigitalOutputDevice (23),
DigitalOutputDevice (18), DigitalOutputDevice (22)]

motor_seq = [
    [1,0,0,0],
    [1,1,0,0],
    [0,1,0,0],
    [0,1,1,0],
    [0,0,1,0],
    [0,0,1,1],
    [0,0,0,1],
    [1,0,0,1]
]

while True:
    for seq_num in range (len(motor_seq)):
        for motor_pin in range (0,4):
            if motor_seq[seq_num][motor_pin] == 1:
                motor_pins[motor_pin].on()
            else:
                motor_pins[motor_pin].off()
        sleep(0.001)
```

GPIO Zero does not include support for the stepper motor, so instead each of the four outputs is controlled as a DigitalOutputDevice (this is the parent of the LED device used previously). The motor_seq holds the sequence that the coils need to be activated. There is an overlap as each coil is activated resulting in the motor moving only a half-step at a time. To reverse the direction, the order of the sequence should be reversed.

More Devices to Connect To

This chapter has covered how you can convert between different voltages, how you can read an analog sensor using an analog-to-digital converter (ADC), and how you can get an analog signal from a digital pin. It has also covered interfacing with three common motors, a DC motor, a servo motor, and a stepper motor.

These circuits can form building blocks for use in other more complicated circuits. They are very useful when you need to interface with real-world sensors which are often analog or that use other protocols such as I²C and SPI. With this additional understanding, it will have significantly increased the number of sensors that you can now connect to the Raspberry Pi.

The main project in this chapter is a true and false game using an LCD display. To expand this, you could look at adding scrolling text for the LCD display (particularly useful if you only have a two-row LCD display) or adding another loop so that the game starts again without needing to restart it. Chapter 12 will show how this can be used to create a complete game by placing it in an enclosure and expanding the function.

The next chapter will look at controlling circuits in Python. It will make use of the DC motor control to show how a model train can be controlled.

CHAPTER 7

Adding Control in Python and Linux

This chapter will be concentrating on the software side of the programs. This includes things you can do within Python programs but also some of the features of Linux that will allow us to start our programs automatically. This will provide some of the techniques you will need for projects in the later chapters. Some of the techniques listed will help add functionality to the disco lights, have a program run automatically, and add a basic graphical interface for controlling electronics projects.

The chapter will also provide automated control of a model train. Even if you are not interested in model trains, this will cover important information relating to using input sensors which is useful in many other projects, in this example, using a reed switch as a sensor to provide a feedback loop.

This chapter will also look at how to control a multi-color LED string, which is good for creating your own lighting displays.

Introduction to Computing

Computers receive information (data), process the data using stored instructions, and then provide an output. The inputs could be a keyboard and mouse or could be some kind of sensor. Likewise, while we may traditionally consider that a computer screen is the usual output device, the output could be in turning on a light or controlling the brakes on a car without having any kind of visual screen. The use of stored programs is the part that turns these electronic circuits into a computer. Sometimes the programs are stored in firmware on the computer, and sometimes these are programs that can be loaded from disk or memory stick.

In the case of the Raspberry Pi, the programs are stored on the SD card. The operating system is a Linux-based distribution, known as Raspberry Pi OS. Most of the

© Stewart Watkiss 2020
S. Watkiss, *Learn Electronics with Raspberry Pi*, https://doi.org/10.1007/978-1-4842-6348-8_7

software created for this book is written in Python, which is a common programming language used in education and industry. One of the benefits of Python is that there are already lots of modules that have been written that make access to the hardware easier.

Taking the Next Steps in Python Programming

Most of the Python programs that have been used so far have been fairly simple. One of the reasons for Python being so simple to use is thanks to the code inside the Python interpreter that hides a lot of the complexity that other programming languages have. It's also thanks to some of the Python modules that others have been written that make interfacing with the hardware so easy.

When creating longer and more complex programs, it is important to structure the programs in a way that makes them easier to understand. This chapter will look at some techniques that will make our programs easier to write and understand.

I will stop short of covering object-oriented programming (OOP) in any detail. OOP is an option in Python but needs a different approach to programming. This is not because of any faults of object-oriented programming, but it would need more than the space I could contribute in this book to cover it properly. I do recommend looking at OOP if you want to take your programming further.

Many of the programs still use some object-oriented programming as most of the modules that are written using object-orientation. Accessing software in this method can make it easier to understand what is happening.

Making Decisions with Python Programming

The example programs so far have already used Python to make decisions or at least to run different parts of a program depending upon certain parameter. These decisions have included whether to turn a light on or off depending upon the value of a sensor and whether a button press was the correct response for a game. You can also include code that determines which way to move a game character based on the movement of a joystick or change the length of a time delay based on the value of an analog input.

Another form of a decision is whether to repeat certain code which is implemented in the form of a loop. These are often implemented using a *for* loop which has repeated a certain number of times or a *while* loop which continues to loop until a certain condition is met. These decisions are key to being able to handle the inputs and outputs from our electronic circuits. Some of these are listed as follows as both a recap for those you may have come across already and perhaps some new ones that can make programming a little easier.

The first is the if statement which performs an action depending upon the result of a comparison, typically looking if a certain variable is equal to, greater than, or less than another value.

```
if myvariable == 10 :
    print ("The value is equal to 10")
```

This compares the value of myvariable looking to see if it is equal to 10. Note that there are two equals characters used; using only a single equals character will result in the value of 10 being stored into myvariable rather than testing to see if something is equal which requires "==". To test for myvariable being higher than 10, you can use the greater than symbol ">", and to test that it is lower than 10, you can use the less than symbol "<". If you would like to check for something being not equal to a certain value, then "!=" should be used in place of the double equal sign used previously.

Using an if statement, you can also run a different action if the condition is not met. The code in the *if* block is run if the condition is met and the *else* block if the condition is not met.

```
if myvariable == 10 :
    print ("The value is equal to 10")
else:
    print ("The value is not equal to 10")
```

In the preceding example, the first print statement is called if the value is equal, but if the value is not equal, then the print statement following the else statement will be called instead.

Another useful technique is to be able to chain events together. While we could do this by having if statements within the else statement, this is easier to follow using an *elif* statement (which is a contraction of else if).

```
if myvariable == 10 :
    print ("The value is equal to 10")
elif myvariable < 10 :
    print ("The value is less than 10")
else :
    print ("The value is greater than 10")
```

In this case, the *elif* statement checks for the value being less than 10. As it has already checked that the value is not equal to 10, anything that doesn't meet the if and elif conditions must be greater than 10.

Another useful thing is to be able to put multiple conditions within a single *if* statement. This can be achieved by using the words "and" or "or" between each clause.

```
if ((button_pressed == True) and (myvariable > 10)) :
    print ("Well done score - you won")
```

In the preceding example, it checks that both button_pressed is True *and* that myvariable is greater than 10. If we wanted this to be run if either condition was met, then we would use *or* instead. I have added brackets around the various parts of the if condition to make it clearer to understand; these are not required, but it can help with understanding what is happening and will avoid any problems due to operator precedence (where certain operators are taken into consideration first).

Loops are another form of decision-making. The while True loop is a common loop which keeps on looping forever or at least as long as the program is running (as the program can be stopped by pressing Ctrl-c, or some other external call). Another way to exit from a forever loop (or any other kind of loop) is to include a break statement. This is often used within an if statement, so that when a certain condition is met, it "breaks" from the loop. It is also possible to return to the start of the loop using a continue statement. The following code shows both these in use:

```
myvariable = 0
while True:
    myvariable = myvariable + 1
    print ("In loop")
    if (myvariable < 10) :
        continue
    break
```

This will print the line "In loop" ten times. It starts by incrementing the value of myvariable. It prints "In loop" and then checks to see if the value of myvariable is less than 10.

If it is, then it continues back to the top of the loop. Once the code has looped ten times, the value of myvariable will be equal to 10 and the code can reach the break which exits from the loop.

An alternative to the while True loop is to use a condition in the while statement.

```
myvariable = 0
while myvariable < 10:
    myvariable = myvariable + 1
    print ("In loop")
```

With this while loop, the program will run as long as myvariable is less than 10. This will give the same output as the previous example.

Python also provides another way of doing this which is easier to understand using a *for range* loop.

```
for i in range (0, 10):
    print ("In loop")
```

Using the for loop, there are only two lines which is much less than the previous examples. It is also easier to read as you can tell from the first line how many times the loop will repeat without having to work through the logic later in the program. The range function creates a list of values starting at 0 and going up to 9. The for loop then iterates over each of these in turn by copying the value from range into the variable i and then running that iteration of the loop. You are not limited to using numbers using the for loop; you could also iterate over any lists.

```
my_list = ["Loop 0", "Loop 1","Loop 2","Loop 3","Loop 4","Loop 5"]
for this_string in my_list:
    print ("In "+this_string)
```

In this example, a list is defined consisting of five entries. The for loop then iterates over each of the elements in the list, putting the value into the variable this_string. Each entry is then printed out, one line at a time.

Creating Python Functions

The programs so far in this book have been written as a sequential block of code designed to be run from the top to the bottom of the file. Loops are used to avoid some repetition, but if you wanted to do something multiple times but elsewhere in the program, it has had to be repeated. This can create duplicate blocks of code, result in very long code, and make it difficult to understand what the code is doing. The solution to this is to move related parts of the code into a function. Then instead of having to copy that same block of code into multiple places, you can just call the function.

To create a function, the block of code starts with a "def" statement along with the name of the function and any parameters, followed by the code inside the function.

For example, if you wanted a function that would read an analog input from a sensor, you may create the following:

```
def read_analog(input):
    # Code for the function goes here
```

In this case, it defines a function called read_analog, which has a single argument called input.

To return information to the code that calls the function, you can add a return statement, followed by the value to return or the name of the variable. The following example shows how we would create a simple function that takes two parameters, input1 and input2, and returns whichever value is the largest (or if they are equal, then the first input):

```
def largest_value (input1, input2):
    if input1 > input2:
        return input1
    elif input2 > input1:
        return input2
    else:
        return input1
```

This can then be called within the main program using

```
largest_value (3, 2)
```

which will return the value 3.

Adding Disco Light Sequences Using Python Functions

As Python functions are so useful, it is worth including a real example using them to control some electronics. This example will revisit the earlier disco lights from Chapter 4 and add some different sequences that can be called from within functions.

If you have created the circuit from Chapter 4, Figure 4-26, then you can use that. Alternatively, Figure 7-1 has a simplified circuit that can be used for testing out these functions.

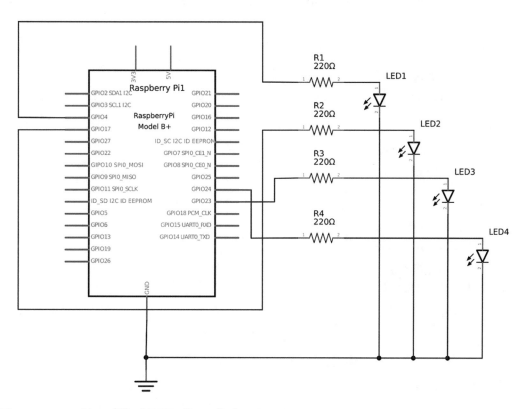

Figure 7-1. *Simplified LED disco light circuit*

This circuit has only four resistors and four standard LEDs. It uses the same GPIO pins as the disco light project and so can be used for testing out the different sequences.

The code for testing the sequences is shown in Listing 7-1. It should be saved as discolight-sequences.py.

Listing 7-1. Light sequences using functions

```
from gpiozero import LED
from time import sleep

# GPIO port numbers for the light
#9 = gnd, 7 = GPIO 4, 11 = GPIO 17, 16 = GPIO 23, 18 = GPIO 24
LED_PINS = [4, 17, 23, 24]
```

```python
# Time between each step in the sequence in seconds
DELAY = 1

lights = [LED(LED_PINS[0]), LED(LED_PINS[1]), LED(LED_PINS[2]),
LED(LED_PINS[3])]

def all_on():
    for x in range (4):
        lights[x].on()

def all_off():
    for x in range (4):
        lights[x].off()

def sequence():
    for x in range (4):
        for y in range (4):
            lights[y].off()
        lights[x].on()
        sleep(DELAY)

def repeat_sequence(num_sequences):
    for x in range (num_sequences):
        sequence()

# Main code starts here
all_off()
sleep(DELAY)
all_on()
sleep(DELAY)
sequence()
sleep(DELAY)
repeat_sequence(6)
```

This program has four functions. The first function called all_on turns all the LEDs on, the next all_off turns all the LEDs off, sequence lights the four LEDs in sequence, and repeat_sequence will repeat the sequence for a number of times as defined in the parameter for the function.

Unlike the code used previously, a function will not run until it is called. After the functions, there is a block of code starting after the comment "# Main code starts here". This is not contained within a function so will run when the program is run. This code calls each function with a delay between each other. The function `repeat_sequence` calls another function `sequence` which allows even further code reuse.

If you look within the functions, several of them reference the variable x. These are created within the function as local variables which only apply within that function. For example, even though repeat_sequence calls sequence and both functions refer to the variable x, these values are independent of each other. The list that holds the lights is created outside of the function and is visible to all the functions without having to create a new copy for each function.

The all_on and all_off functions should be self-explanatory. The sequence function uses a nested loop. The first loop uses the variable x and will be called once for each disco light. The first run within the loop will turn off all the LEDs and then turn the first LED on. The second will turn off all the LEDs and then the second LED on, which continues up to the fourth which turns all the LEDs off and then the fourth one back on. This gives the effect of showing a single LED being lit shifting from left to right. The inside loop is one that turns all the LEDs off. This could have been replaced with a call to the all_off function.

The repeat_sequence function takes a parameter called num_sequences, which should be an integer number. The loop will then call sequence the number of times that num_sequences was set to.

Using a Python Main Function

In addition to using functions for small parts of your code, you can create a special function around the main part of the code. This is a requirement in many other programming languages but is not required in Python although it can be useful. You can do this by creating a function called `main` and calling it when the program is started using the following code:

```python
def main():
    #The main program code goes here

#Run the main function when this program is run
if __name__ == "__main__":
    main()
```

This separates the main function from the rest of the file so that variables within main are local to main rather than global variables. It is generally good practice in programming to avoid using global variables where possible, so this is considered a good thing. You can still include global variables in the program which are defined using a globals statement in the functions where they are needed. This also has the benefit of allowing the program to be used as a module, but also have a main function, so it can be run as a stand-alone program.

Making Python Programs Executable

The programs we have created so far have been executed from within Mu or would need to be run on the command line using

```
python3 myprogram.py
```

It is useful to be able to run the program directly using its name in the same way that other programs can be run from the command line. This can be achieved by adding a shebang entry as the first line in the program. The shebang takes the form of a hash character "#" normally used for comments, followed by an exclamation mark. This is a contraction of hash and bang which are alternative names for those characters. To use Python 3, we put the path to the Python interpreter. On most systems, this is

```
#!/usr/bin/python3
```

The one downside of this is that it may not work across different Unix-like operating systems, including different Linux distributions. This is not going to be a problem for these programs as they will only work with the Raspberry Pi anyway, but you may see a slightly different entry, which is

```
#!/usr/bin/env python3
```

This achieves the same thing, but instead of python3 having to be in a certain directory, the env (environment) command will locate it for you.

The next stage in making a program executable is to tell Linux that it has permissions to run. By default, Linux gives permission so that the user can read and write to the file but not execute it. The chmod command can be used to add executable permissions using +x as shown here:

```
chmod +x myprogram.py
```

After adding a shebang entry and making a program executable, it can be run directly from the command line. The program should be prefixed with ./ (which means run it from the current directory) as this:

```
./myprogram.py
```

This makes the program a little easier to run and looks a bit more professional than having to type python3 before it. It also makes it easier to run the program with command-line options and to run the program automatically.

Handling Command-Line Arguments

The programs so far have either run without any user control or have been dependent on interacting with the user directly or through an electronic circuit. It is useful to be able to tell a program what you would like it to do without needing to interact with it in real time. You can achieve this by adding command-line arguments. For example, with the time delay light, you may want to change the length of time that the light stays on. By adding a command-line argument, you can change the delay when it is run.

The arguments to a Python program are provided as a list called sys.argv. If you only have a simple requirement, then you can just access the list directly, as shown in Listing 7-2. This is named as ledtimer2.py.

Listing 7-2. LED timer program with command-line arguments

```
#!/usr/bin/python3
from gpiozero import LED
from time import sleep
import sys

# Time to keep the light on in seconds
DEFAULT_DELAY = 30

# GPIO port numbers for the LED
LED_PIN = 4

if len(sys.argv) > 1:
    try:
        delay = int (sys.argv[1])
```

```
    except:
        print ("Invalid argument. The argument must be a number.")
        exit (0)

    if delay < 1 :
        print ("Invalid number. The argument must be a positive number.")
        exit (0)
else:
    delay = DEFAULT_DELAY

led = LED(LED_PIN)

while True:
    input_text = input("Press enter to turn the light on for "+str(delay)+"
    seconds")
    if input_text == "q":
        exit(0)
    led.on()
    sleep(delay)
    led.off()
```

This is based on the led timer code used in Chapter 4, but there have been a few changes. Firstly, so that this can be used with the disco light circuit rather than needing the original LED timer circuit, the LED_PIN has been changed to reflect one of the LEDs used in the disco light. I have also removed the need for the button, using the keyboard to activate the light. If you still have the LED timer circuit, then you can change this to pin 22 and reinsert the button code.

Instead of using a constant for the delay, it takes the value from the argument and stores it into a variable called delay. Python doesn't differentiate between the constant and the variable (both are in fact just standard variables), but the convention is that variables written all in uppercase should not be changed one set to an initial value.

To run the program, first add permission to execute using

```
chmod +x ledtimer2.py
```

You can then run the program using

```
./ledtimer2.py
```

You can then add a command-line argument such as the following which will turn the light on for 5 seconds:

```
./ledtimer2.py 5
```

The program can be stopped by pressing q and then Enter or by using Ctrl-c which can be used to stop most command-line programs.

Here is an explanation of the major changes that have been made compared with the previous code from Chapter 4.

The module sys is imported. This is required to access the command-line arguments, which are stored in a list called argv. In this example, I have used the shorter import statement rather than the *import-from* which has been used for gpiozero and sleep modules:

```
import sys
```

Either method could have been used. If you use the import-from method, then you explicitly list the parts of the module that you plan to use, and you can then use them directly. When using import without from, you need to prefix the imports by the module name. For example, LED is explicitly imported from the gpiozero module, so it is referred to as LED without having to say it is from the gpiozero module. Using import without from, you need to explicitly state that argv is in the sys module by prefixing it with sys giving sys.argv. There are pros and cons to both methods. Using it in this way makes it obvious that it is the sys module that contains that list.

Whenever taking user-provided data from the command line or in a user response, it is important to check that value before using it; otherwise, it could cause the program to behave incorrectly or crash. The first step is to check to see if a command-line argument has been provided at all. This is done by checking the length of the argument list:

```
if len(sys.argv) > 1:
```

The reason that this checks for more than one entry is because the argument zero always exists and stores the name of the program that is running. The next thing is to test if the value is an integer number:

```
delay = int (sys.argv[1])
```

This takes the argument number 1 (remember argument 0 is the name of the program) and tries to store it as integer. The attempt is enclosed in a try-except clause.

This is a feature of the Python error handling, whereby if the "try" fails, it then runs the code under the "except" clause. In this case, it prints an error and exits the program.

The final check is to ensure that the number is a positive number by checking it is not less than 1:

```
if delay < 1 :
```

After the checks, there is a while loop which waits for an input from the user. The LED is then turned on for the delay amount (in seconds). The input function used for the response from the user is normally used to get some text from the user. If the user presses q followed by enter, then that will quit the program; otherwise, it will just wait for the user to press the enter key and then continue running the program.

If you want to have multiple arguments, then you could just read them using the sys.argv list as used earlier. If you want to do something more complex like having different arguments which are optional or that can be in a different order, then you may be better off looking at the argparse module which allows for multiple arguments.

Automated Model Train

It is now time for another project to practice some of the techniques covered in this chapter. This project will automate a model train used in a model railroad layout. This could be in your home or a train at a public display where you want to train to automatically stop at a station without having to keep stopping and starting the train manually.

Model trains are normally run using a DC motor. In traditional analog layouts, they are controlled the same as other DC motors, applying an appropriate DC power to the track which gets picked up by the train and supplied to its motors. DCC trains work differently as they provide control signals over the track; this project is just designed for analog trains, although the techniques relating to detecting the train can be used for any kind of train. The DC motor control in this should work for most track-powered trains, although you may need to check what voltage the trains are designed to run at. The photo in Figure 7-2 shows an example train on my outdoor railway.

Figure 7-2. Model train

From AC to DC – Bridge Rectifier

Most analog model train sets have a plug-in power supply, which then connects through a controller, which has a dial to determine direction and speed. While most power supplies for other electronic applications handle the conversion from AC to DC, with model trains, that is usually done in the controller. As a result, if you want to use the same power supply that came with your existing train set (rather than an alternative DC power supply), then you will need to add circuitry to perform the conversion from AC to DC. The simplest way is to use a diode which only allows the current to flow in one direction; this will allow the current to flow through one half of the AC wave and block for the other half. This technique wastes around half the power, so a better solution is a bridge rectifier (also known as a full-wave rectifier).

The diagram in Figure 7-3 shows a transformer, followed by a bridge rectifier. In this diagram, the bridge rectifier is created using 1N4002 rectifier diodes, although you can also buy a bridge rectifier containing all four diodes in a single package such as a 2KBP04 bridge rectifier.

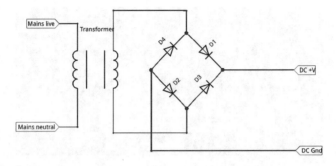

Figure 7-3. *Bridge rectifier*

This works as follows:

> In the first part of the wave, the current flows through D1 as the
> positive DC voltage and returns through D2 from the DC ground.
> The other two diodes are reverse biased and so will not conduct.

> In the second part of the wave, the current is reversed on the AC
> side and so D1 and D2 are now reversed and so will not conduct.
> The current flows through D3 to the positive DC supply and
> returns from the DC ground through D4.

Using the circuit in Figure 7-3, the output voltage will not be smooth as it will
fluctuate in line with the incoming AC as a series of peaks and troughs. For driving
electrical motors, that will not be a problem, but it would likely cause problems if used
as the power supply for microcontrollers or integrated circuits that need a stable power
supply. If that is required, the supply can be smoothed using large capacitors, which
store a charge when the output voltage is high and provide that to the output when the
voltage reduces. The diagram in Figure 7-4 shows an approximate waveform of AC and
DC voltages.[1] As well as smoothing the supply using a capacitor, many circuits, especially
those with ICs, will also need to be supplied through a voltage regulator, which is
covered in Chapter 13.

---

[1]The diagram shows an ideal world waveform. There will be a voltage drop across the diode
with some loss at the bottom of the DC waveform where the voltage is too low for the diode to
conduct.

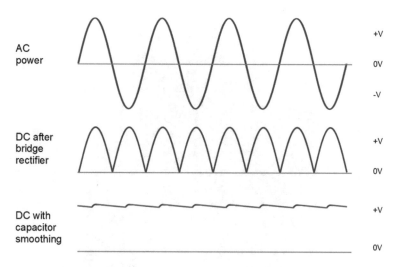

Figure 7-4. *Voltage waveforms for AC and rectified DC*

Controlling the Motors

The motors are controlled using a H-bridge circuit which was covered in Chapter 6. The speed of the motor is controlled by varying the voltage which is achieved using PWM. The choice of H-bridge depends upon the maximum current that the motor will use. In the case of indoor railways such as HO/OO, the SN754410 can handle 1A of continuous current which is sufficient. The SN754410 circuit from Figure 6-22 can be used by replacing the motor with a connection to the track. For outdoor trains such as the G-Scale railway shown in Figure 7-2, you may need a motor controller which can handle a higher current such as the L298N that was used for the stepper motor in Chapter 6. The photo in Figure 7-5 shows a controller board using the L298N. These are commonly available on eBay and can be used for either indoor or outdoor model trains. Unless you are going to integrate the H-bridge into your printed circuit board, I suggest using an L298N motor controller circuit board for controlling a model railway.

Figure 7-5. *L298N-based motor controller*

The output of the bridge rectifier (or DC power supply) should be connected as the supply to the motor controller. The motor controller also needs a 5V power supply. There is a jumper on the board which connects the 12V supply to a voltage regulator; if using a 12V DC supply, you can leave the jumper in place. If you are using a higher voltage for the motor (19V is quite common), then you should remove the jumper and connect the 5V power supply to the Raspberry Pi. Do not connect the 5V connection to the Raspberry Pi if the jumper is still connected as the power draw from the Raspberry Pi could damage the regulator on the motor board.

If using the bridge rectifier circuit, you should also use a large size capacitor such as 2200μF to smooth the power supply. This should be connected directly between the positive and ground outputs from the bridge rectifier. The Raspberry Pi GPIO ports 17 and 18 should be connected as the input to the motor.

Feedback Loop

This automation setup should drive the model train around the track and then stop and pause when it reaches the station. After allowing time for passengers to leave and board the train, it then starts again. In theory, you could do this using timing; you can time how long it takes for the train to reach the station and run the train for that length of time. This does not however work in practice as there are several things that can go wrong.

You could be slightly off with your timing, which works well for the first few laps around the track, but gradually gets worse; or the resistance between the rails and the train may change due to dust or dirt on the track.

Detecting the Train Using a Reed Switch

To accurately stop at the station, each time you need to be able to detect the train approaching. A simple way to detect the presence of the train is to use a magnetic switch known as a reed switch. A reed switch is a switch that instead of using a button to turn it on or off is controlled by a magnet. The switch is normally open when there is no magnetic field nearby and closed when an appropriate magnet comes close to it. A burglar alarm sensor mounted on a doorframe uses the same principle. A photo of a reed switch and magnet is shown in Figure 7-6.

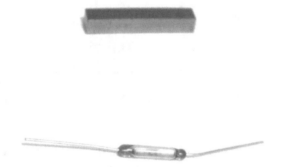

Figure 7-6. *A reed switch with magnet*

The reed switch will pull one of the GPIO input pins down to zero volts the same as used previously using the Button GPIO Zero object. The reed switches do need to be treated carefully as they are usually enclosed in glass which is easily broken. You can also buy reed switches that are more rugged which is recommended for use on an outdoor railway. If you prefer to manually control the stopping of the train, then you could replace the reed switch with a standard push-to-make button switch.

A wiring diagram showing how the components are connected is shown in Figure 7-7. This is not an actual circuit diagram; instead, it is a high-level diagram showing how the connections go between the various parts. In this case, the 2200µF capacitor would be connected within the bridge rectifier block between the +V out and the ground terminals.

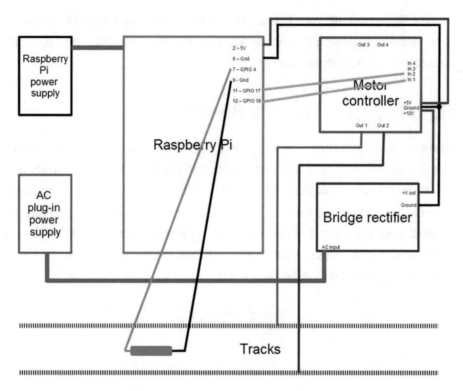

Figure 7-7. *Wiring diagram of Raspberry Pi with motor controller with reed switch*

The reed switch will need to be positioned inside the train track so that the train goes over it, but doesn't interfere with the train. Ideally, the reed switch can be soldered to a long wire, although as soldering is not covered until Chapter 12, you could push the reed switch into a female-to-female jumper lead and push the wire from the reed switch into the connector. The magnet needs to be stuck to the bottom of the train either on the locomotive or one of the carriages; it needs to be positioned close to the track but without risk of hitting anything. In my case, I used Blu Tack (otherwise known as adhesive putty) to hold the magnet in place, or you could use self-adhesive pads or glue for a more permanent fixing.

Software to Control the Train

The Python program will start the train, slowly increasing its speed, run at the maximum speed until the train approaches the station, and then slow the train down to a stop.

The train will pause for a while at the station and then start off again. Rather than just jumping straight to the full speed, I made the train accelerate slowly until it reached full speed and then decelerate slowly back down again.

The best way to understand it is to start looking at the code shown in Listing 7-3, which is saved as traincontrol.py.

Listing 7-3. Model train motor control and reed switch detection

```python
#!/usr/bin/python3
from gpiozero import Motor, Button
from time import sleep

# GPIO numbers for motor
MOTOR_PIN_FWD = 17
MOTOR_PIN_REV = 18
# GPIO pin for reed switch
REED_PIN = 4

# max speed to reduce top speed
# maximum value is 1
MAX_SPEED = 1.0
# How long to wait between speed increases
ACC_DELAY = 0.5
# How long to wait at the station
STATION_DELAY = 10

m1 = Motor (MOTOR_PIN_FWD, MOTOR_PIN_REV)
reed_switch = Button (REED_PIN)

# Go from stop to max speed
def train_speed_up (max_speed):
    speed = 0
    while speed < max_speed:
        speed += 0.1
        if speed >= 1:
            speed = 1
        m1.forward(speed)
        sleep(ACC_DELAY)
```

```python
def train_slow_down (current_speed):
    speed = current_speed
    while speed > 0:
        speed -= 0.1
        if speed <= 0 :
            m1.stop()
        else:
            m1.forward(speed)
        sleep(ACC_DELAY)

while True:
    print ("Leaving the station")
    # Accelerate up to full speed
    train_speed_up(MAX_SPEED)
    # wait until it triggers reed switch
    print ("Going to station")
    reed_switch.wait_for_press()
    print ("Stopping at station")
    train_slow_down(MAX_SPEED)
    sleep(STATION_DELAY)
```

The program starts by defining some constants. In addition to the pin numbers for the GPIO ports, there is a value for the maximum speed in case the top speed is too fast or unrealistic, an acceleration delay (how long to wait between speed increases and decreases), and how long to wait in the station. You can see the motor object created as m1.

The reed switch is created as a button object; other than needing a magnet to close, it is essentially the same as having a button switch. You could replace the reed switch with a button if you wanted to add a bit of human interaction on determining when the train should stop at the station.

Next, there are two functions which provide the smooth acceleration and deceleration of the train, used when it leaves the station when it slows down. The speed change is within a while loop, so it does not return until the desired speed is reached. There is a test if the speed is too fast to ensure it does not exceed 1.0 (which will cause an error) and to call the stop method once the speed is less than or equal to 0.

The main program flow follows the functions. This consists of a while loop that calls the appropriate functions and waits on the reed switch being triggered by the train passing over it.

Using the Internet of Things to Control the Model Train

You've no doubt heard about the Internet of Things (IoT) which is about controlling electronic devices from the Internet. This will look at using IoT to control the model train.

There are different methods which can be used to provide a web interface to control a Python program. One option is to run a traditional web server and have that call the Python code; an alternative is to create a mini-web server in Python.

This project will be based around the Python Bottle module which implements the web server functionality. In addition, there will need to be some HTML code for the website and a bit of JavaScript to make it more responsive. The HTML and JavaScript are outside the scope of this book, so I will just be concentrating on the Python code. If you want to take your IoT projects further, then I'd suggest getting a good book on HTML and JavaScript as well.

This code will no longer use the reed switch but uses the same motor control program used previously.

The Python Bottle module is effectively an entire web server in a Python module. All that is required is to install the module, import it into an application, and then run the appropriate commands.

To get started, you will need to install the module and another file that is required for the JavaScript.

First, install the Python module using

```
sudo apt install python3-bottle
```

Now, create a directory to hold our program, and inside that, create a public folder which holds the files that we will make available through the web server.

```
mkdir ~/iot-train
mkdir ~/iot-train/public
```

The program uses jQuery which makes it easier for JavaScript to interact with the web server without needing to refresh the page. To install jQuery, change to the public directory and download the jQuery file using

```
cd ~/iot-train/public
wget http://code.jquery.com/jquery-3.5.1.min.js
```

Now, change to the iot-train directory which is where the program needs to be stored:

```
cd ~/iot-train
```

Rather than rewrite all the code for controlling the train, this will make use of the code used previously. To make it so that the code can be used for running as a stand-alone program and for inclusion in the web application, we will use the special Python Main Function code that was explained earlier. This is shown in Listing 7-4, which should be saved as a file traincontrol.py.

Listing 7-4. Updated motor control to allow importing

```
#!/usr/bin/python3
from gpiozero import Motor, Button
from time import sleep

# GPIO numbers for motor
MOTOR_PIN_FWD = 17
MOTOR_PIN_REV = 18
# GPIO pin for reed switch
REED_PIN = 4

# max speed to reduce top speed
# maximum value is 1
MAX_SPEED = 1.0
# How long to wait between speed increases
ACC_DELAY = 0.5
# How long to wait at the station
STATION_DELAY = 10

m1 = Motor (MOTOR_PIN_FWD, MOTOR_PIN_REV)
reed_switch = Button (REED_PIN)
```

```python
# Go from stop to max speed
def train_speed_up (max_speed):
    speed = 0
    while speed < max_speed:
        speed += 0.1
        if speed >= 1:
            speed = 1
        m1.forward(speed)
        sleep(ACC_DELAY)

def train_slow_down (current_speed):
    speed = current_speed
    while speed > 0:
        speed -= 0.1
        if speed <= 0 :
            m1.stop()
        else:
            m1.forward(speed)
        sleep(ACC_DELAY)

# Go immediately to set speed
def train_set_speed (speed):
    m1.forward(speed)

def main():
    while True:
        print ("Leaving the station")
        # Accelerate up to full speed
        train_speed_up(MAX_SPEED)
        # wait until it triggers reed switch
        print ("Going to station")
        reed_switch.wait_for_press()
        print ("Stopping at station")
        train_slow_down(MAX_SPEED)
        sleep(STATION_DELAY)
```

```
#Run the main function when this program is run
if __name__ == "__main__":
    main()
```

I've also added a new function train_set_speed() which takes the train straight to that speed without any gradual acceleration or deceleration.

You can give this file executable permission using

```
chmod +x traincontrol.py
```

which will allow you to run it the same as the previous example. The clever thing now is that you can also import it into another program that can use the functions without running the main part of the code. To set the speed to 0.3, we can use the following short piece of code:

```
#!/usr/bin/python3
from traincontrol import *

train_set_speed(0.3)
```

As long as this is in the same directory as traincontrol.py, it will load the existing program as a module and run the train_set_speed() function.

The code to run the Bottle web server and to handle the appropriate requests should be called iot-train.py and be saved in the /home/pi/iot-train directory. The code is shown in Listing 7-5.

Listing 7-5. Web app to control the model train

```
#!/usr/bin/python3
from traincontrol import *
import sys
from bottle import Bottle, route, request, response, template, static_file

app = Bottle()

# Change IPADDRESS if access is required from another computer
IPADDRESS = 'localhost'
# Where the files are stored
DOCUMENT_ROOT = '/home/pi/iot-train'
```

```
# public files
# *** WARNING ANYTHING STORED IN THE PUBLIC FOLDER WILL BE AVAILABLE TO
DOWNLOAD
@app.route ('/public/<filename>')
def server_public (filename):
    return static_file (filename, root=DOCUMENT_ROOT+"/public")

@app.route ('/')
def server_home ():
    return static_file ('index.html', root=DOCUMENT_ROOT+"/public")

@app.route ('/control')
def control_train():
    getvar_dict = request.query.decode()
    speed = int(request.query.speed)
    if (speed >=0 and speed <= 10):
        command_speed = speed/10
        train_set_speed(command_speed)
        return 'Speed changed to '+str(speed)
    else:
        return 'Invalid command'

app.run(host=IPADDRESS)
```

First, this imports the relevant modules, including traincontrol.py file. When importing the Bottle module, I have included a few functions that we won't actually be using in this program, but they can be useful for other programs, so I've left them in.

The app is created as a Bottle, which is in effect a web server. Next is the entry IPADDRESS = 'localhost' which sets the IP address that the web server listens on. With this set to localhost, it will only be possible to access the server from a web browser running on the Raspberry Pi. If you would like to be able to access this from anywhere on the local network (and depending upon your router configuration potentially the Internet), then change this to 0.0.0.0 which means all addresses.

The Bottle module then uses the @app.route entries to determine what to do with incoming requests. The first says that if we get a request for file in the /public folder, then return a static_file (a normal file) from the public directory.

The second @app.route entry relates to "/" which is the web server root directory where we return the default file *index.html*. The final @app.route directive is where the real work happens. This says that if an entry begins with /control, then run the `control_train()` function. In that function, we then get the value of the speed argument from the get request and convert it to an integer using the following lines:

```
getvar_dict = request.query.decode()
speed = int(request.query.speed)
```

To make the application a little more user-friendly, it uses integer values from 0 to 10 to represent the speed. The code checks that the request is valid by making sure it is a number larger than or equal to 0 and smaller than or equal to 10. This is an important step as you should never accept information provided from a web request unless it has been checked first. If this was not the case, then someone could try and insert something inappropriate which could compromise the security of the web server or the computer. The value is then divided by 10 to convert it into the correct range for the motor function. This value is then used to call train_set_speed() and set the speed of the motor.

That function then returns a status message to confirm that the command was successful or not. In this case, it's just a single line of text which we can handle in the web browser using JavaScript.

The final step is to start the web server using

```
app.run(host=IPADDRESS)
```

I have included the host parameter to change the address, as otherwise it will only listen on the localhost. You can also specify a port parameter, but I have left it set at the default port of 8080.

That is the entire web server code. This is in my opinion one of the great things about Python, in that thanks to the use of modules that others have already created you can include an entire web server in less than 40 lines of code.

With the web server part complete, you also need the HTML code and some JavaScript to send the appropriate requests to the web server. This will all be contained within a single file called index.html. The file in Listing 7-6 should be saved in the /home/pi/iot-train/public directory as a file index.html.

Listing 7-6. HTML file for IOT train

```
<!doctype html>
<html lang="en">
<head>
<meta charset="UTF-8">
<title>Model Train Control</title>
<!-- Add Jquery -->
<script type="text/javascript" src="/public/jquery-3.5.1.min.js"></script>
</head>
<body>
<h1>Train Control</h1>

<div id="status">...</div>

<select id="speed">
    <option selected="selected">0</option>
    <option>1</option>
    <option>2</option>
    <option>3</option>
    <option>4</option>
    <option>5</option>
    <option>6</option>
    <option>7</option>
    <option>8</option>
    <option>9</option>
    <option>10</option>
</select>

<script>
// call back function from ajax code
function updateStatus (data) {
    // Update screen with new status
    $('#status').html(data);
}
```

```
function changeSpeed (speed) {
    $.get('/control', 'speed='+speed, updateStatus);
}

$( "#speed" ).change(function() {
    changeSpeed($( "#speed" ).val())
});

</script>
</body>
</html>
```

It is beyond the scope of this book to teach HTML and JavaScript as well, but I will still give a few pointers to how the code works. One of the first things is to load the JavaScript jQuery library using

```
<script type="text/javascript" src="/public/jquery-3.5.1.min.js"></script>
```

This library makes programming in JavaScript much easier and helps to write portable JavaScript that can work across different web browsers.

The next part is very basic html which is not going to look particularly nice (which is best achieved using CSS) but provides a title, a text position that we will use for status messages, and an option allowing the user to select the speed.

The rest is a block of inline JavaScript. For more advanced programs, this would normally be broken out into a separate JavaScript file, but to keep it simple, it has just been included in the HTML file for this example. There are two regular functions, updateStatus which receives the response from the web server and updates the status text and changeSpeed which sends a get request to the web server.

The last block of JavaScript code overrides the change function of the select element, so that whenever it changes, it calls the changeSpeed() function.

To start the server, give it executable permissions using

```
chmod +x iot-train.py
```

Start the application using

```
./iot-train.py
```

You will see a status message which informs you of the address and port the server is listening on. Whenever a new request is received, it will also show a line of text showing what is being requested and the status code.

To access the page, point the web browser at the address of the site followed by :8080 for the port number. This is shown using the default localhost in Figure 7-8.

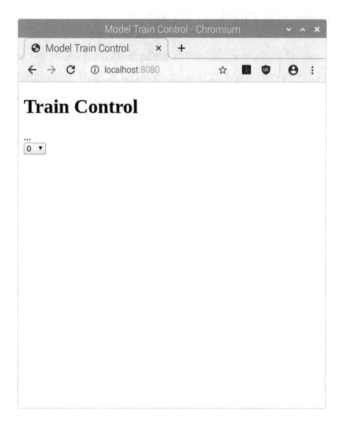

Figure 7-8. *Screenshot of the web page for the IoT train control*

There is no validation or other security checking used in this program. This means that anyone else on the same network can control your model train or, if you forward to the Internet, then anyone around the world. For a hobby train set, that is likely not a concern, but if you are looking at using this to control something more important, then you should add further code to restrict who can use the program.

Caution   If using Python Bottle to control something more important than a toy, then ensure you add appropriate controls so only authorized people can control it.

The program works but is not particularly great to see or use. You may want to look at improving this using graphical buttons or Cascading Style Sheets (CSS).

Running Python Programs As a Service
Starting a Program During Startup

One thing with the model train web browser code is that it needs to be started manually whenever the computer is restarted. If the Raspberry Pi is to be permanently connected to the train setup, then it is much easier if the program starts automatically when the Raspberry Pi is powered on. This can also be useful for any other server type programs. This will look at setting the Internet of Things train program to run during startup, but this can equally apply for other services.

On the Raspberry Pi OS, the startup and running processes are controlled using systemd. This provides a way to start, monitor, and manage background programs. It has a lot of features which can make it complex, but the part we are going to use is straightforward.

To have the program start automatically during the boot process, you need to create a new service file. The service file needs to be stored in the /etc/systemd/system/ directory and end with the suffix ".service". I called this iot-train.service. The file needs to be created as the root user using sudo.

If creating through a graphical screen, then you can use

```
sudo mousepad /etc/systemd/system/iot-train.service
```

Add the details shown in Listing 7-7.

Listing 7-7. Systemd configuration file for IOT train service

```
[Unit]
Description=IOT Model Train Control
Wants=network-online.target
After=network-online.target

[Service]
Type=simple
ExecStart=/home/pi/iot-train/iot-train.py
User=pi
```

```
[Install]
WantedBy=default.target
```

The Unit section provides generic information that applies to the service. The first entry in this section is a description entry which provides a user-friendly description of what the service is used for. The Wants entry will ensure that the network is also started, and the After entry means that this will not start until after the network is online. It is a good idea to include these in for most network applications unless there is a need to wait until another service is started first, in which case enter the name of that service in the After entry instead.

The Service section provides the options related to this service. The option Type=simple is used for a standard program that has not been specifically designed as a server application.

The ExecStart option specifies the command that is run for this service. In this case, it calls our web server application.

The User option gives the username that the program will run under, in this case the user pi.

The Install section includes the WantedBy=default.target entry. This indicates that we want the service to start when the computer is running at the default runlevel.

The service can now be started using the command

```
sudo systemctl start iot-train
```

You can check the status of the program using

```
sudo systemctl status iot-train
```

To set it to start automatically, use

```
sudo systemctl enable iot-train
```

You should now be able to reboot the computer and the service will start up automatically. You just need to point your web browser at http://localhost:8080 and you should be able to control the model train.

Running Programs at a Regular Interval with Cron

Another useful feature is being able to run a program at regular intervals. This is useful to be able to run tasks at set times of each day or to run a command on the same day each week. With the move to the new Systemd scheduling, this can be achieved using that, but this will look at the older and currently better-known method of cron.

Cron is a scheduler that can run commands at regular intervals. It is often referred to as crontab which is a name of its configuration file and the tool used to edit the configuration file.

Each user can have their own list of cron tasks to be run at set times. These can be edited using crontab -e which will load the current crontab entries into the default editor. If you have not yet set a default editor, then it will ask which editor to use recommending nano as the easiest to use. Once opened, the file should be edited to show any tasks that are required, saved (use Ctrl-o from within nano), and then choose exit (Ctrl-x). Upon exiting, the crontab will be loaded and take effect, whenever one of the conditions is met.

An example crontab entry is shown in Listing 7-8.

Listing 7-8. Example crontab file

```
# m h   dom mon dow    command
0 9 * * 6,7 /home/pi/ledtimer.py
30 15 * * 1-5 /home/pi/ledtimer.py
0 11 * * * /home/pi/ledtimer.py
```

Listing 7-8 shows an example crontab edit session showing the relevant part of the file (there are several comment lines above this entry). This example shows the same command being run three times at different days and times.

Each line reflects a single entry which has five time/date fields to specify when the commands are run, followed by the command to execute. Using the preceding abbreviations, these are (in order)

```
m - Minutes - 0 to 59
h - Hours - 0 to 23
dom - Days of Month - 1 to 31
mon - Month - 1 to 12 or JAN-DEC
dow - Day of week - 1 to 7 or MON-SUN (or 0 can be used for Sunday)
```

The fields can have a single value, comma-separated values, range of values, or an asterisk for any value.

To interpret the top entry in the previous example, it will run on the 0 minutes of the ninth hour (9:00 am) on any day of the month and any month of the year, but only on days of the week 6 and 7 (the weekend). The second entry will run at 15:30 on each day of the month and any month of the year, but only on weekdays (1–5). The third entry runs at 11:00 every day.

As well as the time-based entries, there are other special commands that can be used such as @weekly (midnight on Sunday morning), @hourly once an hour, and @reboot which runs when the system is started.

Controlling Color Light Strips Using NeoPixels

Another fun project is using NeoPixel color LEDs. NeoPixels is a name used by supplier Adafruit; these are also known by other suppliers as pixel strips, individually addressable RGB LEDs, or by the code WS2811, WS2812, or WS281x.

These LEDs can be connected together into a long string. I have a flexible strip which has 150 of these LEDs mounted, all of which are controlled by a single data connection, plus the power supply. A picture of a slightly shorter strip of these LEDs in action is shown in Figure 7-9.

Figure 7-9. *Color light strip using RGB LEDs*

The LEDs are available in a variety of different shapes and configurations. These vary from single LEDs designed to be soldered onto a circuit board to circles, strips, and a matrix able to create simple pictures.

For each LED, there is a small IC which is usually mounted underneath the LED or sometimes within the LED itself. The IC used is normally a variant of WS2811 or WS2812. The Raspberry Pi must encode the information with precise timing so that the IC can interpret the data. This is done by the IC reading, taking in the information for all LEDs on the string, removing the information for its own LED, and then passing the rest through to the output. The first in the sequence will need to pass through the information for all other LEDs, whereas the last one only sees the information for its own LED.

The Raspberry Pi GPIO port is 3.3V, but these RGB LEDs work at their brightest when powered from a 5V power supply. The signal should be at least 0.7 times the supply voltage, which is 3.5V. The maximum the GPIO can give is 3.3V, although it can be much lower. If you connect the GPIO output directly to the pixels, then there is a good chance it will work but not always, and therefore a level shifter is needed to increase the output voltage from the GPIO port to 5V. The basic MOSFET circuit is in the previous chapter in Figure 6-2; it is repeated in Figure 7-10 to save you searching back through the book.

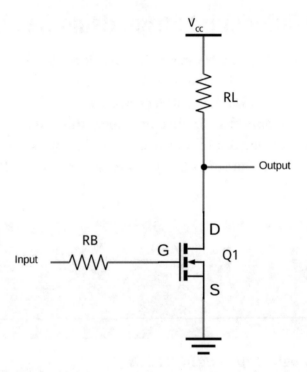

Figure 7-10. *MOSFET level shift circuit for controlling RGB LEDs*

You may recall that this circuit is an inverting buffer, which gives a low output when the input is high and vice versa. This is something that can be resolved by changing a setting in the software. An alternative circuit is to use a 74HCT125 non-inverting buffer IC or a bidirectional level shifter such as the one used for the I²C LCD display in Chapter 6 (only one direction will be used).

The input to the level shifter should be connected to GPIO port 18 on the Raspberry Pi, which is the output that supports hardware PWM.

The components I have used for this circuit are

- RL – 2.2kΩ

- RB – 470Ω

- Q1 – 2N70000

I have shown an example of the circuit using breadboard-mounted NeoPixels in Figure 7-11. This is a good way to get started using NeoPixels. You can then move up to controlling larger strips by replacing the breadboard-mounted NeoPixels with a connection to an external pixel strip.

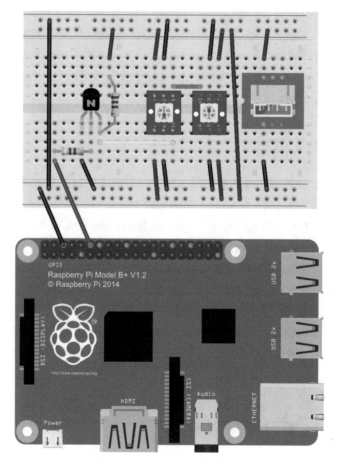

Figure 7-11. *Breadboard version of NeoPixel circuit*

You will notice that there is an external power supply in the form of a micro-USB connector, the same type of connector used to power some models of the Raspberry Pi. This is not required when using only two LEDs, but a more powerful power supply is required for larger LED strips.

Also note that there are two power supply connections from the same power supply to each of the NeoPixels. This is not actually required; there are two +V and two GND connections which are there to make daisy-chaining easier. They have been included here so that you can see which pins are available for connecting to the power supply. You just need to ensure that one +V and one GND connection is connected to the 5V power supply to each NeoPixel.

The LEDs are mounted the opposite way around in the breadboard layout, which means that data out from the left LED is on the same side of the breadboard as data in on the right one. This makes it easier to connect the data out and data in connections together (as shown by the orange wire in the diagram). Normally, there will be multiple LEDs connected in series often on a long LED strip.

Powering RGB LEDs

According to the datasheet for the WS2812, each RGB LED consists of three different LEDs in a single package. Each of these LEDs can use up to 20mA when fully lit. With the color set to white and maximum brightness, these can draw up to 60mA per LED. If you have 150 LEDs, then this needs a 9A power supply. In reality, I found the LEDs that I used actually ran at around half that, but you do need to ensure that you have a fairly substantial power supply which needs to be able to supply sufficient current to all the LEDs without overheating.

The ground connection of the power supply should be connected to the ground of the Raspberry Pi, but the 5V connection from the power supply should not be directly connected to the Raspberry Pi.

Installing the Python Module

There is a Python module which can be used to generate the signal that drives the WS281x ICs. This is available from `https://github.com/rpi-ws281x/rpi-ws281x-python`.

It is also included in the Python PIP libraries. The easiest way to install is using the command

```
sudo pip3 install rpi_ws281x
```

To achieve the specific timing needed, the Raspberry Pi makes use of the PWM clock on the Raspberry Pi. To allow the Raspberry Pi to manipulate this clock, the audio driver needs to be disabled. This prevents you from using the standard audio output.

This is achieved by editing the file /etc/modprobe.d/raspi-blacklist.conf and adding the following entry:

```
blacklist snd_bcm2835
```

The Raspberry Pi will need to be rebooted after adding the sound module to the blacklist.

Controlling RGB LEDs from Python

You can now use the PixelStrip module to control the RGB LEDs. I have created a simple program to test the circuit and to show how to change the color of the LEDs. As this is designed for the circuit in Figure 7-11, it is written for only two LEDs. This is shown in Listing 7-9 named pixel-test.py.

Listing 7-9. Pixel strip test program

```
#!/usr/bin/python3
from rpi_ws281x import PixelStrip, Color
import time

LEDCOUNT = 2          # Number of LEDs
GPIOPIN = 18
FREQ = 800000
DMA = 5
INVERT = True         # Invert required when using inverting buffer
BRIGHTNESS = 255

strip = PixelStrip(LEDCOUNT, GPIOPIN, FREQ, DMA, INVERT, BRIGHTNESS)
# Initialize the library (must be called once before other functions).
strip.begin()
```

```python
while True:
    # First LED white
    strip.setPixelColor(0, Color(255,255,255))
    strip.setPixelColor(1, Color(0,0,0))
    strip.show()
    time.sleep(0.5)
    # Second LED white
    strip.setPixelColor(0, Color(0,0,0))
    strip.setPixelColor(1, Color(255,255,255))
    strip.show()
    time.sleep(1)
    # LEDs Red
    strip.setPixelColor(0, Color(255,0,0))
    strip.setPixelColor(1, Color(255,0,0))
    strip.show()
    time.sleep(0.5)
    # LEDs Green
    strip.setPixelColor(0, Color(0,255,0))
    strip.setPixelColor(1, Color(0,255,0))
    strip.show()
    time.sleep(0.5)
    # LEDs Blue
    strip.setPixelColor(0, Color(0,0,255))
    strip.setPixelColor(1, Color(0,0,255))
    strip.show()
    time.sleep(1)
```

The settings are defined at the top of the file, which among other things define the number of LEDs and brightness. It also sets the invert option which counteracts the inverting nature of the MOSFET circuit. These values are passed to the PixelStrip when creating the strip object.

After creating the strip object, the begin method needs to be run before setting the color of each LED. The method to set the color is setPixelColor, which takes the pixel number and a Color value.

The Color value is created using three colors Red, Green and Blue with values between 0 and 255. Turning them all on (255, 255, 255) turns the LED white, and setting them all to zero (0, 0, 0) turns it off. We then turn only the Red, Green, and Blue parts in turn. Combining these in different amounts can give different colors.

After setting the color for each pixel, strip.show() needs to be called to send the update to the strip.

The NeoPixel library needs to have administrator privileges to access the GPIO ports. The program should therefore be run using sudo which runs it under the root user. I have called the file pixel-test.py so this would be run as

```
sudo ./pixel-test.py
```

Creating a Graphical Application Using Pygame Zero

The final stage for our LED project is to create a graphical application, also known as a graphical user interface or GUI. Creating a graphical program has a bad reputation for being hard to do and needing a lot of code to get started. Unfortunately, this reputation is often deserved as the very nature of graphical applications does involve a lot of code due to the need to create the graphical windows, to handle mouse-clicks, and to keep the program running in the background. Some programming languages have been designed to make this easier for the beginner, but they have not had the access to the hardware that we need for controlling electronics.

Fortunately, Pygame Zero has come to the rescue. In much the same way that GPIO Zero has made programming the GPIO port easier, Pygame Zero is built on top of the Pygame games' programming module, making it easier to create a graphical application. As it is still based on Python, you can use it along with all the GPIO Zero code used previously.

Pygame Zero is useful for creating games, but in this, I have created a very basic program using rectangular buttons to select one of the sequences. This is designed for controlling several LEDs, and while most of it will work with the two LEDs on the breadboard, it is really designed for connecting to a string of LEDs. The basic graphical interface is shown in Figure 7-12.

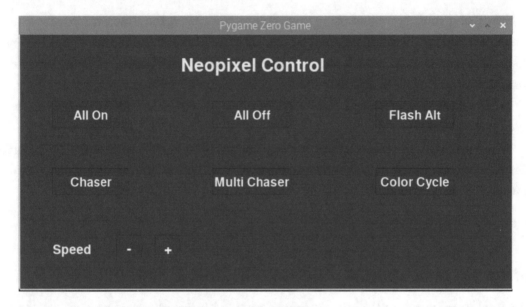

Figure 7-12. *Graphical application for RGB LED control*

I saved the code to a file pixel-gui.py. The code is provided in Listing 7-10, which needs to be run as root using the sudo command.

Listing 7-10. Pixel strip test program

```
#!/usr/bin/pgzrun
from rpi_ws281x import PixelStrip, Color
import time

LEDCOUNT = 10
GPIOPIN = 18
FREQ = 800000
DMA = 5
INVERT = True       # Invert required when using inverting buffer
BRIGHTNESS = 255

WIDTH = 760
HEIGHT = 380

BUTTON_COLOR = 40,40,200
WHITE = 255, 255, 255
```

```
buttonText = (
    u"All On",
    u"All Off",
    u"Flash Alt",
    u"Chaser",
    u"Multi Chaser",
    u"Color Cycle"
)
buttonRect = (
    Rect(50, 100, 120, 40),
    Rect(300, 100, 120, 40),
    Rect(550, 100, 120, 40),
    Rect(50, 200, 120, 40),
    Rect(300, 200, 120, 40),
    Rect(550, 200, 120, 40)
)
minusRect = Rect(150, 300, 40, 40)
plusRect = Rect(210, 300, 40, 40)

# Delay counts is number of updates before change in 60th of a second
delay_counts = 30
seq_number = 0
sequence = "All On" # Start with all lights on
timer = 0

# Setup Pixel Strip
strip = PixelStrip(LEDCOUNT, GPIOPIN, FREQ, DMA, INVERT, BRIGHTNESS)
# Initialize the library (must be called once before other functions).
strip.begin()

def draw():
    screen.fill((80,80,80))

    screen.draw.text(
        "Neopixel Control",
        centerx = 360, top = 30,
        fontsize=40,
```

```python
        color=WHITE
    )

box = []
for i in range(len(buttonRect)):
    box.append(buttonRect[i].inflate (-1, -1))
    screen.draw.filled_rect(box[i], BUTTON_COLOR)
    screen.draw.text(
        buttonText[i],
        centerx = box[i][0] + 60, centery = box[i][1] + 20,
        fontsize=28,
        color=WHITE
    )

screen.draw.text(
    "Speed",
    (50, 310),
    fontsize=28,
    color=WHITE
    )

boxMinus = minusRect.inflate(-1, -1)
screen.draw.filled_rect(boxMinus, BUTTON_COLOR)
screen.draw.text(
    "-",
    centerx = boxMinus[0] + 20, centery = boxMinus[1] + 20,
    fontsize=32,
    color=WHITE
)

boxPlus = plusRect.inflate(-1, -1)
screen.draw.filled_rect(boxPlus, BUTTON_COLOR)
screen.draw.text(
    "+",
    centerx = boxPlus[0] + 20, centery = boxPlus[1] + 20,
    fontsize=32,
    color=WHITE
)
```

```python
def on_mouse_down(button, pos):
    global seq_changed, sequence, delay_counts
    x, y = pos
    # Check position of main buttons
    for i in range(len(buttonRect)):
        if buttonRect[i].collidepoint(x,y) :
            sequence = buttonText[i]
    # Check position of speed buttons
    if minusRect.collidepoint(x,y) :
        delay_counts = delay_counts + 5
    if plusRect.collidepoint(x,y) :
        delay_counts = delay_counts - 5

def update():
    global timer
    global delay_counts
    global seq_number
    timer = timer +1
    if (timer > delay_counts) :
        seq_number += 1
        updseq ()
        timer = 0

def updseq () :
    global sequence
    if (sequence == "All On"):
        seq_all_on()
    if (sequence == "All Off"):
        seq_all_off()
    if (sequence == "Flash Alt"):
        seq_flash_alt ()
    if (sequence == "Chaser"):
        seq_chaser ()
    if (sequence == "Multi Chaser"):
        seq_multi_chaser ()
    if (sequence == "Color Cycle"):
        seq_color_cycle()
```

```python
###### Sequences
def seq_all_on():
    for x in range (LEDCOUNT):
        strip.setPixelColor(x, Color(255,255,255))
    strip.show()

def seq_all_off():
    for x in range (LEDCOUNT):
        strip.setPixelColor(x, Color(0,0,0))
    strip.show()

# Uses 2 seq numbers for odd and even
def seq_flash_alt ():
    global seq_number
    if (seq_number > 1):
        seq_number = 0
    colors = [Color(255, 255, 255), Color(0,0,0)]
    for x in range (LEDCOUNT):
        if (x %2 == 1):
            strip.setPixelColor(x, colors[seq_number])
        else:
            strip.setPixelColor(x, colors[1-seq_number])
    strip.show()

def seq_chaser ():
    global seq_number
    if (seq_number >= LEDCOUNT):
        seq_number = 0
    for x in range (LEDCOUNT):
        strip.setPixelColor(x, Color(0,0,0))
    strip.setPixelColor(seq_number, Color(255,255,255))
    strip.show()

# Needs at least 6 pixels preferably more for this to look correct
def seq_multi_chaser ():
    global seq_number
    if (seq_number >= LEDCOUNT):
        seq_number = 0
```

```python
    colors = [Color(255, 0, 0), Color(0,255,0), Color(0,0,255)]
    for x in range (LEDCOUNT):
        strip.setPixelColor(x, Color(0,0,0))
    # Set current, one before and one after
    # seq number is always valid
    strip.setPixelColor(seq_number, colors[1])
    # Ensure there is one before - if not put it at the end of the row
    if (seq_number > 0) :
        strip.setPixelColor(seq_number-1, colors[0])
    else:
        strip.setPixelColor(LEDCOUNT-1, colors[0])
    # Ensure there is one after - if not put it at the start of the row
    if (seq_number < LEDCOUNT-1) :
        strip.setPixelColor(seq_number+1, colors[2])
    else:
        strip.setPixelColor(0, colors[2])

    strip.show()

def seq_color_cycle():
    global seq_number
    colors = [Color(248,12,18), Color(255,51,17), Color(255,102,68), \
        Color(254,174,45), Color(208,195,16), Color(105,208,37), \
        Color(18,189,185), Color(68,68,221), Color(59,12,189)]
    if (seq_number >= len(colors)):
        seq_number = 0

    # seq number is used to define the first color then we increment
    through the colors
    this_color = seq_number
    for x in range(LEDCOUNT):
        strip.setPixelColor(x, colors[this_color])
        this_color = this_color + 1;
        if (this_color >= len(colors)):
            this_color = 0
    strip.show()
```

Despite this code being much shorter than other GUI programs, it's still quite a lot of code, although some of this is for the LED sequences rather than the GUI program itself. I will not go through the code in detail, but will pick out the important things, especially in how they relate to Pygame Zero.

A first thing to note is that the shebang entry does not call the python3 interpreter, but instead calls pgzrun:

```
#!/usr/bin/pgzrun
```

This still uses Python, but running through pgzrun will perform the steps required to set up the GUI environment.

Next are the usual PixelStrip configuration details. These are the same as used previously, although the LEDCOUNT has been increased to 10. I recommend having an LED strip with at least eight LEDs to be able to see some of the effects.

The next part is a WIDTH and HEIGHT constant, which determine the size of the graphical window. In this case, the size has been chosen because it fits nicely on the official Raspberry Pi touch screen.

```
WIDTH = 760
HEIGHT = 380
```

There are two lists: buttonText which provides the texts for the buttons and buttonRect which provides a rectangle that will be used for creating the buttons. The Rect object is created using x and y as the first two parameters and then the size along the x and y axis for the next two parameters. There are then two more rectangles used for buttons to change the speed.

After setting up a few more variables (which will be used as global variables that can be accessed from the other functions), the PixelStrip object is created and initialized. This is the end of the main part of the code, and the rest of the code are all functions. In a normal Python program, we would need some more code to trigger these functions, but this is handled by Pygame Zero which calls the draw, on_mouse_down, and update functions as appropriate.

The draw function sets up the layout on the screen. You will see screen.draw.text which puts some text on the application and screen.draw.filled_rect which draws a rectangle that is used for the buttons.

The on_mouse_down function is called whenever the mouse button is pressed. The code checks whether the mouse is over a button at the time (using collidepoint), and if so, then it updates the sequence global variable or the speed of the sequence using the delay_counts variable.

The update function is called periodically by Pygame Zero, and it is this function that we use to update the sequence. This function is normally called 60 times each second, which is why our delay_counts variable uses 60th of a second for each delay count. If we are within the current cycle, then we just increment our timer, but once the timer is larger than delay_counts, we update the sequence.

The updseq function is not directly related to Pygame Zero; it is instead one I added myself. It is called once each time we update the pixels. It calls the appropriate sequence function, which is in the section after the line

```
###### Sequences
```

The functions below the sequences update the LED strip based on the sequence number. The seq_all_on and seq_all_off functions are self-explanatory. The seq_flash_alt function uses the modulo operation "%". This performs a division operation and provides the remainder as the result of the operation. In this case, by performing a modulo of two, we will get a 0 for an even number and a 1 for an odd number.

The chaser function turns all the LEDs off and then turns the appropriate LEDs on. The final function is a color cycle function. Rather than calculate the individual colors using sine waves and other mathematical functions, I have stored the colors into a list to make this easier to understand.

Add executable permission using

```
chmod +x pixel-gui.py
```

The program is then launched using

```
sudo ./pixel-gui.py
```

Adding an Icon to the Raspberry Pi Desktop

You can also icon to the Raspberry Pi Desktop menu launcher. That way, the program can be run from the application menu instead of needing to run it from the command line. The Raspberry Pi OS includes a menu editor which can be used to add the program to the start menu.

Launch the configuration tool from the Preferences menu and Main Menu Editor. This is shown in Figure 7-13.

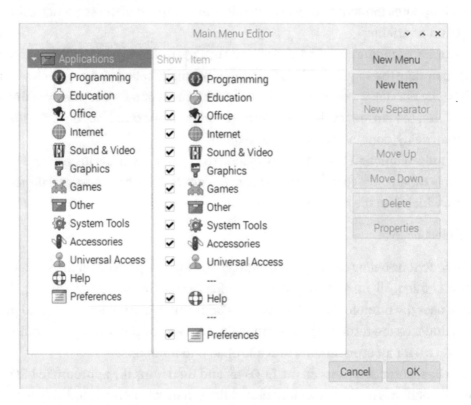

Figure 7-13. *Raspberry Pi Main Menu Editor*

The menu item can be added to one of the existing menus or create a new category using the New Menu button. Some of the menus may not be displayed initially as they will only show if they have an active item in the menu. After choosing the other menu from the left, choose the New Item button on the right. This is shown in Figure 7-14.

Figure 7-14. *Raspberry Pi adding a new application icon*

Give the application a name that is used on the menu. In the command, enter the full command as it would be executed from the terminal, including the sudo command. A comment can also be added if you wish. To change the icon, click the box on the left-hand side and then find an appropriate icon image from your computer. A suitably sized .gif or .png file works well, and the one I used is included in the source code. After you click OK, the menu should update to show the new application. If the menu does not appear, then you may need to reboot the Raspberry Pi.

More Linux and Programming

This chapter has covered some Python programming that can be used to control electronics connected to the Raspberry Pi. It covered basic Python concepts such as making decisions within programs and how you can create functions to make coding easier and facilitate code reuse. It then went on to show how to create a web application using Python Bottle and a GUI application using Pygame Zero.

This has been based around automated control of a model railway and the use of PixelStrips which can be used to create impressive lighting displays. This now gives the skills to create bigger and more complex programs.

The techniques covered in this chapter should give you the ability to improve these and other programs. Some suggestions are to add more sequences to the disco and pixel strip lights and to write a graphical program to control the model train using a touch screen. You could also look at improving the web interface for the IoT train so that it changes speed in a more realistic way.

This chapter has also covered some aspects of the operating system that can be used for your programs. This includes how to add software, how to register it as a service, having it start up at boot time, run at set times, and adding a menu entry for a GUI application.

The next chapter will look at the Raspberry Pi camera and how it can be controlled using electronic sensors.

CHAPTER 8

Using the Raspberry Pi Camera

In this chapter, we will look at the Raspberry Pi camera and how it can be controlled using electronic sensors. This will look at using the camera to take photographs automatically based on a PIR sensor and how to use the camera for creating stop frame animation.

Cameras Available for the Raspberry Pi

This will start by setting up the Raspberry Pi camera by connecting it to the camera connector directly on the Raspberry Pi. This camera connector has been included on all versions of the Raspberry Pi, except for the early versions of the Pi Zero.

At the time of writing, there are three different official cameras. The camera module V2, the Pi NoIR module V2, and the Raspberry Pi high-quality camera. The first two modules have an 8-megapixel sensor with a fixed focus. The standard module is useful for most general use; the Pi NoIR camera is the same but without the infrared filter suitable for night photography using infrared lighting. The high-quality camera is a 12.3-megapixel camera which needs a separate C- or CS-mount lens to be attached; it provides better quality photos but needs the user to manually adjust the aperture and focus.

All the official cameras use the camera connector. The camera connector provides direct access between the camera and the processor which is more efficient than using a webcam which connects using the USB protocol.

To connect the camera, lift the tab on the connector next to the HDMI connector (HDMI 1 on the Raspberry Pi 4). Insert the ribbon cable into the connector with the blue side facing away from the HDMI connector. Push the tab back down which should hold the camera cable firmly into place. Figure 8-1 shows a Raspberry Pi with the camera module connected.

© Stewart Watkiss 2020
S. Watkiss, *Learn Electronics with Raspberry Pi*, https://doi.org/10.1007/978-1-4842-6348-8_8

Figure 8-1. *Circuit diagram for the infrared receiver circuit*

The camera module needs to be enabled through the Raspberry Pi configuration tool. From the menu, choose Preferences and then Raspberry Pi Configuration. The camera is enabled through the Interfaces tab. This is shown in Figure 8-2. After enabling the camera, you will need to reboot before you can use it.

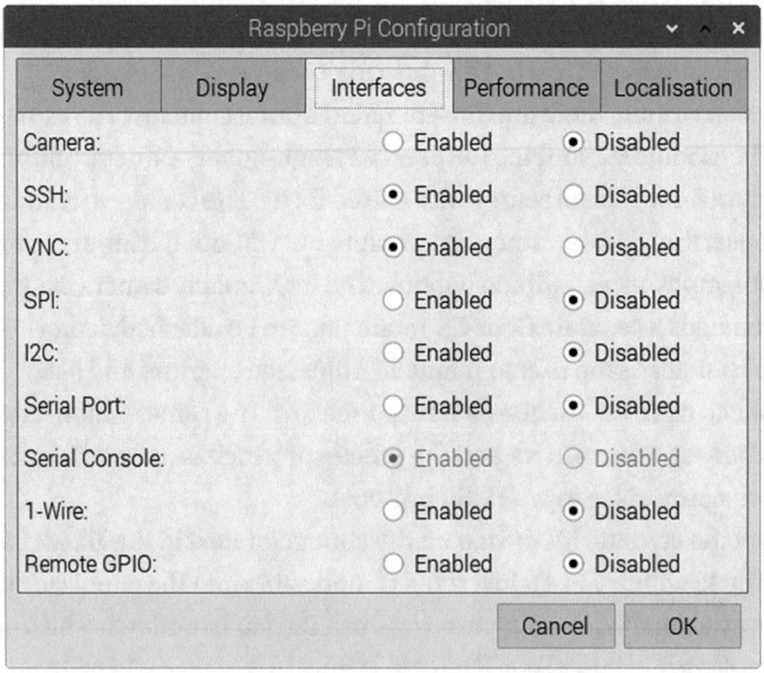

Raspberry Pi Configuration				⌄ ^ ✕
System	Display	Interfaces	Performance	Localisation
Camera:		○ Enabled	◉ Disabled	
SSH:		◉ Enabled	○ Disabled	
VNC:		◉ Enabled	○ Disabled	
SPI:		○ Enabled	◉ Disabled	
I2C:		○ Enabled	◉ Disabled	
Serial Port:		○ Enabled	◉ Disabled	
Serial Console:		◉ Enabled	○ Disabled	
1-Wire:		○ Enabled	◉ Disabled	
Remote GPIO:		○ Enabled	◉ Disabled	
			Cancel	OK

Figure 8-2. *Configuration screen to enable the Raspberry Pi camera*

Once connected and enabled, you can test if the camera works using the raspistill command:

```
raspistill -o photo1.jpg
```

This will take a photograph and store it as photo1.jpg. If you have a screen directly connected to the HDMI port, then you will see a preview prior to the photograph being taken; otherwise, you will just notice a delay before the photo.

Assuming this command works, you can now proceed to controlling the camera through Python. First is a simple program that takes a photograph and saves it to the local computer. This is shown in Listing 8-1 and is called picamera-test.py in the source code.

Listing 8-1. Simple program to test the Raspberry Pi camera

```
import picamera

camera = picamera.PiCamera()

camera.capture('/home/pi/photo1.jpg')
camera.close()
```

This is a simple program which should be easy enough to follow. The first line imports the picamera module. In earlier examples, the *from* keyword was used which meant that we could use the imported module without referring to the module. In this case, the standard import keyword has been used. This means when you create your object from the picamera module, you need to prefix the instruction with the module name which is picamera.

The code then creates an instance of the picamera object called camera. You can then call the camera methods using this object. The first is called capture. As you can probably guess, this captures a photograph and saves it in a file called photo1.jpg. Finally, the close method is called to clean up the resources that were allocated.

This code has used the same filename as the previous command, so it will overwrite the file created previously. If creating multiple photos, then you will need a way of giving each file a new name. There are two simple ways we could do this. The first is to add a unique number which is incremented for each new file. This involves keeping track of the number. The alternative is to add the date and time to each file, which will make it easy to create the filename. Both options have their pros and cons; I think that using the date is a good way of doing this. This will use the time module and the strftime method which formats the time into a readable date format. The date format used is the ISO

8601 date format, which formats the date in order of the most significant part of the date first. This provides the date in the form of *year-month-day*T*hour:minutes:seconds*. The advantages of this date format are that ordering the files by filename will put them into chronological order and that it is a date format that is recognized anywhere around the world. The method time.gmtime() can be used to get the current time, which is in seconds since the UNIX epoch (1970). This is converted to a string which is stored in timestring. It is then included in the filename.

The updated code is shown in Listing 8-2 and saved as camera-unique.py.

Listing 8-2. Saving camera photos as a unique name

```
import picamera
import time

camera = picamera.PiCamera()

timestring = time.strftime("%Y-%m-%dT%H:%M:%S", time.gmtime())

camera.capture('/home/pi/photo_'+timestring+'.jpg')
camera.close()
```

There is a potential problem with this solution. The Raspberry Pi does not include a real-time clock. If the Raspberry Pi has a network connection (wired or wireless), then it will update the time of the Raspberry Pi using network time servers. If the Raspberry Pi does not have a network connection (such as an outdoor sensor to monitor wildlife), then the date and time may not be correct. If that is the case, the files can be renamed when they are transferred to another computer for later viewing.

Using the PIR Motion Sensor to Trigger the Camera

Chapter 5 showed how a PIR motion sensor could be connected to the Raspberry Pi to detect when someone passes nearby. This can be used in conjunction with the camera to take a photo of the person as they walk near so that you know who has been entering a certain area. It can also be used for detecting and taking photographs of wildlife.

To use the next project, the PIR should be connected to the GPIO as in the diagram in Figure 5-2. The next program will combine the code form the earlier PIR sensor with the camera code. This will wait for motion to be detected and then capture a photo of whoever or whatever triggered the sensor. The files will have the date and time included in the filename.

The complete source code for this is in Listing 8-3 which you can name camera-pir.py.

Listing 8-3. PIR triggered camera

```
from gpiozero import MotionSensor
import picamera
import time

# PIR sensor on GPIO pin 4
PIR_SENSOR_PIN = 4
# Minimum time between captures
DELAY = 5

# Create pir and camera objects
pir = MotionSensor(PIR_SENSOR_PIN)
camera = picamera.PiCamera()

while True:
    pir.wait_for_motion()
    timestring = time.strftime("%Y-%m-%dT%H:%M:%S", time.gmtime())
    print ("Taking photo " +timestring)
    camera.capture('/home/pi/photo_'+timestring+'.jpg')
    time.sleep(DELAY)
```

This code is primarily a merge of the PIR and camera programs listed previously. The main change is for the camera code to be included in the while loop. The camera. close entry has also been removed, as it will continue capturing photos. Ideally, the close should still be called when the program is terminated; however, this code runs continuously (unless it is stopped from Mu or Ctrl-c is pressed), so the close has been removed.

The print statement shows the time that the photograph is taken. This is useful during testing but can be removed once the program is proved to be working correctly.

The code is saved as camera-pir.py which can then be run from the command line. You may want to look at this code running automatically when the Raspberry Pi is started, which was explained in Chapter 7.

Stop Motion Videos

A popular use of the Raspberry Pi and the camera module is in creating stop motion videos. This is where you create a video story by taking photographs for each frame in the video. For a professional video, you may look at taking around 24 photographs for each second of video; for a home video, around ten frames per second would be a good figure. This still needs a lot of photographs to be taken, so to make this easier, this will show how you can add a simple push button to take the photos and then how they can be combined into a video.

Crimp Connections

The buttons used so far have been mounted on a breadboard, but for this, it is easier to have a button on a lead so that it can be placed in a more convenient position. The push button that I chose has the option for soldering on the connector tabs, or they can instead be connected using a 2.8mm female spade connector. A wire can be crimped to the space connector using a crimp tool, which removes the need for soldering. Crimp connectors are available with insulation on (often used in car electrics) or uninsulated. The uninsulated ones are better for use with the thin wires I have used. A photograph of the crimp tool and suitable connector is shown in Figure 8-3.

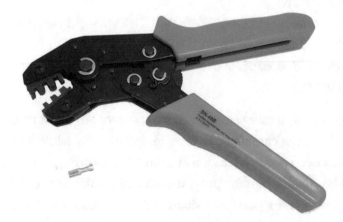

Figure 8-3. *Crimp tool with female spade connector*

I have placed the crimp connectors on male-to-female 12-inch (30cm) long jumper leads. This allows the female end to be connected directly to the GPIO ports of the Raspberry Pi and gives a reasonable amount of flexibility for positioning the button. This is shown in Figure 8-4.

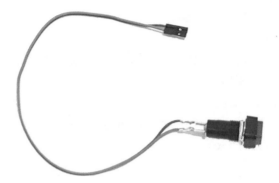

Figure 8-4. *Push-button switch with crimped jumper wires*

The button can be connected to GPIO port 10 (physical pin 19) and Ground (physical pin 6) the same as the push-button switch used in Chapter 3. The code is based on the picamera code used previously, now using the bottom and sequential number of the files. This is shown in Listing 8-4, called camera-stopmotion.py.

Listing 8-4. Stop motion camera program code

```python
#!/usr/bin/python3
from gpiozero import Button
import picamera
import os

# PIR sensor on GPIO pin 4
BUTTON_PIN = 10

image_dir = '/home/pi/film/'

# Create pir and camera objects
button = Button(BUTTON_PIN)
camera = picamera.PiCamera(resolution=(720,576))
camera.hflip=True
camera.vflip=True

image_number = 1

while True:
    filename = "{}frame{:03d}.jpg".format(image_dir, image_number)
    # Loop to ensure that filename is unique
```

```
while os.path.isfile(filename):
    image_number += 1
    filename = "{}frame{:03d}.jpg".format(image_dir, image_number)
camera.start_preview()
button.wait_for_press()
print ("Taking photo {}".format(image_number))
camera.capture(filename)
image_number += 1
```

The code uses sequential numbering of the files, which makes it easier for combining these into a video. To prevent overwriting an existing file, it has an additional while loop to check that the file doesn't already exist. If the file exists, then it increments the image number until there is no matching file. This uses os.path.isfile which will identify if the filename matches a file.

You will also see that the filename is made up using a complex string. This uses the string.format method. The curly braces {} in the first part of the string are replaced with the arguments passed to the format method. The entry {:03d} ensures that there are always three decimal places in the number which is prefixed with zeros as required.

The directory image_dir will be used to store the files. This needs to be created before running the program using

```
mkdir /home/pi/film
```

There are a couple of changes made to the way that the images are taken. The first is to reduce the resolution of the camera to 720 x 576 pixels. This creates smaller files which are easier to merge into a video. This can be left to the default but will create larger files and take longer to process. The other is required because the camera mount I used holds the camera in the upside-down position (with the cable entering from the top). The hflip and vflip attributes have been set to True to turn the camera the correct way around. This is only required if the camera is mounted upside down with the cable coming from above.

The start_preview method is also used to show a preview of the image on the screen before the button is pressed. This is so that you can see what the camera is looking at prior to taking the photograph. One restriction for the preview is that it will only show on a screen physically attached to the Raspberry Pi (e.g., through the HDMI port or if using a Raspberry Pi screen connected to the display adapter). If you want to preview the images through VNC, then you need to enable direct capture mode on the VNC server on the Raspberry Pi.

If you run the program, then it will show a preview and wait for the button to be pressed before capturing the image.

Creating the Film

Now that we have the hardware ready, it's time to focus on creating the story. Professional stop frame animation normally uses expensive flexible models. A good example of this is the *Wallace and Gromit* film, which uses models made partly out of clay. If you are good with modeling, then feel free to make your own clay models, but a good way of creating a simple animation on a small budget is to use existing toys such as Lego models. I have used a combination of Lego City and some Lego Friends, although these are not quite to the same scale, they are close enough using the Lego Friends model in the background. You can use any other kinds of models or toys, such as action figures, dolls, puppets, or plasticine monsters.

I also made some backdrops using photos of places that I've visited and different colored papers and cards for the base. You could also create model and landscapes using craft materials.

Editing the Video

You should now have a series of files starting with frame0001.jpg up to whatever number of photos that you have taken. These still images can be combined into a video using a script on the Raspberry Pi or by transferring it to another computer first. I will show you how these can be combined into a video on the Raspberry Pi, which is useful if you want to automate the creation of a video, but most likely, you will want to transfer this to a PC or laptop which will provide more flexibility.

This book is about the hardware and software used to capture the photographs rather than being a guide to video editing, but I will provide some of the basics to get you started and some suggestions for special effects.

Creating the Video on a Raspberry Pi

First, we will look at how we can combine the photos into a video using the Raspberry Pi.

The files can be converted to a video using the ffmpeg command-line program. Change to the directory holding the images and then run the following command.

```
ffmpeg -framerate 10 -pattern_type glob -i "frame*.jpg" -c:v libx264 video.mp4
```

As long as the images were padded with the zeros, this will create an MP4 video using the frames in numerical order. This is at a frame rate of ten frames per second, so you will need a lot of frames to create a reasonable length video.

You will also need a player to play back your video. If you don't have one already installed, then I recommend VLC which is available from the software manager or through

```
sudo apt install vlc
```

Editing the Video Using OpenShot

The command-line tools such as ffmpeg are OK for automatically combining videos into a sequence, but they don't offer the same flexibility as a graphical non-linear editor. Fortunately, there is a free editor called OpenShot which can be used either on the Raspberry Pi or on a PC. If running on a Raspberry Pi, then I recommend using a Raspberry Pi 4, preferably with 4GB or more memory. If your Raspberry Pi isn't powerful enough, then you may prefer to transfer the files to a PC and edit it there.

To install on the Raspberry Pi (or Debian-/Ubuntu-based Linux), you can install using

```
sudo apt install openshot
```

For OS X or Windows, you can download the program from the following link:

```
www.openshot.org/download/
```

When I installed OpenShot on the Raspberry Pi, it created a launch icon, but for some reason, that is not displayed. That can be fixed by deleting and re-adding the icon through the menu editor, or it can be launched using openshot-qt on the command line.

If you have already converted your photos to a video, then after launching OpenShot, the video can be imported using the *Import Files* option on the *File* menu or by dragging the file into the *Project Files* area. The video can then be dragged from the *Project Files* area onto one of the tracks in the timeline area at the bottom of the screen. This is shown in Figure 8-5.

Figure 8-5. *OpenShot with a simple video file*

You can combine this video with other video files or photos and then export it in a suitable format.

If you only have the still photos and haven't yet converted them to a video file, then you can import them directly into OpenShot. This is achieved using Import Files on the File menu. Select all the image files and then click Yes when asked if you would like to import the files as an Image Sequence. This will add the photos but also add a video named frame%03d.jpg. You may need to change the frame rate through file properties, and you can rename the file to something easier to remember. The %03d part of the filename is similar to using :03d in the Python string format. Unfortunately, there are different ways of representing string values in different programming languages or even within the same programming language.

The OpenShot video editor is a fully featured editor which allows you to add other photographs and video, music, or voice over. You will need to use an external microphone (such as a USB microphone) if you want to record voice directly on the Raspberry Pi.

Pan and Tilt Camera

A useful thing for the Raspberry Pi is to have the ability to change the direction that the camera is pointing. This can be achieved using servo motors, which have already been covered in Chapter 6. There is a pan and tilt unit which uses two servo motors that can be connected to the Raspberry Pi. The one used here is created by Pimoroni which is available through several Raspberry Pi suppliers. There are alternatives available, and it is possible to create your own through 3D printing, but this will concentrate on the Pimoroni model.

The pan-tilt module is available with or without a HAT for connecting to the Raspberry Pi. The HAT provides a way to communicate with the servos through I²C as well as provides an output which can be used to connect to LEDs or WS2812 LEDs. This example uses the HAT which uses an I²C interface to control the servos. An alternative is to connect the servos direct to the Raspberry Pi as previously covered in Chapter 6. I have found that the HAT is more reliable in positioning the servos compared to driving the servos directly from the Raspberry Pi using software PWM. The pan-tilt module and HAT are shown in Figure 8-6, which also includes an optional NeoPixel lighting strip.

Figure 8-6. *Pan-tilt HAT with Raspberry Pi camera module and NeoPixel light*

The pan-tilt module consists of two SG90 servo motors. There is one which connects to the base which provides the pan and one that connects to the clamp for the camera module which provides the tilt capability.

There is a Python module that is available for controlling the pan-tilt HAT. If not already installed, this can be installed using

```
sudo apt install python3-pantilthat
```

When installed, this can be imported into a Python program. The commands are easy to use. An example that moves the camera around is shown in Listing 8-5.

Listing 8-5. Test program for the pan-tilt HAT

```
#!/usr/bin/python3

import pantilthat
from time import sleep

while True:
    # pan from one side to another
    pantilthat.pan(-90)
    sleep (5)
    pantilthat.pan(90)
    sleep (5)
    # pan to the middle
    pantilthat.pan(0)
    sleep (5)
    # tilt up
    pantilthat.tilt(-90)
    sleep (5)
    # tilt down
    pantilthat.tilt(90)
    sleep (5)
    # tilt to center
    pantilthat.tilt(0)
    sleep (5)
```

This can be saved as pan-tilt-test.py and when run will move the camera from side to side and top to bottom.

Using Motion to Stream Video

There are a few different ways that video from the camera can be streamed to a web browser. The one used here is called motion, which is free software available at `https://motion-project.github.io/`.

The operating system needs to be told about the video driver. Set up the camera v4l (video for Linux) driver:

```
sudo modprobe bcm2835-v4l2
```

Install motion using

```
sudo apt install motion
```

Enable the daemon by editing the file /etc/default/motion and changing the entry to

```
start_motion_daemon=yes
```

Then update the configuration file /etc/motion/motion.conf and change the appropriate settings. The following are recommended as a minimum:

```
daemon on
stream_localhost off      # allow remote viewing

rotate 180

webcontrol_port 8082
```

The reason for changing the port for webcontrol is so that it doesn't conflict with port 8080 which will be used for the web page for the user to connect to. There are lots of other settings in the file, most can be left at their default values, but you may want to change the width and height for a higher resolution.

After configuring motion, it can be started using

```
sudo systemctl start motion
```

Set motion to start automatically at reboot using

```
sudo systemctl enable motion
```

You can test that motion is working correctly by visiting `http://127.0.0.1:8081/` from a web browser on Raspberry Pi. You can also connect from another computer on the same network by using the IP address of the Raspberry Pi.

Adding a Web Interface

Finally, you can add a web interface to allow the camera to be controlled and viewed from a computer on the network. This will use the same technique as used in Chapter 7 to provide a web interface for the model train.

If you haven't already installed Python Bottle, it can be installed using

```
sudo apt install python3-bottle
```

You will also need to create directories /home/pi/camera and /home/pi/camera/ public (or if using a different directory, you will need to update the source code accordingly). Then download the jQuery file using

```
cd ~/camera/public
wget http://code.jquery.com/jquery-3.5.1.min.js
```

There are two files that need to be added, the source file pantiltcamera.py which is in Listing 8-6 and index.html which is in Listing 8-7.

Listing 8-6. Web application for pan-tilt camera

```
#!/usr/bin/python3
from gpiozero import Servo
from time import sleep
import sys
import pantilthat
from bottle import Bottle, route, request, response, template, static_file

app = Bottle()

STEP_SIZE = 5

# Change IPADDRESS if access is required from another computer
IPADDRESS = '0.0.0.0'
# Where the files are stored
DOCUMENT_ROOT = '/home/pi/camera'

#Setup lights as NeoPixels
pantilthat.light_mode(pantilthat.WS2812)
pantilthat.light_type(pantilthat.GRBW)
```

```python
# public files
# *** WARNING ANYTHING STORED IN THE PUBLIC FOLDER
# WILL BE AVAILABLE TO DOWNLOAD
@app.route ('/public/<filename>')
def server_public (filename):
    return static_file (filename, root=DOCUMENT_ROOT+"/public")

@app.route ('/')
def server_home ():
    return static_file ('index.html', root=DOCUMENT_ROOT+"/public")

@app.route ('/move')
def move_motor():
    getvar_dict = request.query.decode()
    pantilt = request.query.pantilt
    direction = int(request.query.direction)

    if pantilt == "pan":
        pan_value = pantilthat.get_pan()
        if direction == -1:
            if pan_value - STEP_SIZE >= -90:
                pantilthat.pan (pan_value - STEP_SIZE)
                return ("Pan right")
            else:
                return ("Pan right limit reached")
        elif direction == 1:
            if pan_value + STEP_SIZE <= 90:
                pantilthat.pan (pan_value + STEP_SIZE)
                return ("Pan left")
            else:
                return ("Pan left limit reached")
        else:
            return ("Invalid direction")
    elif pantilt == "tilt":
        tilt_value = pantilthat.get_tilt()
```

```
        if direction == -1:
            if tilt_value - STEP_SIZE >= -90:
                pantilthat.tilt (tilt_value - STEP_SIZE)
                return ("Tilt up")
            else:
                return ("Tilt up limit reached")
        elif direction == 1:
            if tilt_value + STEP_SIZE <= 90:
                pantilthat.tilt (tilt_value + STEP_SIZE)
                return ("Tilt down")
            else:
                return ("Tilt down limit reached")
        else:
            return ("Invalid direction")
    else:
        return ("Invalid command")

@app.route ('/light')
def set_light():
    getvar_dict = request.query.decode()
    set = request.query.set
    if (set == "on"):
        pantilthat.set_all(0,0,0,255)
        pantilthat.show()
        return ("Light On")
    else:
        pantilthat.clear()
        pantilthat.show()
        return ("Light Off")

app.run(host=IPADDRESS)
```

Listing 8-7. Index.html file for the web camera

```html
<!doctype html>
<html lang="en">
<head>
<meta charset="UTF-8">
<title>Raspberry Pi Camera</title>
<!-- Add jQuery -->
<script type="text/javascript" src="/public/jquery-3.5.1.min.js"></script>
</head>
<body>
<h1>Raspberry Pi Camera</h1>

<iframe src="http://192.168.0.153:8081" style="width:400px;height:300
px;"></iframe>

<div id="status">...</div>

<p>
<button onclick="moveCamera('tilt', -1)">Up</button>
<br />
<button onclick="moveCamera('pan', 1)">Left</button><button
onclick="moveCamera('pan', -1)">Right</button>
<br />
<button onclick="moveCamera('tilt', 1)">Down</button>
</p>
<p>
<button onclick="setLight('on')">Light On</button><button
onclick="setLight('off')">Light Off</button>
</p>

<script>
// call back function from ajax code
function updateStatus (data) {
    // Update screen with new status
    $('#status').html(data);
}
```

```
function moveCamera (pantilt, direction) {
    $.get('/move', 'pantilt='+pantilt+'&direction='+direction,
    updateStatus);
}

function setLight (set_status) {
    $.get('/light', 'set='+set_status, updateStatus);
}

</script>
</body>
</html>
```

These files are based on the pan-tilt test program and the web part from the IoT model train code in Chapter 7.

As well as controlling the motor, this code and html file include support for an RGBW light module. This is optional and if not included will have no effect.

More Video Editing

This chapter has given some examples of things that can be done using electronics combined with the Raspberry Pi cameras. It's looked at using infrared to trigger the Raspberry Pi camera. It then covered stop motion animation, taking photographs using a switch as a trigger and then merging the still photos into a video using the command line and OpenShot.

Another example is in creating a CCTV-style web interface, providing pan and tilt capability using the pan-tilt HAT.

Once you have made your first video, it can be fun to try different techniques and see how they look. You can find that it takes up a lot of time as hand-editing individual frames can be quite time-consuming, but the results can be very rewarding.

You could also look at improving the web interface for the pan-tilt camera such as being able to move to specific scenes. You may also want to add a capture button to save a static picture.

The next chapter will look at creating a robot with the Raspberry Pi.

## CHAPTER 9

Rolling Forwards: Designing and Building a Robot

This chapter will look at creating a robot vehicle. This will involve selecting and making a chassis, adding motor control, and writing some software that makes it all work. Rather than being followed step by step, this should be considered a guide to how this works and an inspiration for creating your own personalized robot to suit your budget, time, and equipment available.

Selecting or Making a Robot Chassis

The first thing you are going to need is a chassis to provide a study frame for the robot. There are a variety of different robot chassis that can be used, with more coming out all the time. The chassis can vary greatly in cost from upcycling of junk parts to some costing over $100 for just a base and wheels.

The basic requirement for a chassis is a base which is used to mount the motors, batteries, processor (such as a Raspberry Pi), and a motor controller. Several different examples will be covered in this chapter.

The decision about the chassis needs to go together with the type of wheel configuration. So if you have a preference for a certain chassis that may determine what wheel options you can use or if you have a specific wheel configuration in mind, then that may influence your choice of chassis. I have listed some of the different wheel configurations as follows along with some advantages and disadvantages of each model.

© Stewart Watkiss 2020
S. Watkiss, *Learn Electronics with Raspberry Pi*, https://doi.org/10.1007/978-1-4842-6348-8_9

Two Motorized Wheels and Omnidirectional Wheel

These are typically three-wheel motors, with two of them powered and the other able to move freely in any direction. These feature two motors with built-in gears connected directly to large wheels, with an omnidirectional wheel (at either the front or rear) which is unpowered. The omnidirectional wheel often uses a large ball bearing, although some use a caster instead.

The main advantages of having two motorized wheels are that they are normally low cost and the control circuit and software are easier to implement. The main disadvantage is that this is only suitable for driving on flat smooth surfaces.

Four Motorized Wheels

To overcome the problems with the omnidirectional wheel, it is also possible to have four wheels with one at each corner. This can make negotiating gentle slopes easier but does need some additional circuitry. It also goes against the principle of car steering as it means that some of the motors are going against the direction of travel, making it more difficult to control.

Caterpillar Tracks

Vehicles with caterpillar tracks can usually negotiate rough terrain. They are often controlled by a motor for each side, so the control circuitry is the same as the two-motor circuit. The main disadvantage is that these tend to be more expensive than the simpler chassis.

Wheels That Steer

Another alternative is to design a robot whose wheels can move similar to how car wheels do. This would be useful if you wanted to experiment with self-driving cars. This does however require a complex mechanical mechanism to turn the wheels as well as needing more space to turn.

Mecanum Omnidirectional Wheels

Mecanum wheels are a novel design which have rollers around the outside of the wheel. These have the advantage of allowing the robot to move in any direction including sideways. The motor control is more complicated as the four different wheels need to be controlled in different directions, which may not align with the desired direction of movement. This is easiest to understand through a practical explanation which will be covered in this chapter.

Buying a Kit or Making Your Own

There are a variety of different robot kits available. I have listed a few examples as follows, but there are lots of other kits available:

- The CamJam Robotics kit (EduKit 3) provides the motors, wheels, controller circuit, and some sensors. It does not include a chassis (although you can use the supplied box). It is mainly available in the United Kingdom, but you can create the same yourself buying the components separately.

- The STS-Pi is an inexpensive robot kit. As such, it is a good starting point for those wanting to start with Raspberry Pi robots. It is widely available.

- T200 Robot Tank Chassis provides a chassis with 12V motors and caterpillar tracks.

There is a selection of other robot chassis kits that you can buy you could make your own. If you have access to a laser cutter or 3D printer, then you can build a robot to whatever design you wish. If you don't have access to that kind of equipment, then you could make your own using a cardboard box or made out of wood. The main criterion is to have somewhere that the motors and wheels can be mounted that won't buckle when used. I have created my own chassis using a 3D printer which is covered in more detail later.

CamJam Robotics Kit

Although the CamJam kit doesn't include a chassis, the box that it comes in is quite sturdy and can be used to create a complete robot. The photograph in Figure 9-1 shows the CamJam box used as the chassis with the two motors mounted at one end and an omnidirectional wheel at the other end. This box is big enough to house the motors, a 4 x AA battery pack, and a Raspberry Pi Zero with add-on motor controller board. You still need to supply your own Raspberry Pi, but otherwise most components are included.

Figure 9-1. *CamJam Robotics kit, with box used as a robot chassis*

The motor controller used on the CamJam kit is based around a DRV8833 controller. This provides a dual H-bridge driver in a surface mount IC, which is soldered onto a Raspberry Pi header board. This is like the SN754410 covered in Chapter 6 using a service mount IC on a printed circuit board. Motor A is connected to GPIO pins 10 and 9, and motor B uses GPIO pins 8 and 7.

STS-Pi Kit

The STS-Pi is shown in Figure 9-2. This kit includes the chassis and motors but does not include a motor controller. The recommended motor driver is the Explorer HAT, Explorer HAT Pro, or Explorer pHAT. These include a motor controller, and in the case of the Explorer HAT and Explorer HAT Pro, they also include a small breadboard. In the case of the Explorer HAT, the motor control is through ULN2003A Darlington transistors; the Explorer HAT Pro and Explorer pHAT use the same DRV8833 IC as used in the CamJam kit. Motor 1 uses GPIO pins 19 and 20, and motor 2 uses GPIO pins 21 and 26.

Figure 9-2. *STS-Pi Raspberry Pi robot*

T200 Robot Tank Chassis

The T200 does not include any kind of motor controller. It is a basic chassis with motors and caterpillar track wheels. There are holes included in the top layer to allow circuit boards to be mounted on the top. The chassis is shown in Figure 9-3 with the Raspberry Pi and motor controller on it, and the battery is mounted underneath the chassis.

Figure 9-3. *The T200 robot chassis*

The motors in the T200 run at 12V and need to support a higher current than the small motors used in the other kits. I have used a L298N which is available pre-soldered to a motor controller board as shown in Chapter 7, Figure 7-5.

The T200 chassis has various holes for mounting components. It is possible to mount components directly to these using appropriate PCB stands and screws. To provide more flexibility, I have created my own mounting brackets to hold a 12V battery under the chassis and to mount the Raspberry Pi and other components on top of the chassis. These were designed in FreeCAD and printed on a 3D printer. I have included the

233

STL files in the source code if you would like to print the same, although they are not necessary if you don't have access to a 3D printer.

As the battery is rated at 12V, I have used a buck converter to convert the 12V supply to 5V which can be used by the Raspberry Pi. Power supply options are covered further in Chapter 13.

Mecanum Robot

The final robot I will cover is a homemade robot using Mecanum wheels. I have used the TB6612FNG for controlling that robot. This is a surface mount IC but is available soldered to a breakout board by SparkFun. This robot is different to the others, so it is covered in more detail later in the chapter.

Choosing a Raspberry Pi

When buying a Raspberry Pi, I normally recommend getting a recent Raspberry Pi model B. The current version at the time of writing is the Raspberry Pi 4. While that is a powerful computer with good performance and memory that comes at the cost of power and size, the Raspberry Pi Zero is less powerful, but its reduced power requirements make it my first choice for battery-powered projects.

An alternative is one of the older models of the Raspberry Pi such as the Raspberry Pi 2 or Raspberry Pi 3+. These are larger and use more power than the Raspberry Pi Zero, but much less than the Raspberry Pi 4. I have used a Raspberry Pi 2 on the 12V robot where there is more power available and on the STS-Pi as that is designed specifically for a full-size Raspberry Pi.

The Raspberry Pi Zero is available in different models. I recommend the Raspberry Pi Zero W (with wireless) or the Raspberry Pi Zero WH (with wireless and pre-soldered headers). The latter is useful if you don't want to solder wires or a header onto the Raspberry Pi yourself. I will assume you are using a Raspberry Pi Zero WH, but you can solder the headers onto the Raspberry Pi if you have a different model.

Connecting the Motors

These examples use a motor controller board (either on the Raspberry Pi or separately), so it is mostly a case of wiring them up between the Raspberry Pi and the motors.

Powering the Motors and the Raspberry Pi

When creating a robot, you need to look at power to the motors as well as the Raspberry Pi. The Raspberry Pi GPIO ports cannot provide sufficient power for the motors, so a separate motor controller is needed. The controller can be powered from a different power supply to the Raspberry Pi or using a single power supply which is connected to both the motor controller and the Raspberry Pi. There are advantages and disadvantages to both options.

One advantage to having separate power supplies is that it would then be possible to run the motors at a higher voltage. Many motors are designed for up to 6V, and with the losses in the H-bridge, they can be connected to a supply of up to 7V, whereas the Raspberry Pi needs a stable 5V power supply. Most 6V motors will work well with a 5V supply; however, you could potentially get a little better performance out of the motors if we used a higher-voltage power supply compared to the Raspberry Pi. If using a higher-power motor, such as 12V motors, you will need to use two different power supplies or drop the voltage for the supply to the Raspberry Pi which is covered in Chapter 13.

One reason for using a separate power supply is that motors can introduce electrical noise onto the power supply, which can cause problems with sensitive electronics such as the Raspberry Pi.

The advantages to using a single power supply are the cost, the space, and the convenience of not needing to charge or replace two different sets of batteries. I normally use a single power supply for both the Raspberry Pi and the motors. If you do come across power-related problems with the robot, then you may want to consider different power supplies.

A USB power bank can be used to provide a 5V power supply, which is suitable for the Raspberry Pi and 6V motors. Another option is to create a power supply using four AA batteries. I don't recommend disposable batteries, except for occasional use (from an environmental and cost point of view), but they have a nominal voltage of 1.5V, each giving a total of 6V, although in use, this is usually a little lower. High-capacity NiMH rechargeable batteries have a nominal voltage of 1.2V which gives 4.8V. Either of these will work, but the rechargeable batteries are only just enough to power up the Raspberry Pi. It can mean that if the voltage dips a little when the motors are in use, then the supply voltage to the Raspberry Pi may dip. Using high-capacity rechargeable batteries appears to work well; however, when I tried with cheaper batteries, I have found that during a motor stall (when the robot crashed), the power would drop and the wireless network connection would disconnect.

It is possible to connect power to the Raspberry Pi through the GPIO connector using the 5V pin, but for most purposes, I recommend that you connect through the normal USB connector on the Raspberry Pi. Using the USB power supply passes through the voltage protection circuitry of the Raspberry Pi.

Caution   Care must be taken if connecting power through the GPIO port as it bypasses the polyfuse included used to protect the power coming from the micro-USB port. If connecting power directly to the GPIO port, you should ensure it is a stable power supply of around 5V.

You can use a USB breakout connector or wire a USB connector direct to the power supply. The photo in Figure 9-4 shows a micro-USB connector that can be used to take power from a terminal connector to the Raspberry Pi power supply. There are four wires in a USB cable; it is only the power wires that are required which are normally colored red (+5V) and black.

Figure 9-4. *Micro-USB connector with bare wires for connecting to a power supply*

One thing to be aware of is that the position of the motor wires may need to change to ensure that they are both going in the right direction. This will depend upon the motors and the direction that they are facing when mounted inside the robot. It is also possible to just change this around in the code or swap the wires around on the motors.

Controlling the Robot Using Python

This will look at a few different ways to control the robot. The first will be a simple program that runs on the command line. The program will look for certain keys being pressed and act accordingly. For the direction control, I have used the numbers from the numeric keypad on a keyboard as they are arranged in a convenient grid. If you are using a compact keyboard that doesn't include a numeric keypad, then you may want to change these to use appropriate letters instead.

The numeric keypad and the directions are shown in Figure 9-5.

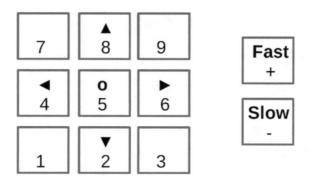

Figure 9-5. *Direction keys for the robot*

The number 0 is also used to have the camera take a photo and q is used to exit (quit) from the program.

This will be using GPIO Zero to control the robot. The code will set the speed and direction and then wait for a key to be pressed which will be used to update the speed or direction as appropriate. The code for this is included in the source files, called robotcontrol.py, included in Listing 9-1.

Listing 9-1. Keyboard control for two motor robots

```
#!/usr/bin/python3
import sys, tty, termios
import picamera, time
from gpiozero import Robot

# Pin numbers
# CamJam 10,9 - 8,7
# STS-Pi 19,20 - 21,26
robot = Robot(left=(19, 20), right=(21, 26))
camera_enable = False
```

```python
try:
    camera = picamera.PiCamera()
    camera.hflip=True
    camera.vflip=True
    camera_enable=True
except:
    print ("Camera not found - disabled");

photo_dir = "/home/pi/photos"

# get a character from the command line
def getch() :
    fd = sys.stdin.fileno()
    old_settings = termios.tcgetattr(fd)
    try:
        tty.setraw(sys.stdin.fileno())
        ch = sys.stdin.read(1)
    finally:
        termios.tcsetattr(fd, termios.TCSADRAIN, old_settings)
    return ch

# list to convert key into motor on/off values to correspond with direction
# direction based on number keypad
# 8 = fwd, 4 = left, 5 = stop, 6 = right, 2 = rev
# the key for the list is the character
direction = {
    # number keys
    '2' : "backward",
    '4' : "left",
    '5' : "stop",
    '6' : "right",
    '8' : "forward"
}

current_direction = "stop"
# speed is as a percentage (ie. 100 = top speed)
# start speed is 50% which is fairly slow on a flat surface
speed = 50
```

```python
print ("Robot control - use number keys to control direction")
print ("Speed " + str(speed) +"% - use +/- to change speed")

while True:
    # Convert speed from percentage to float (0 to 1)
    float_speed = speed / 100
    if (current_direction == "forward") :
        robot.forward(float_speed)
    # rev
    elif (current_direction == "backward") :
        robot.backward(float_speed)
    elif (current_direction == "left") :
        robot.left(float_speed)
    elif (current_direction == "right") :
        robot.right(float_speed)
    # stop
    else :
        robot.stop()

    # Get next key pressed
    ch = getch()

    # q = quit
    if (ch == 'q') :
        break
    elif (ch == '+') :
        speed += 10
        if speed > 100 :
            speed = 100
        print ("Speed : "+str(speed))
    elif (ch == '-' ) :
        speed -= 10
        if speed < 0 :
            speed = 0
        print ("Speed : "+str(speed))
```

```
    elif (ch in direction.keys()) :
        current_direction = direction[ch]
        print ("Direction "+current_direction)
    elif (ch == 'O' and camera_enable == True) :
        timestring = time.strftime("%Y-%m-%dT%H.%M,%S", time.gmtime())
        print ("Taking photo " +timestring)
        camera.capture(photo_dir+'/photo_'+timestring+'.jpg')
robot.close()
```

The code uses a robot object from the gpiozero library. This takes the GPIO pins for the left and right motors. These are the pins that go to the appropriate inputs on the H-bridge motor controller.

If the robot includes a camera, then that can be used to take still photos when requested. If you try and access the camera on a robot without a camera connected, then it triggers an error (known as an exception). To handle this, the camera instance is created in a try block to gracefully handle any errors. If this did not include the try statement and if the camera was not found, then the program would give an error message and stop. The camera is mounted upside down on my robot (with the cable coming from the top), so it is flipped horizontally and vertically after creating the camera object.

I've also added a getch() function. The name stands for get character, which is taken from the name of a similar function in C. The reason this function is required is that Python normally reads key presses from the standard input device. This is a buffered device which will hold all the characters until Enter is pressed and then send them all the program as a line. That would mean the user would have to press Enter after each command, which is not so easy to use. This function sets the input to raw mode so that each key press can be read individually. After the key is read, it restores the input back to standard mode; otherwise, this may mess up the terminal when you exit the program.

The direction keys are stored as a list; if you would like to add more keys to this list, you can do so as long as they have the same value as the existing ones. For example, if you wanted to add wasd (common key controls used in games), then you could add the following entries into the list:

```
'w' : "forward",  'a' : "left", 's' : "stop", 'd' : "right",
```

The current_direction starts with the default of stop and the speed to 50%. This speed was chosen as it is a slow speed but is still sufficient for the STS-PI robot to be able to move forward. This allows the user to get used to the controls before increasing speed. You may need to change this up or down depending upon your robot. The value is stored as a percentage in the speed variable; however, GPIO Zero expects a number between 0 and 1; the value is divided by 100 and stored as a floating-point number in variable float_speed.

Setting the robot in motion is as simple as calling robot.forward(), robot.backward(), robot.left(), and robot.right(). The optional parameter is the speed which sets the PWM ratio. There is also robot.stop() which stops both motors.

Upon exit, robot.close() is called to clean up.

This should be saved onto the Raspberry Pi on the robot. It could be controlled directly using a wireless keyboard on the robot, but then that would need the program to be started whenever the robot was powered on, and without a screen, performing a clean shutdown or restarting the program would be difficult. It is perhaps more convenient to run this over a wireless network connection using SSH.

If you find that the wrong motor turns when the appropriate key is pressed or that the robot moves in the wrong direction, then this can be rectified by swapping the wires going to the motors or by changing the pin settings when the robot object is created toward the start of the code.

The preceding code uses the generic robot within the GPIO Zero library. There are some comments in the file showing the pins for other robots which can be substituted as required.

The Mecanum Robot

This next robot is based around Mecanum wheels. Mecanum wheels are a novel design which have rollers around the outside of the wheel. As well as steering, they allow the robot to move directly sideways.

One feature of using Mecanum wheels is that it needs four wheels, each of which needs to have their own motor. To accommodate this, I created my own chassis, which I designed in FreeCAD, shown in Figure 9-6. This chassis was 3D printed, and the STL files are included in the source code, which you can use if you have access to a 3D printer. If you do not have a 3D printer, then it is possible to create your own chassis using acrylic sheets or thin wood.

Figure 9-6. *3D printed Mecanum robot*

The motors are small 6V motors with a 298:1 ratio gearbox. These are available as ones that you need to solder yourself or ones with a push header shim to save soldering. These motors can be driven using any of the motor boards previously discussed, although with four motors it is going to need double the number of H-bridges. In this case, I have used the TB6612FNG H-bridge IC. This is a surface mount IC which would be good for creating a permanent controller board. Surface mount ICs are normally difficult to use for testing, but fortunately, it is also available pre-soldered to a breakout board by SparkFun. Using the breakout board, I have mounted it on a breadboard and cabled that back to the Raspberry Pi. The cabling between the Raspberry Pi and the motor boards is shown in Figure 9-7.

Raspberry Pi GPIO (pin number)	Motor Board	Function
+5V (4)	Vcc and Stby	Power and enable
Ground (6)	Ground	
18 (12)	PWM (all)	Speed
2 (3), 3 (5)	Left AI1, AI2	Front left motor
14 (8), 15 (10)	Left BI1, BI2	Rear left motor
22 (15), 23 (16)	Right AI1, AI2	Front right motor
24 (18), 24 (22)	Right BI1, BI2	Rear right motor

Figure 9-7. *Table of GPIO ports for the Mecanum robot*

The code provides keyboard control for the robot which is included in Listing 9-2.

Listing 9-2. Keyboard control for Mecanum robot

```python
#!/usr/bin/python3
import sys, tty, termios
from gpiozero import PWMOutputDevice, Motor

pwm_pin = 18
m_f_l = (2,3)
m_f_r = (22,23)
m_r_l = (14,15)
m_r_r = (24,25)

motors = [
    Motor(m_f_l[0], m_f_l[1], pwm=False),
    Motor(m_f_r[0], m_f_r[1], pwm=False),
    Motor(m_r_l[0], m_r_l[1], pwm=False),
    Motor(m_r_r[0], m_r_r[1], pwm=False)
    ]

pwm_out = PWMOutputDevice (pwm_pin)

# get a character from the command line
def getch() :
    fd = sys.stdin.fileno()
    old_settings = termios.tcgetattr(fd)
    try:
        tty.setraw(sys.stdin.fileno())
        ch = sys.stdin.read(1)
    finally:
        termios.tcsetattr(fd, termios.TCSADRAIN, old_settings)
    return ch

# list to convert key into motor on/off values to correspond with direction
# direction based on number keypad
# 8 = fwd, 4 = left, 5 = stop, 6 = right, 2 = rev
# the key for the list is the character
```

```python
direction = {
    # number keys
    '1' : "turn_left",
    '2' : "backward",
    '3' : "turn_right",
    '4' : "left",
    '5' : "stop",
    '6' : "right",
    '7' : "diagonal_left",
    '8' : "forward",
    '9' : "diagonal_right"
}

current_direction = "stop"
# speed is as a percentage (ie. 100 = top speed)
# start speed is 50% which is fairly slow on a flat surface
speed = 50
pwm_out.value = speed/100

print ("Robot control - use number keys to control direction")
print ("Speed " + str(speed) +"% - use +/- to change speed")

while True:
    # Convert speed from percentage to float (0 to 1)
    if (current_direction == "forward") :
        motors[0].forward()
        motors[1].forward()
        motors[2].forward()
        motors[3].forward()
    # rev
    elif (current_direction == "backward") :
        motors[0].backward()
        motors[1].backward()
        motors[2].backward()
        motors[3].backward()
```

```
elif (current_direction == "left") :
    motors[0].backward()
    motors[1].forward()
    motors[2].forward()
    motors[3].backward()
elif (current_direction == "right") :
    motors[0].forward()
    motors[1].backward()
    motors[2].backward()
    motors[3].forward()
elif (current_direction == "turn_left") :
    motors[0].backward()
    motors[1].forward()
    motors[2].backward()
    motors[3].forward()
elif (current_direction == "turn_right") :
    motors[0].forward()
    motors[1].backward()
    motors[2].forward()
    motors[3].backward()
elif (current_direction == "diagonal_left") :
    motors[0].stop()
    motors[1].forward()
    motors[2].forward()
    motors[3].stop()
elif (current_direction == "diagonal_right") :
    motors[0].forward()
    motors[1].stop()
    motors[2].stop()
    motors[3].forward()
# stop
else :
    motors[0].stop()
    motors[1].stop()
    motors[2].stop()
    motors[3].stop()
```

```
# Get next key pressed
ch = getch()

# q = quit
if (ch == 'q') :
    break
elif (ch == '+') :
    speed += 10
    if speed > 100 :
        speed = 100
    pwm_out.value = speed/100
    print ("Speed : "+str(speed))
elif (ch == '-' ) :
    speed -= 10
    if speed < 0 :
        speed = 0
    pwm_out.value = speed/100
    print ("Speed : "+str(speed))
elif (ch in direction.keys()) :
    current_direction = direction[ch]
    print ("Direction "+current_direction)
```

Most of the code is repeated from the previous robot code. This is based around the GPIO Zero Motor class instead of the Robot class used previously. This gives more control over the four different motors. The motors are now in a list so that they can be addressed individually.

In addition to adding the extra motors, additional direction keys have been added to demonstrate some of the additional functionality available for the Mecanum wheels. Turn left and right has been moved to the bottom left and right keys (keys 1 and 3 on the numeric keypad), which operate the wheels in a conventional way driving one side forward and the other backward. Keys 4 and 6 have been changed to move sideways. This uses a feature of the Mecanum wheels where driving the front and the back wheels in opposite directions results in the rollers turning which moves the robot sideways. Keys 7 and 9 have diagonally opposite wheels turning which causes the robot to move in diagonal direction.

The Mecanum robot still uses pulse-width modulation to vary the speed, but this is applied using a single pin on the Raspberry Pi which is connected to the PWM pin for each of the H-bridge configurations. This means that all the motors run at the same speed, which is the easiest way to control this robot. If you wanted to vary the speed separately, which would give a higher degree of control for changes in direction, then you can allocate a separate pin for each H-bridge.

Measuring the Distance Using an Ultrasonic Range Sensor

Once you have the robot working, there are other sensors that can be added to provide an increasing amount of automation. The first one considered here is an ultrasonic range sensor, otherwise known as a distance sensor. As its name suggests, this can be used to measure the distance from an object. In this case, it can be used to determine when the robot is getting close to a wall or other obstacle. The ultrasonic distance sensor is shown in Figure 9-8; this works in a similar way to the parking sensors on cars. It sends out an ultrasonic signal and then times how long it takes for that signal to reach an object and be reflected back to the sensor.

You will need to find a way of mounting this on the robot. In the case of the STS-Pi, I have created a 3D printed bracket to hold the sensor; on other robots, you may need to get creative with cardboard and tape.

Figure 9-8. *Ultrasonic distance sensor*

There are four connections to the sensor. Two of these are for a 5V power supply and ground. The other two connections are for the trigger signal and the echo response. The sensor is designed for a 5V signal. In the case of the input to the ultrasonic sensor, the 3.3V from the Raspberry Pi is sufficient to trigger the outgoing signal, but connecting the sensor output direct to a GPIO pin could damage the Raspberry Pi. This can be handled using a simple voltage divider circuit covered in Chapter 5. The voltage divider reduces the voltage down to a safe level for the Raspberry Pi GPIO. This is shown in the circuit diagram in Figure 9-9.

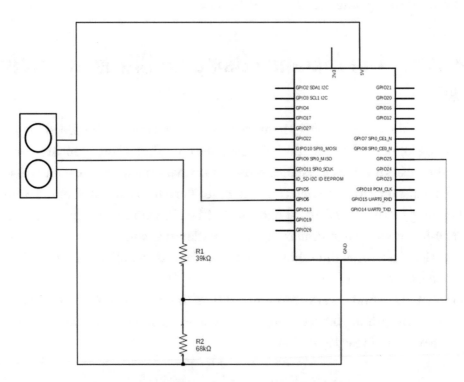

Figure 9-9. *Circuit diagram for ultrasonic distance sensor*

The circuit diagram only shows the ultrasonic distance sensor part; this assumes that the motor control circuit is still in place. The trigger pin is connected to GPIO 6 and the echo response to GPIO 25. These have been used as they are made available on the Explorer HAT Pro as output 1 and input 4, respectively. If you are not able to use these ports, then you could change to other GPIO ports as appropriate. If using the Explorer HAT Pro, then the two resistors are not needed as the inputs are configured to be 5V safe.

Before creating the full program to control the robot, it can be useful to test that the ultrasonic circuit is working correctly. First, I created the code distance.py shown in Listing 9-3.

Listing 9-3. Code to detect distance using ultrasonic distance sensor

```
#!/usr/bin/python3
from gpiozero import DistanceSensor
from time import sleep

sensor = DistanceSensor(25, 6)

while True:
    print('Distance is ' + str(sensor.distance) + 'm')
    sleep(1)
```

This uses the GPIO Zero library which added the distance sensor since the previous version of this book. This has greatly reduced the amount of code needed.

Behind the scenes, in the GPIO Zero library, the code works by first turning the trigger off and waiting for the sensor to settle. A pulse is sent to the sensor's trigger pin to send an ultrasonic signal. It then measures how long for the ultrasonic signal to travel to an object and return to the sensor. Multiplying the time taken by the speed of sound gives double the distance to the object. This is divided by two and then returned as the distance. The calculated value is then printed in meters.

The distance sensor is fairly accurate for distances of between 5cm and 1m. The next program is called robot-distance.py which drives the robot forward until it gets within 13cm of an obstacle and then turns right. If the robot then has space to move, it will move forward again; otherwise, it will move right some more. The value of 13cm was based on experimentation and allows for the motor continuing to move forward for a short while after reading the distance and is enough to prevent it getting stuck into a corner. The distance and the speed of the robot may need to be adjusted for different robots and motor configurations. The full code to control the robot using the distance sensor is provided in Listing 9-4.

Listing 9-4. Controlling a robot based on an ultrasonic distance sensor

```
#!/usr/bin/python3
import time
from gpiozero import Robot, DistanceSensor
```

```
# Pin numbers
# CamJam 10,9 - 8,7
# STS-Pi 19,20 - 21,26
robot = Robot(left=(19, 20), right=(21, 26))
distance_sensor = DistanceSensor(25, 6)

min_distance = 0.13
speed = 0.5

while True:
    distance = distance_sensor.distance
    print ("Distance "+str(distance))
    # if we are close to a wall then turn right
    if (distance < min_distance) :
        print ("Too close turning")
        robot.right(speed)
    else :
        robot.forward(speed)
    time.sleep(1)
```

As you can see, this code makes use of the GPIO Zero robot library to control the motors and distance sensor. In practice, the range finder worked well on walls and large objects but is not able to see certain obstacles that are too high or low compared with the position of the sensor. This needs to be considered when creating a course for the robot to navigate through.

Following a Line Using a Line Sensor

Another useful sensor is an infrared proximity sensor, which can be used to detect a line on the floor to follow. This is inspired by real robots that may navigate around a factory using floor markings. A popular sensor is the TCRT5000 infrared proximity sensor which consists of an emitter and receiver in a single module. There is a barrier between the two so that the sensor only sees signals that are reflected back to it from a nearby surface. These are available individually, but in my case, I have bought three sensors mounted to a single board. This is shown in Figure 9-10.

Figure 9-10. *Line following sensor*

Using infrared, the line follower is normally used for a robot to follow a dark-colored line on a light-colored floor. When the sensor is over a dark line, the infrared is not reflected. It is possible to follow a line using one, two, or three sensors. Using one sensor needs only one pin on the GPIO but means that the robot needs to scan side to side when it loses the line. Having two sensors helps the robot to move in the correct direction by knowing which way it needs to turn to correct itself. With three sensors, the robot can drive in a straight line when the center sensor detects the line and then knows which way to correct if it sees the line through one of the side sensors.

The sensors can be connected to any available GPIO port. In the example code, I have used GPIO 22, 23, and 24 for left, right, and center. The code for the line following program is named line-follower.py, included in Listing 9-5.

Listing 9-5. Robot line follower code

```
#!/usr/bin/python3
from gpiozero import Robot, LineSensor
from time import sleep

sensor_left = LineSensor(22)
sensor_center = LineSensor(23)
sensor_right = LineSensor(24)

# Pin numbers
# CamJam 10,9 - 8,7
# STS-Pi 19,20 - 21,26
```

```
# pins reversed as this robot goes the opposite direction
robot = Robot(right=(7, 8), left=(9, 10))

current_direction = "forward"
# speed is as a percentage (ie. 100 = top speed)
# start speed is 50% which is fairly slow on a flat surface
speed = 20

while True:
    # Convert speed from percentage to float (0 to 1)
    float_speed = speed / 100

    # Center detected - go forward
    if sensor_center.value == 1:
        robot.forward(float_speed)
    # Otherwise see if too far left or right
    if sensor_left.value == 1:
        robot.right(float_speed)
    elif sensor_right.value == 1:
        robot.left(float_speed)
    # Otherwise drive forward
    else:
        robot.forward(float_speed)
```

This is only a starting point for the code. The speed has been dropped to 20% which just about worked with my robot, but it would still sometimes overshoot a corner. You may want to look at the robot turning more slowly when it no longer detects the line with the center sensor.

To try this out, you can print your own circuit using plain white paper with a 1cm (1/2 inch) wide line printed in black ink.

Using a Wireless USB Controller

The programs created previously were based around keyboard control. This is not the easiest way to control a robot, as even with a wireless keyboard, it is challenging to balance a keyboard while controlling a moving robot.

A more natural interface is to use a USB joypad controller. One option which allows you to use the existing program is to use a separate utility program called QJoyPad. QJoyPad converts the signals from the controller into key presses to the program. This technique will work with a variety of different controllers including wired and wireless controllers, although wireless is likely to be the most useful for controlling a robot around the floor. I have used an inexpensive wireless USB controller as shown in Figure 9-11.

Figure 9-11. *Wireless USB controller*

QJoyPad is a program which needs to be installed and configured separately. First, install QJoyPad using

```
sudo apt install qjoypad
```

After installing, there should be an icon installed on the Games menu, or it can be run from the command line as qjoypad. This will add a controller icon to the menu bar where you can configure the mappings from the controller to the keyboard. The easiest way to do this is to use the Quick Set option and press the button on the controller, followed by the keyboard button you would like to map it to. Then click Add to save it as robot.

Both the robot program and qjoypad need to be set to automatically start when the Raspberry Pi boots up. This is achieved by adding a desktop file for each of the programs into the directory /home/pi/.config/autostart.

First, create the directory if it doesn't already exist:

```
mkdir ~/.config/autostart
```

Then add the files robotcontrol.desktop and qjoypad.desktop which are included in Listings 9-6 and 9-7.

Listing 9-6. Auto-start desktop file for robotcontrol.py

```
[Desktop Entry]
encoding=UTF-8
Version=1.0
Type=Application
Exec=lxterminal -e "/home/pi/robotcontrol.py"
Terminal=true
Name=Robot Control
Comment=control a robot
```

Listing 9-7. Auto-start desktop file for qjoypad.py

```
[Desktop Entry]
encoding=UTF-8
Type=Application
Exec=/usr/bin/qjoypad robot
Terminal=false
Name=QJoyPad
Comment=Controller support
```

The program will now start when the Raspberry Pi boots up so that it is possible to control the robot without first needing to connect a keyboard or screen.

More Robotics

This chapter has covered creating robots using chassis kits or by creating one from scratch. It has looked at different motor and wheel configurations, including two powered wheels and an omnidirectional wheel, tank track wheels, and the Mecanum wheels.

Some automation has been provided using an ultrasonic distance sensor and infrared line following sensors. For a future development, you may want to look at combining the two and having the robot follow a line but stop if there is an obstruction in the way. It has also looked at how you can use a wireless USB game controller to control the robot.

This is just a small taste of what could be achieved with a Raspberry Pi-powered robot. If you are interested in robots, then you may want to look for robotics clubs in your area who may run challenges or competitions.

The next chapter will look at computer gaming. It will cover how you can interface a joystick with the Raspberry Pi to create a simple game console. It will also look at APIs (application programming interfaces) and how they can be used to control Minecraft using the joystick and buttons.

## CHAPTER 10

Customize Your Gameplay: Minecraft Hardware Programming

This chapter will look at how electronics can be integrated with other programs through an API (application programming interface). It will also create a game console–type device complete with joystick and arcade buttons. This is based around the API for Minecraft Raspberry Pi edition, which is available for free for the Raspberry Pi.

Minecraft is a block-based construction game where you can make buildings and other objects. It is a popular game available for PC and consoles and as Minecraft Pocket Edition for tablets and phones. It is also available as a special Minecraft Pi Edition, which is a version with reduced functionality specifically for the Raspberry Pi; in particular, it only comes with creative mode. The Raspberry Pi edition includes an API which provides a way to interface with Minecraft using Python. This can be used to interface with the electronics sensors and outputs that can connect to the Raspberry Pi. This project adds a joystick controller and buttons to the Raspberry Pi. The joystick can be used to move the Minecraft character Steve around the world. The buttons will each provide a specific function in the Minecraft game.

Creating a Game Console

There are already game consoles available which use the Raspberry Pi, often as a retro game console. While you can buy a pre-made console or a kit such as the Picade, this will show how you can create your own using a box, joystick, and arcade buttons. In the case of the Picade, a separate HAT is used which can be used to connect to the GPIO and adds

© Stewart Watkiss 2020
S. Watkiss, *Learn Electronics with Raspberry Pi*, https://doi.org/10.1007/978-1-4842-6348-8_10

audio support. Rather than need the Picade HAT, this connects switches directly to the GPIO on the Raspberry PI. You can do the same using the Picade HAT, although you will need to update the code to use the different GPIO pin-out.

The first thing is to create a box to house the electronics and mount the buttons. In electronics terms, this is known as an enclosure. I used a *Really Useful Box*, which is a brand name for some strong plastic boxes. It is possible to get cheaper boxes, but it is worth paying a little extra for a good quality box if it is going to take some knocks from fast gameplay. As the box is made from plastic, it's easy to make holes for the switches and for the connections to the Raspberry Pi. I mounted the Raspberry Pi to the bottom of the enclosure using 2.5mm PCB mounts. To create the holes, I used a 16mm hole saw for the joystick and a 25mm hole saw for the giant button, but was unable to find a hole saw for the buttons, so I used a 28mm wood drill bit instead. For the USB and HDMI access, I used a small drill and a needle file to shape the hole. The finished enclosure with joystick and buttons is shown in Figure 10-1.

Figure 10-1. *Enclosure with joystick for the game console*

The photo in Figure 10-2 shows the inside of the game console enclosure. This uses ribbon cable to make the wiring look neater, but there is plenty of space in the enclosure for adding a breadboard or other electronics if required.

Figure 10-2. *Inside the joystick enclosure*

Joystick and Switches

I used a joystick, five arcade buttons, and a giant button, which gives a good flexibility for creating custom games. There are two kinds of joystick, digital ones which have a switch indicating which direction the joystick is pushed and analog ones whose resistance changes as the joystick is moved. This uses a digital joystick one that has four micro-switches. The micro-switches are pressed into the closed position as the joystick moves. This type of joystick can normally be found searching for micro-switch joysticks from your favorite electronic supplier.

A micro-switch is a small switch similar in action to the push-button switches but designed to be pushed by a mechanical device. These are often found in safety guards on machines or incorporated into other devices such as the joystick and the button switches. The buttons, even the giant button, are all based around micro-switches, which are mounted underneath the mechanical switch.

Wiring the Switches

The circuit for this project is simple. Each switch is connected between a GPIO input port and ground. This is the same as when switches have been used previously using the pull-up resistors within the Raspberry Pi; when they are not pressed, they give a logic high through the pull-up resistor, and when they are pressed, they connect to ground giving a logic low.

The micro-switches have male terminal spade connectors. These are designed to be connected to 4.8mm female spade crimp connectors. Using spade connectors makes it is to reuse the switches in future compared to soldering directly to the switch. A suitable crimp tool is required to crimp the spade connectors such as the SN-48B shown in Figure 10-3. This is the same as the one used in Chapter 8.

The connection at the Raspberry Pi end is a bit more challenging. In Chapter 8, the other ends of the wires were pre-terminated, but the cables for this need to be a bit longer than are generally available. The technique I used is to use ribbon cable and crimp the wires to 2.54mm female header pins (sometimes referred to as Dupont connectors). This allows the wires to be connected directly to the GPIO connector on the Raspberry Pi. To attach these connectors to the wire needs a different crimp tool to the one used previously as they are too small for that tool. A suitable crimp tool is the SN-2, also shown in Figure 10-3. While crimping to the spade connectors is quite straightforward, due to the small size, crimping the connectors for the Raspberry Pi end is very fiddly and takes quite a bit of practice.

One alternative is to buy pre-made cables (which normally have a male connector for connecting to the Picade HAT). As these have male connectors, they would need to be connected to a breadboard before using jumper wires to connect to the Raspberry Pi.

Another alternative is to use solid core wire crimped onto the space connectors at the switch end and then pushed directly into the breadboard. This still needs crimping for connecting to the switches, but avoids the fiddly crimp needed for the smaller connectors.

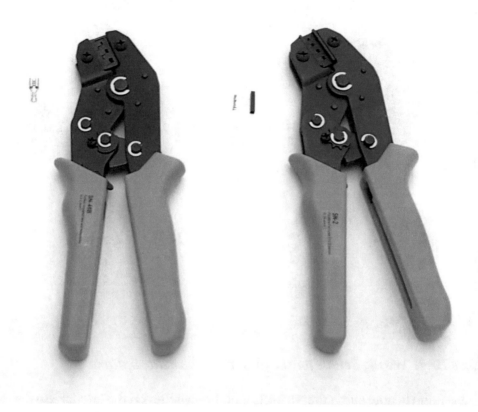

Figure 10-3. SN-48B crimp tool with female spade connector and SN-2 tool with Dupont-style connector

All the switches need to have one side of the switch connected to ground. This is done by having a wire from the ground connection on pin 6 which is then daisy-chained to one side of each switch. The normally open terminal of each switch is then connected to the appropriate GPIO port, shown in Figure 10-4.

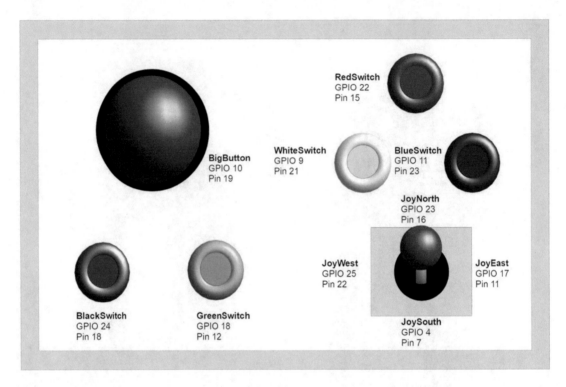

Figure 10-4. *Wiring details for the joystick and arcade buttons*

One thing to note about the wiring is that the switches on the joystick are physically located in the opposite positions to those shown in the diagram. The diagram is based on the direction of the joystick. When the joystick is pushed forward (JoyNorth), the bottom of the joystick pushes in the opposite direction.

Once this is wired up, you can use the buttons as GPIO Zero inputs in your own games or for use in an arcade game emulator such as RetroPie. There is a short test program in Listing 10-1, which can be used to test the buttons. This is called buttons-test.py.

Listing 10-1. Test program for game buttons

```
from gpiozero import Button
from time import sleep

button_pins = {
    'JoyNorth' : 23,
    'JoyEast' : 17,
    'JoySouth' : 4,
```

```
    'JoyWest' : 25,
    'RedSwitch' : 22,
    'BlueSwitch' : 11,
    'WhiteSwitch' : 9,
    'GreenSwitch' : 18,
    'BlackSwitch' : 24,
    'BigButton' : 10
    }

buttons = {}

for button_name, gpio_num in button_pins.items():
    buttons[button_name] = Button (gpio_num)

while True:
    for button_name, this_button in buttons.items():
        if (this_button.is_pressed):
            print ("Button {} is pressed".format(button_name))
    sleep(0.2)
```

This uses a dictionary of the button names to GPIO numbers. It then creates another dictionary which has the GPIO Zero button objects. It then loops through all the objects and prints the name of any buttons that are pressed. There is a sleep of 0.2 seconds; this is only a short period of time so it's likely that it will print an output twice for even a fairly short press.

Connecting to Minecraft with Python

Now that you know the buttons are wired correctly, it can be used to interface with Minecraft. The Minecraft application programming interface (API) makes it easy to interact with Minecraft from Python. This can be used in conjunction with GPIO Zero to take an input from the joystick or buttons and use that to control action in the game.

Minecraft is included in the full install of Raspberry Pi OS or can be installed using

```
sudo apt install minecraft-pi
```

Minecraft needs to be running first. It can be found under games on the start menu. You should choose Start Game and then Create new to build your first world. You can pause the game using the Esc key, which will allow you to move the screen or switch to your Python program. Clicking Back to game will then return you into the game mode. To switch from Minecraft to another program without pausing, use the Tab key.

Tip   Minecraft Pi Edition draws directly to the screen memory which is not always captured when using VNC. If you cannot see the Minecraft screen, enable direct capture mode through the Raspberry Pi VNC options.

You will be in the game controlling the Steve character, carrying a sword. In the game, you can move around using the WASD keys (W for forward, A for left, S for backward, and D for right). The space key is used to jump, or a double press of the space key will allow Steve to fly. The E key will bring up the inventory, allowing you to change tool/weapon or use another item from the inventory. The mouse will allow you to look around, and the mouse button uses the current tool.

Once you familiarized yourself with moving around Minecraft, you can create our first program. This can be written using the Mu editor in Python 3 mode. The first test code minecraft-test.py is shown in Listing 10-2.

Listing 10-2. Test program for Minecraft Pi API

```
from mcpi.minecraft import Minecraft
mc = Minecraft.create()
mc.postToChat("Hello Minecraft World")
```

After importing the Minecraft library, a Minecraft object is created which is named mc. The postToChat displays a message on the screen. This is shown in Figure 10-5.

Figure 10-5. *Hello Minecraft World message*

As well as sending information to Minecraft, the API can provide the status of your current position in the Minecraft world. The following script minecraft-status.py in Listing 10-3 will provide information about your position in Minecraft.

Listing 10-3. Program to get status in Minecraft Pi API

```
from mcpi.minecraft import Minecraft

mc = Minecraft.create()

position = mc.player.getTilePos()

print ("X position :"+str(position.x)+", Y position :"+str(position.y)+", Z
position:"+str(position.z))
```

When this is run, it displays your position within the Minecraft world. Minecraft is a 3D environment and so there are three values to show the position.

The x position is the longitude (east-west position). As the character moves further east, the x position increases, and as the character moves west, the x position decreases. The position is relative to the starting position and so goes negative when moving west compared to the starting position.

The y position is the altitude (height relative to sea level). As the character moves upward (up a hill or into the sky), the y position increases, and as the character moves down, it decreases. As the character goes underground, the y position goes negative.

The z position is the latitude (north-south position). As the character moves north, the z position decreases, and moving south, the value of z increases. This is relative to the start position of the character. The output to the print statement is shown in the Mu run window as shown in Figure 10-6.

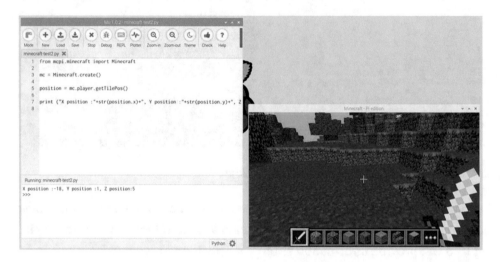

Figure 10-6. *Finding our location in Minecraft*

As well as reading the position, you can change the position of the character using setPos. The program in Listing 10-4 will return to the start position.

Listing 10-4. Program to return to start position in Minecraft

```
from mcpi.minecraft import Minecraft
mc = Minecraft.create()
mc.player.setPos(0, 0, 0)
```

If you run this, then you may find a problem. The character always starts with x = 0 and z = 0, but it starts at the normal ground level for that position. Unless the start position happened to be at sea level (y = 0) or in a valley, Steve could be trapped underground and won't be able to move. To fix this, you can check what kind of block is at that position to ensure it is not a solid block.

The next bit of code will check to see what kind of block is at that position. If it's an air block, then it decreases Y to find the first solid block to stand on, and if it's a solid block, then we will increase Y to find the nearest air block. This uses the getBlock from the mcpi.block module to find the type of block at a particular position. This has been put into a function so it can be used in future programs. It is shown in Listing 10-5 and saved as minecraft-safe.py.

Listing 10-5. Program to safely return to the start position in Minecraft

```
from mcpi.minecraft import Minecraft
import mcpi.block as block

# Find nearest empty block based on an x, z position
def getSafePos(x_pos, y_pos, z_pos):
    block_id = mc.getBlock(x_pos, y_pos, z_pos)
    # If y position is in the air then move down to find the first
    non-air block
    if (block_id == block.AIR.id):
        while (block_id == block.AIR.id):
            y_pos = y_pos - 1
            block_id = mc.getBlock(x_pos, y_pos, z_pos)
        # we have found the first solid block - we want to go one above
        that on the first air block
        y_pos = y_pos + 1
    # If y position is underground then count up to find the first air
    block
    else :
        while (block_id != block.AIR.id):
            y_pos = y_pos + 1
            block_id = mc.getBlock(x_pos, y_pos, z_pos)
    # Return full address
    return (x_pos, y_pos, z_pos)

mc = Minecraft.create()
mc.player.setPos(getSafePos(0, 0, 0))
```

This tests to see if the block is of type block.AIR.id, which indicates that it is free space. There is a constant of each type of block, such as block.WOOD.id, block. COBBLESTONE.id, and block.GLASS.id.

Moving Around Using a Joystick

You should now have an idea of how you can use Python to talk to Minecraft. This can now be combined with Pygame Zero to detect the joystick or button presses and move the character accordingly. One thing to consider is the previous problem of trying to move into a solid block. This also needs to be applied if there is a block in the way of where the character will move. To overcome this, there needs to be a button to act as a jump button. I have also configured two further buttons, one of which is auto-jump which will automatically move up one block and long jump which will climb or safely fall any number of blocks in a single move. The code to do this is in Listing 10-6 saved as minecraft-move.py.

Listing 10-6. Program to move around Minecraft using a joystick

```
# Move around in Minecraft using a joystick
from mcpi.minecraft import Minecraft
import mcpi.block as block
from gpiozero import Button
import time

# Setup various buttons and connect to minecraft
mc = Minecraft.create()

JOY_NORTH = 23
JOY_EAST = 17
JOY_SOUTH = 4
JOY_WEST = 25

BTN_JMP = 22
# use to enable automatic jump by a single block
BTN_AUTOJMP = 9
# Jump, or safely fall any number of blocks
BTN_LGEJMP = 11

# Time to wait before moves
DELAY = 0.2
```

```python
# Main loop to monitor buttons
def main():

    joy_north = Button(JOY_NORTH)
    joy_east = Button(JOY_EAST)
    joy_south = Button(JOY_SOUTH)
    joy_west = Button(JOY_WEST)

    btn_jmp = Button(BTN_JMP)
    btn_autojmp = Button(BTN_AUTOJMP)
    btn_lgejmp = Button(BTN_LGEJMP)

    # Autojump setting
    auto_jump = False

    while True:
        # jump status can be 0 = no jump, 1 = jump now, 2 = autojump, 3 =
        long_jump
        jump = 0
        # check for each button and set appropriate status
        if (btn_jmp.is_pressed) :
            jump = 1
        # toggle auto jump status
        if (btn_autojmp.is_pressed) :
            if (auto_jump == True):
                auto_jump = False
                mc.postToChat("Auto jump disabled")
            else :
                auto_jump = True
                mc.postToChat("Auto jump enabled")
        if (auto_jump == True):
            jump = 2
        if (btn_lgejmp.is_pressed):
            jump = 3

        # Don't check it's a safe position to move to - we test that later
        # Get current position and apply joystick movement
        position = mc.player.getTilePos()
```

```python
        if (joy_north.is_pressed):
            position.z = position.z - 1
        if (joy_south.is_pressed):
            position.z = position.z + 1
        if (joy_east.is_pressed):
            position.x = position.x + 1
        if (joy_west.is_pressed):
            position.x = position.x - 1

        if (jump == 2):
            # Jump only if next position is solid
            block_id = mc.getBlock(position)
            if (block_id != block.AIR.id):
                position.y = position.y + 1
        # Now apply appropriate jump to new position
        if (jump == 1):
            # Jump regardless
            position.y = position.y + 1
        # auto jump uses getSafePos
        if (jump == 3):
            position = getSafePos(position.x, position.y, position.z)

        # Now we have the position to move to, check it's not a solid block
        block_id = mc.getBlock(position)
        if (block_id == block.AIR.id):
            mc.player.setTilePos(position)
        # Otherwise not a valid move so ignore

        # Delay before next instruction
        time.sleep(DELAY)

# Find nearest empty block based on an x, z position
def getSafePos(x_pos, y_pos, z_pos):
    block_id = mc.getBlock(x_pos, y_pos, z_pos)
    # If y position is in the air then move down to find the first non-air
    block
```

```
    if (block_id == block.AIR.id):
        while (block_id == block.AIR.id):
            y_pos = y_pos - 1
            block_id = mc.getBlock(x_pos, y_pos, z_pos)
        # we have found the first solid block - we want to go one above
        that on the first air block
        y_pos = y_pos + 1
    # If y position is underground then count up to find the first air
    block
    else :
        while (block_id != block.AIR.id):
            y_pos = y_pos + 1
            block_id = mc.getBlock(x_pos, y_pos, z_pos)
    # Return full address
    return (x_pos, y_pos, z_pos)

#Run the main function when this program is run
if __name__ == "__main__":
    main()
```

This uses a combination of GPIO Zero and the Minecraft API.

One issue with the joystick is that it always moves according to the compass directions. If Steve is facing north, then this works well, but if not, then it may not feel natural. This is a limitation of Minecraft Pi Edition as unfortunately there is no way to determine which direction you are facing.

There are three more buttons left on the console. One will be used to show the current location, the second to create a new house, and the third (our big button) to transport us to the most recent house – just the sort of things that would be useful if you were in survival mode and wanted to escape from a danger (although it is only creative mode on the Raspberry Pi).

Our complete console will then look as in Figure 10-7.

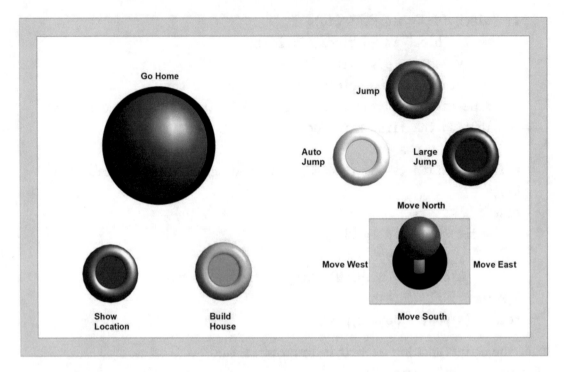

Figure 10-7. *Joystick and button functions for use in Minecraft*

Building a House in Minecraft

One of the good things about writing code is that you can use it to automate things that would otherwise take much longer to do manually. Building a house is a good example of this, as instead of placing each brick individually, a for loop can be used to automate the placement of the blocks for the walls.

Before creating the walls, the code must create the space for our house to go; otherwise, it could end up with the ground coming up inside of the house. It would take a lot of calls do this a block at a time, but fortunately, there is a quicker way using setBlocks. The setBlocks method can be used to set an area of blocks to a particular block.

The code then creates four walls and a roof. Initially, the walls will be plain, but the code then adds a door and windows afterward. The code to build a house is called minecraft-house.py, shown in Listing 10-7.

Listing 10-7. Build a house in Minecraft

```
# Build a house in Minecraft
import mcpi.minecraft as minecraft
import mcpi.block as block
from mcpi.minecraft import Minecraft
from gpiozero import Button
import time

# Setup various buttons and connect to minecraft
mc = Minecraft.create()

# Green button
BTN_HOUSE = 18

# House size
house_size_x = 16
house_size_y = 6
house_size_z = 10

# Save position of house here
# allows us to go to it later
# if not defined then leave at 0,0,0
# vec3 allows us to create a position vector
house_position = minecraft.Vec3(0,0,0)

# Time to wait before moves
DELAY = 1

# Main loop to monitor buttons
def main():
    btn_house = Button(BTN_HOUSE)

    while True:
        if (btn_house.is_pressed) :
            # Set position to current location
            # This will be the center of the house
            house_position = mc.player.getTilePos()
            build_house(house_position, house_size_x, house_size_y, house_
            size_z)
```

```python
        # Delay before next instruction
        time.sleep(DELAY)
    time.sleep (0.2)

def build_house (house_position, house_size_x, house_size_y, house_size_z):
    # clear blocks where the house is to be built
    mc.setBlocks (
        house_position.x - (house_size_x / 2),
        house_position.y,
        house_position.z - (house_size_z / 2),
        house_position.x + (house_size_x / 2),
        house_position.y + house_size_y,
        house_position.z + (house_size_z / 2),
        block.AIR.id)
    # Build floor
    mc.setBlocks (
        house_position.x - (house_size_x / 2),
        house_position.y - 1,
        house_position.z - (house_size_z / 2),
        house_position.x + (house_size_x / 2),
        house_position.y - 1,
        house_position.z + (house_size_z / 2),
        block.COBBLESTONE.id)
    # build front wall - north wall
    mc.setBlocks (
        house_position.x - (house_size_x / 2),
        house_position.y,
        house_position.z - (house_size_z / 2),
        house_position.x + (house_size_x / 2),
        house_position.y + house_size_y,
        house_position.z - (house_size_z / 2),
        block.BRICK_BLOCK.id)
```

```python
# build rear wall - south wall
mc.setBlocks (
    house_position.x - (house_size_x / 2),
    house_position.y,
    house_position.z + (house_size_z / 2),
    house_position.x + (house_size_x / 2),
    house_position.y + house_size_y,
    house_position.z + (house_size_z / 2),
    block.BRICK_BLOCK.id)
# build side wall - east wall
mc.setBlocks (
    house_position.x + (house_size_x / 2),
    house_position.y,
    house_position.z - (house_size_z / 2),
    house_position.x + (house_size_x / 2),
    house_position.y + house_size_y,
    house_position.z + (house_size_z / 2),
    block.BRICK_BLOCK.id)
# build side wall - west wall
mc.setBlocks (
    house_position.x - (house_size_x / 2),
    house_position.y,
    house_position.z - (house_size_z / 2),
    house_position.x - (house_size_x / 2),
    house_position.y + house_size_y,
    house_position.z + (house_size_z / 2),
    block.BRICK_BLOCK.id)
# Build roof
mc.setBlocks (
    house_position.x - (house_size_x / 2),
    house_position.y + house_size_y + 1,
    house_position.z - (house_size_z / 2),
    house_position.x + (house_size_x / 2),
    house_position.y + house_size_y + 1,
    house_position.z + (house_size_z / 2),
    block.WOOD.id)
```

```python
        # Frame of house now built - add doors and windows
        # Make doorway out of air block
        mc.setBlocks (
            house_position.x,
            house_position.y,
            house_position.z - (house_size_z / 2),
            house_position.x + 1,
            house_position.y + 2,
            house_position.z - (house_size_z / 2),
            block.AIR.id)

        # Add 2 windows
        mc.setBlocks (
            house_position.x + (house_size_x / 4),
            house_position.y + (house_size_y / 2),
            house_position.z - (house_size_z / 2),
            house_position.x + (house_size_x / 4) + 2,
            house_position.y + (house_size_y / 2) + 2,
            house_position.z - (house_size_z / 2),
            block.GLASS.id)

        mc.setBlocks (
            house_position.x - (house_size_x / 4),
            house_position.y + (house_size_y / 2),
            house_position.z - (house_size_z / 2),
            house_position.x - (house_size_x / 4) - 2,
            house_position.y + (house_size_y / 2) + 2,
            house_position.z - (house_size_z / 2),
            block.GLASS.id)

#Run the main function when this program is run
if __name__ == "__main__":
    main()
```

This looks a lot of code, although that is partly because each setBlocks command uses eight lines as the command is split across multiple lines to make it easier to read.

This is not required, but by having each one on its own line, it makes it easier to see how each of the x, y, and z positions are calculated.

A bit of care needs to be taken when deciding on where to position the house in the Minecraft world. While the code will carve out the space needed for the house, it would look odd if much of the house was in the air or if the door is inaccessible. Ideally, the house should be on a level area. Also, if the wall with the door is positioned in the side of a hill, then you may need to dig yourself out.

If you want to teleport yourself to the house in future, the big button is reserved for this, and then the position is saved in the house_position variable, so that can be used with setTilePos().

The finished house is shown in Figure 10-8.

Figure 10-8. *Minecraft house built using code*

The program has used inputs from the joystick and buttons. It's also possible to use Minecraft to give outputs. You could, for example, have an LED light up depending upon the proximity to certain resources or create a game which activates an LED when a certain objective is achieved.

More Minecraft Hardware Programming

This chapter has created a game console that can be used for interacting between the user and computer software. This is not too different from how a USB joystick works, although in the case of a USB joystick there is additional hardware to convert the signals before sending them to the Raspberry Pi. You could use this console to create your own games that interact with the joysticks and buttons or configure it for use with RetroPie.

The console has then been used to demonstrate the use of an API using the popular game of Minecraft. The electronics has been kept simple in this chapter to focus on the interaction with the Minecraft API, but that does not need to be the case. You could also use any of the other sensors from the earlier chapters or used the movement in Minecraft to send instructions to a robot created in the previous chapter.

If you are interested in doing more in Minecraft Pi, then there is more information on the API at `www.stuffaboutcode.com/p/minecraft-api-reference.html`.

The next chapter will look at logic gates and digital electronics to provide an understanding on how computers and digital systems work.

CHAPTER 11

Understanding Digital Logic

Digital logic is the basis around how all digital electronics work including the basic building blocks for creating a computer such as a Raspberry Pi. It's an interesting subject, but there is too much to cover just using practical projects. This chapter is therefore going to be more about the theory rather than learning through practical projects. At the end of the chapter, there will still be a practical element, which is based around 7-segment LED displays.

Some of the concepts on here are better explained through animation. I have created some videos which explain some of these concepts, which are on my website at www. penguintutor.com/electronics/digital.

Digital Logic and Binary

When talking about digital electronics, such as microprocessors and computers, information is represented by switches that turn the voltage between high and low. This has already been covered when using the GPIO ports where the output has been turned on or off which represent the high and low states. On the Raspberry Pi, there is no way of turning a GPIO port partway on; PWM was used to create the illusion of the port being partly turned on, but that was actually achieved by turning the output high and low quickly.

With only a single output, it is only possible to hold a tiny amount of data, but when multiple outputs are used together or a switch is turned on and off in a specific sequence, this can be used to represent anything you want. To provide meaningful data, the information is stored and manipulated using the binary numeral system.

© Stewart Watkiss 2020
S. Watkiss, *Learn Electronics with Raspberry Pi*, https://doi.org/10.1007/978-1-4842-6348-8_11

Binary is a base-two number system with each digit either a 0 (which is represented in electronics as a logic low, such as 0V) or a 1 (which is represented in electronics as a logic high, such as 3.3V). Within processors, the information is grouped into multiple bits; it was common to have 8 bits which makes a byte, although most computers now are either 32-bit or 64-bit. Using a single byte which is 8 bits long, it is possible to represent up to 256 different values, which go from 00000000_2 (decimal 0) to 11111111_2 (decimal 255). Showing each entry as individual bits takes up a lot of characters, so it is common to show these as hexadecimal values, where 4 bits is replaced by a single hexadecimal character from 0 to F (where letters are used for values above 9). The maximum 8-bit number of is 11111111_2, represented as FF_{16}. You may have already used hexadecimal values when dealing with colors in HTML.

The information in the binary numbers can be in parallel, which is across multiple wires known as a bus, or transmitted as a serial signal over a single wire. A bus is used internally within a processor and for connecting to memory, whereas serial transmission is normally used for connecting to external devices such as over USB.

Logic Gates

The basic building blocks used to create digital circuits are logic gates. There are four primary logic gates – NOT, AND, OR, and XOR, which can then be combined to create more complicated circuits. These are represented by circuit symbols used in schematic diagrams, as with other symbols, there are different standards. There are two shown for each, one of which is based around a distinctive shape for each gate and the other is based on a rectangular block. The logic gates are available packaged in integrated circuit (typically, 4 to 8 in a single IC) or are incorporated into more complicated circuits, which use the logic gates as building blocks.

NOT Gate (Inverter)

A NOT gate is also known as an inverter. It changes a low signal to a high signal and vice versa. The common circuit symbols are shown in Figure 11-1. In these symbols, the circle on the output indicates that these are inverting. An alternative symbol uses the same rectangular block as the symbol on the right but with a triangle in place of the circle.

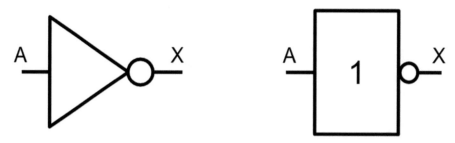

Figure 11-1. *Circuit symbols for a logic NOT gate*

The truth table is used to indicate the status of the output based on the inputs. In the case of the NOT gate, there are only two different states, which are shown in Figure 11-2.

A	X
0	1
1	0

Figure 11-2. *Truth table for a NOT gate*

The truth table shows all possible inputs (A) and the corresponding outputs (X). The inputs are denoted by letters from the start of the alphabet, whereas the outputs are denoted by letters near the end of the alphabet; this is a convention that makes it easy to understand the difference between inputs and outputs.

A NOT gate can be created using a MOSFET. A basic inverting circuit has already been covered in Chapter 6 when creating a MOSFET buffer. When used previously, the inverting aspect was a side effect of the way the MOSFET worked rather than something we wanted. In this case, it is the desired effect. The basic circuit is shown in Figure 11-3.

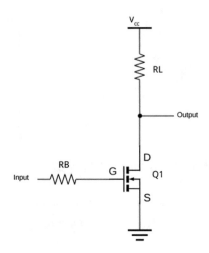

Figure 11-3. *Example circuit for a MOSFET NOT gate*

When the input is low, the MOSFET is switched off. The output is pulled high through resistor RL. When the input is high, the transistor switches on pulling the output low.

The circuit shown is just an illustration of how a NOT gate can be created. The circuit within a logic gate IC is more complicated than this. The output stage normally includes a p-type MOSFET in place of the resistor RL. The p-type MOSFET would operate the opposite to the n-type MOSFET. This means that the output is actively pulled up and pulled down instead of using a passive pull-up resistor. This allows the output to drive a bigger load and maintains the logic levels better. Using a n-type and p-type MOSFET in this way is known as CMOS (complementary metal-oxide-semiconductor). The input stage may also include additional components such as additional diodes to protect against a higher input voltage or static electricity.

AND Gate

The next logic gate is the AND gate. The AND gate has at least two inputs and only gives a high output when all the inputs are high. The logic symbol is shown in Figure 11-4.

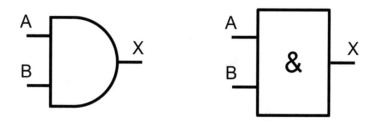

Figure 11-4. *Circuit symbols for a logic AND gate*

The truth table is shown in Figure 11-5. As you can see, the output is 0 for all inputs, except where A AND B are both 1.

A	B	X
0	0	0
0	1	0
1	0	0
1	1	1

Figure 11-5. *Truth table for an AND gate*

The diagram in Figure 11-6 shows a circuit which can act as an AND gate. This is a conceptual circuit to demonstrate how an AND gate functions; an actual logic gate is more complex. As you can see from the diagram, to complete the path between the supply voltage at the top and the output X, both MOSFETs need to be switched on; therefore, both A and B must be high.

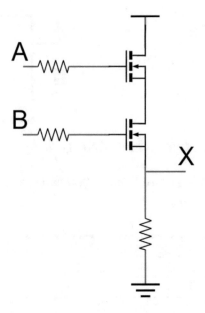

Figure 11-6. *Circuit demonstrating how an AND gate works*

OR Gate

The OR gate has two or more inputs and has a high output if one or more of the inputs is high. The logic symbols for the OR gate are shown in Figure 11-7.

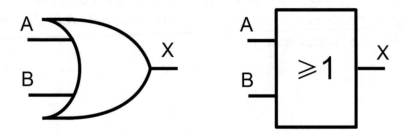

Figure 11-7. *Circuit symbols for a logic AND gate*

The truth table for the OR gate is shown in Figure 11-8.

A	B	X
0	0	0
0	1	1
1	0	1
1	1	1

Figure 11-8. *Truth table for an OR gate*

The diagram in Figure 11-9 shows a circuit which can act as an OR gate. This is a conceptual circuit to demonstrate how an OR gate functions; an actual logic gate is more complex.

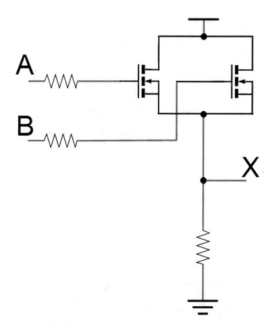

Figure 11-9. *Circuit demonstrating how an OR gate works*

As you can see from this diagram, there are two paths between the positive supply and the output. If either of the MOSFETs is turned on, then the output is high.

XOR Gate

The XOR gate is an abbreviation of exclusive OR. This will provide a high output when only one of the inputs is high. The symbols for the XOR gate are shown in Figure 11-10.

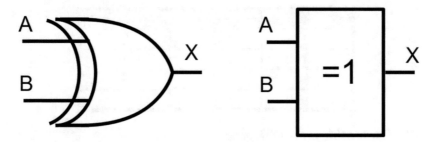

Figure 11-10. *Circuit symbols for a logic AND gate*

The truth table is shown in Figure 11-11, which shows a high output when A or B is high but not if both A and B are high.

A	B	X
0	0	0
0	1	1
1	0	1
1	1	0

Figure 11-11. *Truth table for an XOR gate*

Although previously I included XOR as a primary logic gate, it can actually be made up using other logic gates. This is shown in the circuit in Figure 11-12, which shows an XOR gate made up of NOT, AND, and OR gates.

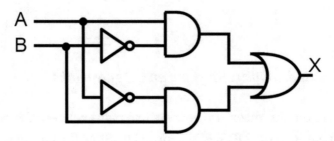

Figure 11-12. *Logic circuit for an XOR gate using NOT, AND, and OR gates*

This logic circuit diagram is significant as it shows how more complex operations can be made by joining logic gates together. In this case, the top AND gate has a high output if A is high and B is low. The bottom AND gate has a high output if A is low and B is high. Then the OR gate gives a high output if either of the two AND gates is high. This way, the output X is high when one input is high and the other is low.

NAND and NOR

Previously, I listed the four primary logic gates as NOT, AND, OR, and XOR; however, perhaps more important are the NAND and NOR gates. The NAND gate is effectively an AND gate, followed by a NOT gate, and the NOR gate is an OR gate, followed by a NOT gate. These are known as the complements of the AND and OR gates. These were made popular because they could be created more simply, but also could mimic the other logic gates. In that way, it is possible to take a circuit that uses any of the four logic gates and replace it with a circuit that uses just NAND or NOT gates. This was significant when circuits were created using logic ICs.

The circuit symbols are the same as the AND and OR gates, but with a circle or sometimes a triangle on the output. Some common symbols for the NAND are NOR gates, shown in Figure 11-13.

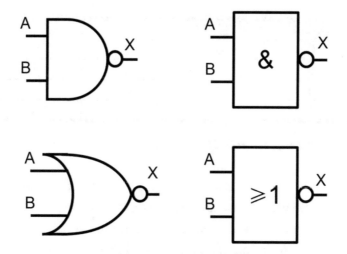

Figure 11-13. Circuit symbols for logic NAND and NOR gates

Creating Logic Circuits – Adder

Using the different logic gates, it is possible to combine them into a more complicated circuit. An important function in microprocessors is the ability to add numbers together.

Addition forms the basis of many mathematical operations in a computer and is also needed for counters which keep track of whereabouts the next instruction is in the program code.

The most basic form of adder circuit is known as a half adder. This is shown in Figure 11-14 created using an XOR and a AND gate.

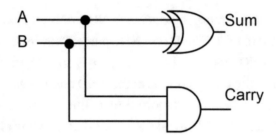

Figure 11-14. *Half adder circuit*

If both A and B are low, then both outputs are low. If one is high and the other low, then the sum is high, and carry is low. If both inputs are high, then the sum is low, but the carry is high. This is shown in the truth table in Figure 11-15.

A	B	Carry	Sum
0	0	0	0
0	1	0	1
1	0	0	1
1	1	1	0

Figure 11-15. *Truth table for a half adder*

The reason that this is known as a half adder is because while there is a carry out, there is no carry in. If we want to use this on a more inputs (such as an 8-bit number), then there needs to be some way of including the carry in from the lower bit.

The improved circuit to support carry in as well is the full adder with the circuit shown in Figure 11-16.

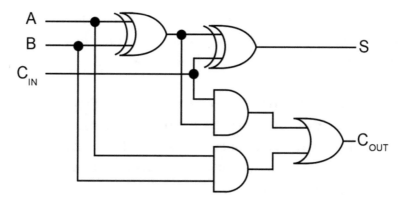

Figure 11-16. *Full adder circuit*

The full adder circuit is labeled with C_{IN} for carry in, S for the sum, and C_{OUT} for carry out. If an 8-bit adder is needed, then that can be created by copying this diagram eight times and adding the carry out of each lower bit to the carry in of the next higher bit. If you create that circuit diagram, you would have to put 20 logic symbols. If you want to create an adder for larger numbers such as 16-bit, 32-bit, or 64-bit numbers, then the circuit diagrams are going to be very large. Fortunately, this can be simplified. Just like we use a logic symbol to hide the complexity of the actual transistors inside the gate, you can simplify an adder to a single symbol. The symbol for a full adder is shown in Figure 11-17.

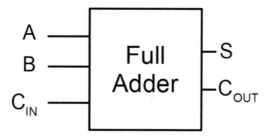

Figure 11-17. *Circuit symbol for a full adder*

As you can see, the complexity of the previous circuit is hidden in a single rectangle, which is labeled with the function of the circuit. This is commonly used for many different circuits to make it easier to understand and reduce the size of the diagrams.

In the case of an 8-bit adder, the symbol could be replaced with a single block with the single input A replaced with inputs A_0–A_7 and the same for the B inputs and the sum outputs. There will only be one carry in and carry out as the others are used internally.

This technique for simplifying circuit diagrams can be used for any level of complexity even to the point where it is used to represent the entire computer. This has already been used in numerous diagrams in this book where the Raspberry Pi is shown as a single block.

Using multiple full adders to create an adder does have a disadvantage when it comes to speed. Logic circuits act very quickly, but when chained together, the small delays can add up. In the case of the adder, the least significant bit performs the add before passing the carry out to the next stage. The output of the next stage in the adder is dependent upon that carry out from the first stage. This is known as a ripple carry adder. It is possible to instead have a fast adder which can calculate each bit of the number simultaneously, although the circuitry is increasingly complex.

Flip-Flops

The adder circuit is an example of a combinational logic circuit. This means that (except for the delay in updating the outputs) the logic output is entirely dependent upon the inputs at the time. It is sometimes necessary to store information either as a form of short-term memory (such as a register in a processor) or so that the information is presented to other stages of the circuit when they are ready to receive it. This needs sequential logic, of which the most basic form is the flip-flop. There are several different types of flip-flops, three of which are explained as follows.

Basic Flip-Flop

The basic flip-flop can be made up using two NOR or NAND gates with feedback between the output and input. The NOR and NAND gate circuits work in a similar way, although the NOR-based circuit is triggered by a high logic signal, whereas the NAND-based circuit is based on a low logic signal. The NOR circuit is a little easier to understand, so that is the one used here. The circuit is shown in Figure 11-18.

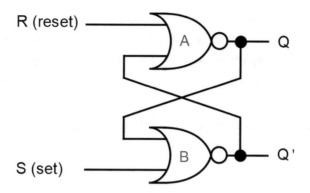

Figure 11-18. *Basic flip-flop with NOR gates*

The flip-flop has two inputs, called set and reset. There are two outputs Q and Q';
these are complementary outputs. The Q is the data output and Q' the complement
(opposite) of that output. The set input is used to set the flip-flop to the set state (Q=1),
and the reset puts the flip-flop into the reset state (Q=0). I have labeled the NOR gates as
A and B; this is purely to make the explanation easier.

The output from each of the NOR gates is used as an input to the opposite gate. This
is feedback used to maintain the state of the flip-flop.

The initial state cannot be determined until either set or reset is taken high. When set
is taken high (S=1), at least one input of B is 1 and then the output of the B=0. Assuming
R=0, the output of the A depends upon the output of B. With B=0, A=1 and so the output
Q=1. If set goes to 0, then gate B still has a high input from the output of A and so B=0. As
such, the flip-flop maintains the set state and Q=1.

If set is at 0 and reset is set to 1, then A=0, which sets the output Q=0. As both inputs
to B are now 0, B=1. If the reset now goes to 0, then the reset state is maintained by the
feedback.

If you want to get a better understanding of how a flip-flop works, then this is shown
in the truth table in Figure 11-19.

S	R	Q	Q'	
1	0	1	0	
0	0	1	0	If Q = 1
0	1	0	1	
0	0	0	1	If Q = 0
1	1	0	0	

Figure 11-19. *Truth table for a basic NOR flip-flop*

This truth table is different from the previous ones, in that there are now two lines with the same inputs (S=0 and R=0) but different outputs. This is because they are dependent upon the previous state. The final entry, where set and reset are both high, is invalid as both Q and its complement are the same. This state should be avoided when using flip-flops.

This basic flip-flop is useful for understanding how a flip-flop works, although the flip-flops that are normally used also include a clock signal.

SR Flip-Flop

The basic flip-flop provides the set and reset function that the SR flip-flop uses. The flip-flops that are used in most circuits had the added ability to determine at what point in time the data is stored into the flip-flop. This is done by adding either an enable signal (which is triggered by logical level) or a clock signal (which is edge triggered), so that the state of the flip-flop only changes when ready.

This is important when the flip-flop takes an input from a previous stage where there may be a delay before the data is valid. For example, with the ripple adder, there is a state where the output may change based on its inputs, but because the carry has not yet rippled through, the output is incorrect. In this case, the enable or clock signal would only be triggered after there has been time for the adder to complete its calculation.

The circuit symbols in Figure 11-20 show three different symbols based on different types of enable or clock signal.

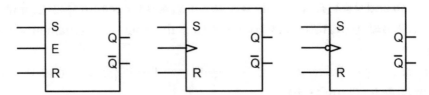

Figure 11-20. *SR flip-flops with different enable and clock types*

The symbol on the left is based on an enable input. The state of the flip-flop can change only when the enable (E) is high. If that signal is set permanently high, then it will operate the same as the basic flip-flop.

You will also note that the complementary output Q' is shown as Q with a line over it. These mean the same thing, that the output is the opposite of Q. The line above the output is often used in diagrams but is difficult to include in printed text so is sometimes replaced with Q'. It is also common to see inputs with a line over them, particularly the enable pin; this indicates that the input is based on the enable being low instead of high.

The other symbols show an arrow to indicate it is an edge-triggered clock signal. The default is for a positive edge trigger (when the clock changes from low to high), and the circle denotes a negative edge trigger (when the clock changes from high to low).

Note   You may also see reference to an RS flip-flop. The RS flip-flop is the same as the SR flip-flop in normal operations. They behave differently in the condition where set and reset are high. If this condition is triggered, then with the SR flip-flop the set takes precedent and with the RS flip-flop the reset takes precedent.

D Flip-Flop

The SR flip-flop is useful if you have a separate set and reset signal. It is often the case that you have a single input based on the output of a previous logic circuit. In that case, a D flip-flop is used, where D stands for data. The D flip-flop will store the data on its input based on the clock trigger. The symbol for a D flip-flop is shown in Figure 11-21.

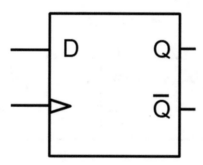

Figure 11-21. *Symbol for a D flip-flop*

One side effect of the D flip-flop is that it no longer has the invalid state, where both set and reset are triggered together. It does still have the state at the beginning when the status is undetermined.

Other Flip-Flops

There are other flip-flops and variations on the ones already shown. Some flip-flops have both enable and clock inputs allowing the clock to be connected to the system clock but only updating when enabled. Some also have additional inputs to set the flip-flop to a pre-determined state to avoid the unknown state when first turned on.

Connecting eight flip-flops side by side but sharing a single clock is known as an 8-bit latch, also known as an 8-bit register. Registers are a fundamental part of how computers work, allowing data to be held temporarily when retrieving from memory or for use as the input or output of any calculations within the processor.

Shift Register

Another use of flip-flops is to create a shift register, which is useful for converting serial data to parallel data. This will be used in an example circuit to reduce the number of pins needed to connect 7-segment LED displays to the Raspberry Pi GPIO.

To create the shift register, multiple D flip-flops are connected, with the output from one stage becoming the input to the next stage. This is shown in Figure 11-22.

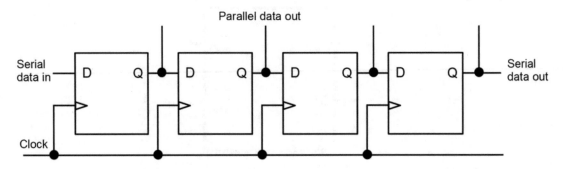

Figure 11-22. *Shift register circuit*

The example shows four stages in the shift register, although I will describe this in terms of an 8-bit shift register, which will be used for the practical example. As you can see, each of the flip-flops is connected using the output from the previous (Q) as the input to the next stage (D). They all share a common clock, so data is transferred simultaneously at each stage. The serial data goes into the first D flip-flop and is saved on the first clock pulse. The serial input is then set to the next bit of information, and on the next clock pulse, the data that is on the first flip-flop is passed to the next one and the new data is stored on the first flip-flop. This continues until all the data is shifted in; for an 8-bit shift register, this takes eight clock pulses. At that point, parallel out is now a parallel version of the serial data. There is also a serial data out which can be used for connecting to another shift register. This allows multiple shift registers to be connected without needing any additional outputs from the Raspberry Pi (or other driving circuit), but that is at the cost of time as that means that more data needs to be shifted through the shift registers.

In most circumstances, you would not want to see the data going through the shift register, so the parallel output should not change until all 8 bits have been sent through the register. To do this, we need an output register, or a latch, which is another use of the D flip-flop. In effect for each bit of data, there will be one D flip-flop for shifting the data in and one D flip-flop for latching that data to the output. A second clock is needed for the output, but that only triggers once for every eight pulses of the serial clock.

This is shown in Figure 11-23, which shows a high-level representation of the components.

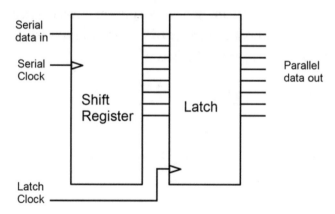

Figure 11-23. *Shift to parallel shift register with latch*

This diagram shows the shift register used to convert the serial data into parallel data, which is then fed into the latch. The shift register and latch have their own clock signal so that the latch only updates the parallel data out when the latch clock is triggered.

If you are looking to buy a shift register as an integrated circuit, then you do not need to buy the latch separately as the IC will include both. It may also have additional circuitry for output enable and sometimes an additional output buffer stage for driving large currents. One such example is the TPIC6B595 8-bit shift register, which is used in the next circuit.

Shift Register LED Circuit

After covering the theory of digital logic, it is now possible to put that into practice in a useful circuit. This will be a shift register that will provide eight outputs from the Raspberry Pi using only three pins from the GPIO. This will be used to drive LEDs.

The shift register will be provided by an integrated circuit, TPIC6B595. This is a shift register with built-in latch. One of the intended uses of this IC is in automobile dashboard displays, where it can be used to drive the LED warning lights. This is achieved through an open-drain output on the parallel data outputs. An open-drain output is where instead of having a push-pull output that is used for many CMOS logic gates, the outputs do not have any connection to the positive voltage but have MOSFET between the output and ground. This allows it to handle a larger current but cannot be used to drive other logic circuits without having a pull-up resistor (except for serial data out). Figure 11-24 shows a simplified version of an open-drain output, which would typically also include some protection diodes.

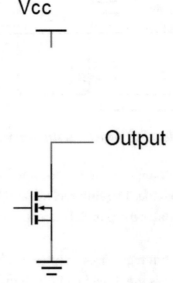

Figure 11-24. *Open-drain output*

Another benefit to having an open-drain output is that a different supply voltage can be used for the load. This is useful if switching loads that need a different voltage.

The circuit diagram for the LED circuit is shown in Figure 11-25.

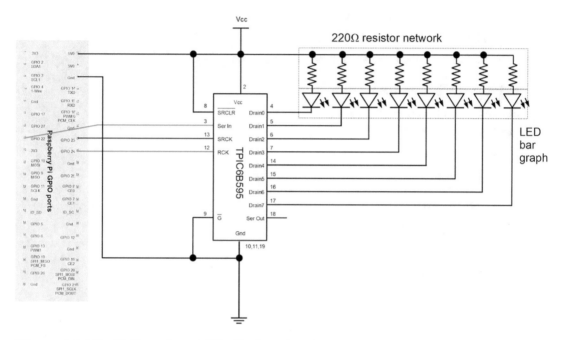

Figure 11-25. *Shift register LED display circuit*

For this circuit, I have used a resistor network, which is eight resistors in a single package with a common connection. I have also used an LED bar graph display. The LED has ten LEDs in a single module, although I am only using eight of the LEDs for this circuit. The LED display and resistor network are for convenience, and to make it easier to see the individual lights, these can be substituted for standard 220Ω resistors and normal LEDs instead.

The program provided for this is a demonstration program to show how the shift register works. This is included in Listing 11-1, saved as shiftreg-demo.py.

Listing 11-1. Shift register demonstration program

```
from gpiozero import DigitalOutputDevice
from time import sleep
```

```python
serial_pin = 22
serial_clock_pin = 23
register_clock_pin = 24

serial_out = DigitalOutputDevice(serial_pin)
serial_clock = DigitalOutputDevice(serial_clock_pin)
register_clock = DigitalOutputDevice(register_clock_pin)

def shift_bit (bit_value):
    serial_out.value = bit_value
    serial_clock.on()
    sleep(0.001)
    serial_clock.off()

def register_update ():
    register_clock.on()
    sleep(0.001)
    register_clock.off()

def shift_byte (byte_value):
    # shift data 1 bit at a time
    for i in range (0,8):
        # shift out 1 bit
        bit_value = byte_value & 0b00000001
        shift_bit (bit_value)
        byte_value >>= 1
    register_update ()

def slow_shift_byte (byte_value):
    # shift data 1 bit at a time
    for i in range (0,8):
        # shift out 1 bit
        bit_value = byte_value & 0b00000001
        shift_bit (bit_value)
        byte_value >>= 1
        register_update ()
        sleep(0.5)
```

```
print ("Resetting shift register")
shift_byte (0b00000000)
sleep(0.5)

print ("Slow shift to 00000001")
slow_shift_byte (0b00000001)
sleep(2)

print ("Slow shift to 10101011")
slow_shift_byte (0b10101011)
sleep(2)

print ("Shifting in 11001100")
shift_byte (0b11001100)
sleep(1)
print ("Shifting in 00110011")
shift_byte (0b00110011)
```

The code has four functions. The first is shift_bit, which shifts a single bit of data into the serial port. It does this by setting the serial output to the value and then sending a 1ms pulse on the serial clock signal. The next function is register_update, which sends a 1ms pulse on the register clock signal to send the value in the shift register to the output register. Using these two functions, you can manually send a bit at a time to the shift register. The next two are used to send a word at a time. The function shift_byte is the normal operation of a shift register sending 8 bits of serial data. It uses a bitwise AND (&) to extract the least significant bit and send that to the shift register. It then uses the bitwise right shift (>>=1) to shift the variable along one bit. Once all 8 bits have been sent, it calls register_update. The final function slow_shift_byte is similar to the shift_byte, but it runs register_update after each bit and has a delay, so you can see as each bit is shifted through the shift register.

The rest of the code provides a short demonstration – first resetting the shift register to all zeros and then running two slow shift examples so you can see the individual bits being pushed through the shift register. It then has two examples using normal operation where the output of the shift register does not change until all 8 bits have been sent.

The code uses binary notation (prefixed with 0b) for the demonstration, but it can be passed an integer instead and will work correctly. You can have the code run through an example of counting in binary by replacing the demonstration part of the code with the following:

```
print ("Counting in binary")
for i in range (0, 256):
    shift_byte (i)
    sleep (0.3)
```

This will count from 0 to 255, which is the full range of values that can be stored in an 8-bit number.

Logic Levels

If you build the circuit in Figure 11-25, then it will almost certainly work. However, note that I said "almost certainly"; it is technically an invalid design, so there is a chance it will not (although I expect only a slim chance it will not work). The reason that the design is invalid is because the Raspberry Pi GPIO and the TPIC6B595 are designed for different logic voltage levels. The Raspberry Pi GPIO is designed for 3.3V, whereas the TPIC6B595 for 5V. There is no danger of damage to the components, as the output is lower than the expected voltage, which may not be the case if it was the other way around. If you put the output from a 5V circuit into a 3.3V Raspberry Pi pin configured for input, then there is a high possibility you will damage the Raspberry Pi.

To understand this in detail, you need to look at the specification for both components. These details are normally taken from the datasheet, which will be explained further in Chapter 13. The details needed are the outputs from the Raspberry Pi GPIO ports and the inputs on the TPIC6B595. The table in Figure 11-26 shows these based on the relevant specifications.

Raspberry Pi GPIO Output				TPIC6B595 Input		
V_{OL}	Output low voltage	VDD IO = 3.3V	Max 0.14V	V_{IL}	Low-level input voltage	Max 0.15 V_{CC}
V_{OH}	Output high voltage	VDD IO =3.3V IOH = 2mA	Min 3.0V	V_{IH}	High-level input voltage	Min 0.85 V_{CC}

Figure 11-26. *Table showing specified logic voltage levels*

The values on the left show the logic level output from the Raspberry Pi. In the case of a logic low, the value will be no more than 0.14V and in a logic high (assuming 2mA output) will be at least 3.0V. The inputs to the TPIC6B595 are provided in terms of the supply voltage V_{CC}. This says the input for a logic low should be no more than $0.15 \times V_{CC}$ and the input for a logic high should be at least $0.85 \times V_{CC}$. With the supply voltage as 5V, this means that a low input must be no more than 0.75V (so the Raspberry Pi low signal is compatible) and a high voltage of at least 4.25V (of which the Raspberry Pi GPIO value is too low).

Looking at the input to the TPIC6B595, there is a range of voltages from 0.75V to 4.25V where the input voltage is out of the specified range. What happens if the voltage is in that unspecified area? In actual use, you will find that the shift register accepts a voltage much lower than the 4.25V as a high signal, but that is not guaranteed. Likewise, the Raspberry Pi GPIO high output is most likely higher than the 3.0V, nearer to 3.3V, but again that is not guaranteed.

There are different approaches that can be taken regarding this potential problem.

First, the option I have taken here is test it and see if it works. In this case, despite being out of the design specification, it does work, and it provides what I needed for this demonstration. There are several problems with this approach. Different ICs may have a different tolerance, and under different conditions, the voltage from the GPIO may be different, so it is possible for it to work on one setup, but not on another. It can also be very difficult to debug if it doesn't work. This option of leaving the circuit as it is does however have the advantage of simplicity and so is something you may want to consider, especially if it's just a personal project or a prototype to be developed further.

Another approach may be to reduce the voltage of the supply. As the minimum logic level is related to the supply voltage, it may be possible to reduce the supply voltage of the shift register. In the case of this IC, it can run as low as 4.5V, which gives a minimum input voltage of 3.8V. It is still not within the guaranteed output of the GPIO, but it has brought it closer and so more likely to work reliably.

If you still want to use this IC and want to ensure if it meets the design tolerances, then the last option is to increase the voltage from the GPIO using a buffer or level shifter. This has already been explained in Chapter 6, and a suitable circuit has been included in Figure 6-2. There are only three connections from the Raspberry Pi to the shift register, so that will need three MOSFETs and associated resistors.

The alternative is to look at an alternative IC, combination of ICs, or other circuit. I looked around and could not find a suitable shift register with open-drain outputs that is compatible with the 3.3V GPIO of the Raspberry Pi. I did however find a shift register with latch that is compatible with the 3.3V supply of the Raspberry Pi, which is the SN74HC595. The SN74HC595 can be run with a supply voltage of between 2 and 6 volts. Using it at 3.3V is fully compatible with the voltage level from the Raspberry Pi GPIO port. There is however one problem in that it does not have the same open-drain output and can only drive loads of around 5mA compared to the 20mA which is used for a suitable brightness from the LEDs (due to the use of extra-large LED displays). This can be resolved by adding another driver stage using either MOSFET switches or Darlington transistors as previously covered in Chapter 4. The Darlington transistors are also available in an IC, such as the ULN2803A, which has eight pairs within a single package. There are different variants of the 7N4HC595 some of which can handle larger currents and could drive the LEDs directly. The particular ones I found are surface mount devices which are not suitable for use on a breadboard, but they could be used on a PCB.

Shift Register 7-Segment LED Display Circuit

This can now be put to practical use in a circuit designed to display numbers on a 7-segment display. This could be a useful addition to the game console created in Chapter 10.

7-segment LED displays have seven rectangular LEDs, which are lit appropriately to create the image of a number. Often, they have one or more additional LEDs for showing a decimal point or a colon when used in a clock display. The eight outputs from the shift register are sufficient for showing a number and one decimal point.

The layout of a 7-segment display is shown in Figure 11-27.

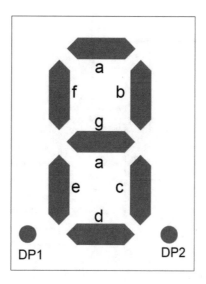

Figure 11-27. *7-segment LED display*

There are two types of LED display. The common anode has a single pin for the positive terminal (the anode), whereas the common cathode has a single pin for the negative terminal (the cathode). As these will be driven by a Darlington transistor, they need to be the common anode type. You should check the datasheet for the displays you use to check the pin-out. In my case, I used extra-large displays which have the pins on the side, whereas the smaller displays often have the pins on the top and bottom.

The circuit will use two 7-segment displays, each with their own shift register and Darlington driver ICs. They also need a resistor for each of the segments of the display. As a result, the circuit diagram is going to be quite big. The size of circuit diagrams is not really a problem as long as you are able to print it at a reasonable size or have the ability to zoom in. Unfortunately, that is not as easy when published in a book, so I have therefore split it across two diagrams. The first diagram in Figure 11-28 shows the shift registers and Darlington drivers, and the second diagram in Figure 11-29 has the 7-segment LED displays and resistors. I have used the connector symbol (circle) to indicate where the two diagrams join.

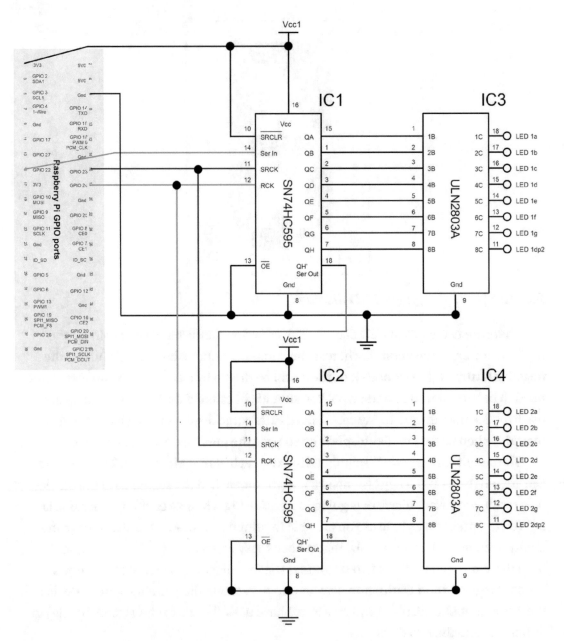

Figure 11-28. *7-segment LED circuit, part one*

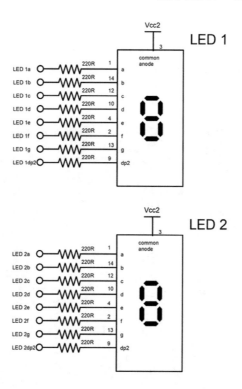

Figure 11-29. *7-segment LED circuit, part two*

Looking at the diagrams, there are two ground symbols, two $V_{CC}1$ power supply labels, and two $V_{CC}2$ labels. Where the power labels have the same reference, they are connected. This avoids having to have lines crossing the diagram, showing the power supply connection. If a separate power supply is used that is not connected, then that should be labeled different, such that Vcc1 and Vcc2 are different power supplies. In this case, Vcc2 should be a 5V supply; with only two 7-segment displays, these can be taken from the GPIO 5V ports; if more are connected, then it may need an external power supply.

You should be able to follow the rest of the diagrams as they follow the same principles as Figure 11-25, although this uses a different IC, the pins are labeled and numbered differently. The SN74HC595 datasheet uses Q for the outputs, which is fairly common, and then the serial output is marked as QH' which I've also labeled as Ser Out. The serial output connects to the serial input of the next shift register IC2, but the same clock signals are used, so both shift registers update at the same time. The datasheet for the Darlington driver IC (ULN2803A) labels the inputs as B and the outputs as C. There is also a common connection which can be used when switching inductive loads (such as motors), but it is not required in this case, so it is left unconnected.

I have created this on a large breadboard as shown in Figure 11-30. You will see that rather than use the jumper wires, I have used solid core wire cut to the exact length required. This takes much longer to do but becomes important when creating larger circuits.

Figure 11-30. *7-segment LED circuit on a breadboard*

I have created code which counts from 00 to 99. The displays could be used separately, such as a score value for player 1 and player 2, or as a single number. The counter displays all the different number combinations that can be displayed. This is saved as 7segment-counter.py, shown in Listing 11-2.

Listing 11-2. Shift register demonstration program

```python
from gpiozero import DigitalOutputDevice
from time import sleep

serial_pin = 22
serial_clock_pin = 23
register_clock_pin = 24

serial_out = DigitalOutputDevice(serial_pin)
serial_clock = DigitalOutputDevice(serial_clock_pin)
register_clock = DigitalOutputDevice(register_clock_pin)

number_values = [0b11111100, 0b01100000, 0b11011010,
    0b11110010, 0b01100110, 0b10110110, 0b10111110,
    0b11100000, 0b11111110, 0b11110110 ]

def shift_bit (bit_value):
    serial_out.value = bit_value
    serial_clock.on()
    sleep (0.001)
    serial_clock.off()

def register_update ():
    register_clock.on()
    sleep (0.001)
    register_clock.off()

def shift_byte (byte_value, update=True):
    # shift data 1 bit at a time
    for i in range (0,8):
        # shift out 1 bit
        bit_value = byte_value & 0b00000001
        shift_bit (bit_value)
        byte_value >>= 1
    if update == True:
        register_update ()
```

```
for i in range (0, 100):
    # tens value
    # No error checking - only works with 0 - 99
    digit_tens = i // 10 % 10
    digit_units = i - (digit_tens * 10)
    shift_byte (number_values[digit_units], False)
    shift_byte (number_values[digit_tens], True)
    sleep(0.5)
```

To create the number digits in terms of the 7-segment display, a dictionary is created, called number_values. These are the binary bit values to turn on the appropriate LED segments to create the digits from 0 to 9.

The code to send the data to the shift register is similar to the code in Listing 11-1. While using a different type of shift register, the code required to send the serial data is the same. The function shift_byte has an extra optional parameter so that the register_ update can be called after both bytes have been sent.

When counting through the values, the number needs to be split into two separate digits for each display which is handled by dividing the value by 10 (using // rounds the number down) and modulo.

The one thing that isn't included is the decimal point, which can be added by adding a 1 to the value in the number_values dictionary.

Summary

This chapter has shown the basics of digital logic gates and how they can be used to create more complicated combinational logic circuits as well as sequential logic. These are the basic building blocks of logical circuits. This also covers some of the key components that are used in a processor, including additional and registers.

The practical project has shown this can be used to expand the GPIO on the Raspberry Pi by using only three data lines to send serial data to an external shift register. This has been used to drive a bar graph LED display and then a pair of 7-segment LED displays.

The next chapter will look at how circuits can be made more permanent.

CHAPTER 12

Making Your Circuits Permanent

Most of the circuits we have made so far have been built using a breadboard. Creating circuits on breadboard is particularly useful when designing a new circuit as it allows for easy modifications to the design and reuse of the components. It does not work so well for permanent circuits as components and wires can get accidentally pulled out of the breadboard. This chapter will look at how to make circuits permanent so that they can survive a reasonable amount of use without the wires falling out. It will also enable you to use components that cannot be connected directly to a breadboard or components that need header pins to be soldered on before they can be connected to a breadboard. This includes many of the NeoPixels that were covered in Chapter 7.

This will involve soldering, which can sound daunting if you haven't done any before but is a useful skill and not as difficult as you may think.

It will also take a brief look at how to create a more professional looking product by placing the circuit into an enclosure and a look at some simple diagnostic tools if the circuit doesn't behave quite as it should.

Soldering

Soldering is a technique to join two metal objects by adding a metal filler. In the case of electronic circuits, this is a process commonly used to join an electronic component to a layer of copper on a printed circuit board or to join a wire to the lead of a component.

The metal used to form the join is known as solder. It has a lower melting point than the components to be joined together, which allows you to melt the solder which can then flow around the joint which then sets hard when allowed to cool. A good way to practice soldering is with a simple electronic kit. These don't need to be Raspberry

© Stewart Watkiss 2020
S. Watkiss, *Learn Electronics with Raspberry Pi*, https://doi.org/10.1007/978-1-4842-6348-8_12

Pi based, although there are some good ones that can be used with the Raspberry Pi. An electronics kit will often include a printed circuit board (PCB) along with some components that need to be soldered into place.

In addition to the kit, you are going to need a few tools to get started with. The minimum is a soldering iron with stand, a pair of wire cutters (preferably side cutters), and a reel of solder, although there are other tools that can make soldering a little easier.

Essential Soldering Tools

While it is possible to buy a basic soldering iron that is connected directly to a mains electrical plug, it is useful to buy one with temperature adjustment. The one that I use includes a digital temperature control, which is shown in Figure 12-1. The digital display is a nice luxury, but when starting out a less expensive one with a simple temperature control knob would be adequate.

Figure 12-1. *Temperature-controlled soldering iron*

Soldering irons also have a power rating. This does not necessarily mean that a soldering iron with a higher power rating will be at a higher temperature than one with a lower power rating. A soldering iron with a higher power rating (such as 50W or higher) will heat up quicker and will maintain the temperature better. This is most important when soldering to a thick gauge wire which can absorb a lot of heat from the soldering iron. For soldering on a PCB, the power rating is usually less important.

Most soldering irons have interchangeable tips with different shaped tips for different types of soldering. I normally use a chisel-shaped tip which makes it easier to get a good contact with the component and PCB. See Figure 12-4 later in this chapter for an example of the tip that I normally use. An alternative is a pointed tip that can be useful for soldering small components.

A soldering iron stand is essential to store the soldering iron when not in use. These usually include a sponge that should be kept moist for cleaning the tip between each use. An alternative to using a sponge is to use a tip cleaner made of brass shavings, which avoids the need to regularly moisten the sponge.

A pair of wire cutters is essential for cutting wires and removing the excess from component leads. They can also be used for stripping the insulation from wires if you don't have dedicated wire strippers. A sharp pair of wire cutters should make it much easier to strip the insulation from a wire than blunt ones.

Tip   Don't be tempted to use your teeth as wire strippers. A pair of wire strippers is much cheaper to replace than the potential damage you could do to your teeth.

A side cutter such as the one shown in Figure 12-2 is most useful as it has a flat side allowing you to cut close to the joint.

Figure 12-2. *Pair of side cutters*

Solder

A good quality solder intended for hobby electronic circuits is normally an alloy made up of a mix of silver, copper, and tin. It normally includes a non-corrosive flux often made from rosin. The flux prevents oxidization during soldering and helps form a clean joint.

In the past, solders often contained lead, but due to concerns about health and the environment, these have become less popular. Some countries have imposed restrictions on the use of lead in commercial products. While some people prefer to use a lead-based solder, a good quality lead-free solder is easy enough to use for most purposes.

Although there is no lead in lead-free solder, there are still many other toxins that can cause serious health problems. Those involved in soldering on a regular basis should use a fume extraction system, which may be mandatory if using at work. A proper fume extraction system may be prohibitively expensive for hobby use. I have a simple fume disperser (sometimes referred to as a fume absorber), which is shown in Figure 12-3. These fume dispersers will not remove the toxins in a rosin-based flux but instead draw the fumes away from the person soldering and dispersing them around the room. These should only be used for occasional use, in a well-ventilated area where the fumes will be able to disperse outside and where other people will not breathe the air coming out the rear.

Figure 12-3. *Bench top fume disperser*

Safety Tips when Soldering

While the idea of holding a hot soldering iron may sound dangerous as long as basic safety precautions are followed, it is relatively safe activity. The following are some basic precautions that should be taken when soldering.

Hot Soldering Iron

It goes without saying that an iron that is hot enough to melt solder could easily burn skin. Accidentally touching your finger with a soldering iron can leave a small burn with no long-lasting effects, but grabbing the end of the soldering iron could cause a more substantial burn. For this reason, it is important to place the soldering iron into a holder and ensure that the wire is not going to get pulled by mistake. Also remember that a soldering iron will remain hot for a long time after it has been switched off or unplugged.

If you do burn yourself, then flood the area with water and leave under running cold water for at least 10 minutes. Any concerns then seek professional medical advice.

Soldering Iron Stand

Always place the soldering iron in a suitable stand when not in use.

Solder Fumes

Breathing in solder fumes regularly can cause serious health problems. Always solder in a well-ventilated area or using appropriate fume extraction (see earlier).

Protect Your Eyes

When cutting leads from components, beware of any ends that may fly off and go in your eye. This can be avoided by holding the loose end leads in one hand when snipping them off or by wearing appropriate eye protection.

Never Solder a Live Circuit

Always remove power from a circuit board prior to any soldering. This is important to protect the power supply (or battery) and components, and from a safety point of view.

Adult Supervision

Soldering is not a difficult activity and can be undertaken by children of an appropriate age as long as it is under appropriate adult supervision.

Soldering to a Printed Circuit Board

One of the easiest ways to start soldering is using a printed circuit board (PCB). These often have the component positions marked on the top so that the component can be easily inserted and then soldered on the bottom of the board. When soldering, you usually want the component to be as close to the PCB as possible. Perhaps the biggest challenge is keeping the circuit board still and ensuring that the component stays in the right place when soldering; this can be tricky particularly with large components. To make this easier, start with the smallest components first and support the rest of the PCB with padding. I will sometimes use a piece of Lego, or similar, to support the PCB.

Once you have the component in place, follow these steps:

- Place the tip of the hot soldering iron so it is in contact with both the pad on the PCB and the lead of the component.

- Bring the solder in and allow sufficient solder to melt to form the joint.

- Remove the solder but leave the soldering iron in place for a few seconds to allow the solder to flow around the pad and the component's lead.

- Remove the soldering iron and allow the joint to cool.

- Ensure that the solder had made a good joint (if not repeat).

- Check that the solder does not expand beyond the pad causing a bridge to any other components or pads.

- Snip off the excess wire from the component.

The photo in Figure 12-4 shows the soldering iron touching both the PCB pad and the component lead.

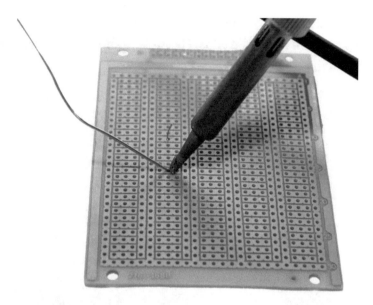

Figure 12-4. *Soldering iron just before making a solder joint*

Soldering is a skill best learned through practice. So, don't get too disheartened if your first solder joint looks a bit untidy. Try again with more circuits and your skills will improve over time.

Here are a few additional hints and tips when soldering:

- Regularly clean the tip, wiping it on a damp sponge or using a brass tip cleaner.

- Tin the tip of the soldering iron using a small amount of solder on the tip.

- Avoid using too much solder.

- Always check for any stray bits of solder and short circuits before connecting the circuit to your Raspberry Pi or power supply.

Soldering Direct to Leads

Soldering leads and wires directly together can be a little more difficult, mainly because the wires don't stay where you need them to. This is where a set of helping hands can be very useful. A traditional helping hand has two crocodile clips mounted on a stand often with a magnifying glass attached. I personally prefer the SparkFun Third Hand which comes with two crocodile clips on flexible stands. I have added two additional crocodile clips to mine, two of which are padded with heat shrink tubing and the other two are bare crocodile clips. Figure 12-5 shows my setup with a wire ready to be soldered to an LED.

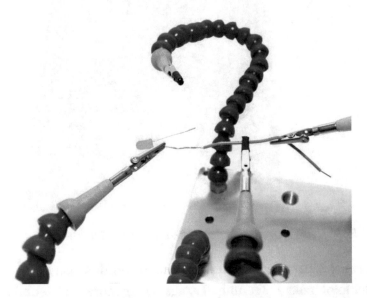

Figure 12-5. *SparkFun Third Hand used to solder a wire to an LED*

With careful positioning, it should be possible to touch the soldering iron to both the LED and wire and then apply the soldering along the two to form a joint. If you need to insulate the leads, then some heat shrink tubing can be placed over the wire before soldering and then moved into position.

Heat shrink tubing is hollow tubing that can be placed over a wire and will shrink when heated. A hot air gun (such as the ones used as paint strippers) should be used to shrink the tubing.

Stripboard

The next chapter will look at making a custom PCB, but when getting started, stripboard is often cheaper and easier. Stripboard (also known under the brand name Veroboard) is a circuit board with copper strips or pads on one side of the board. These are like a permanent equivalent of the breadboard, and in fact, stripboard is available that follows a similar layout to the breadboard we have been using. Figure 12-6 shows some stripboard in a variety of shapes and sizes.

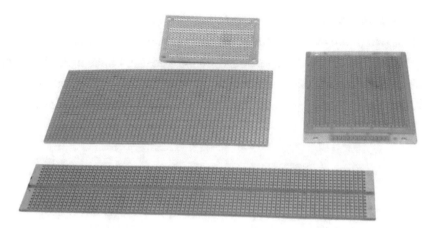

Figure 12-6. *Stripboard*

The components are positioned across the rows much like you would create your breadboard circuit, but with soldering required to join each component to the copper strip. Some designs of stripboard have strips that are broken in a central row which is good for mounting integrated circuits; alternatively, a stripboard cutter can be used to create breaks in the track. A stripboard cutter is a hand tool which looks like a drill with a screwdriver handle. These can be twisted against the track to remove the copper strip over one position at a time.

Perfboard

Perfboard is like stripboard, but without any of the copper pads joined together. The copper pads can be used to hold the components in position, but then wires need to be added joining the components. I personally recommend stripboard over perfboard as I find it can be difficult to get tidy joints when using perfboard.

Raspberry Pi Prototyping Boards

One drawback of stripboard and perfboard is that they don't lend themselves to mounting on top of the Raspberry Pi. One problem is that the connector to fit on the GPIO connecting needs to be mounted on the underside, but it's also difficult to get it positioned just right. They are useful for circuits that are mounted away from the Raspberry Pi and can still be connected to the Raspberry Pi using wires or a cobbler.

A better solution is a prototyping board designed to connect on top of the Raspberry Pi. I have taken two of the circuits used previously and mounted them on top of a prototyping board. The first uses a perboard-based add-on. I have used this to create a version of the NeoPixel MOSFET–based circuit from Chapter 7. This is shown in Figure 12-7, and the underside shows why I am not such a fan of perfboards.

Figure 12-7. *NeoPixel MOSFET circuit on a perfboard add-on board*

My preferred prototyping board is the Adafruit Perma-Proto Pi HAT. This is designed specifically for the Raspberry Pi B+ or later. Figure 12-8 shows the infrared receiver and transmitter circuit from Chapter 5. You will see that I have squeezed the components up to one end to allow space to add some sensors to the rest of the board in future.

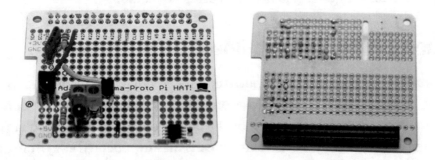

Figure 12-8. *Perma-Proto Pi HAT with infrared transmitter and receiver circuit*

Cases and Enclosures

Once you have your permanent circuit, it is often a good idea to put it into a box to protect the circuit and make it look a little more professional. We call this an enclosure or less formally a case. If you have access to a 3D printer, then you can print your own case, or you can make use of standard enclosures. Usually, these are available following a simple box shape, although I've also used a metal rack–mounted enclosure for my own version of the disco light project from Chapter 4.

The easiest material to use for an enclosure is plastic as that can be easily cut and shaped to fit the required components. I have created an enclosure for the True or False game from Chapter 6, which is shown in Figure 12-9.

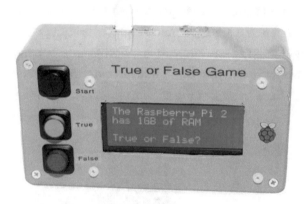

Figure 12-9. *Finished True or False game*

This is based around a cuboid box with a Pi Zero inside. The level shifter is wired directly to the GPIO connector. The Pi Zero is attached inside the case using double-sided sticky pads and holes made into the box for the power lead as well as the HDMI connector. I replaced the mini buttons from the breadboard circuit with panel-mounted push buttons which fitted into holes I drilled into the front panel. The hole for the LCD display was cut using an electric rotary tool. It has been finished off with labels from a Brother labeling machine.

Test Tools

Hopefully, most of the circuits have worked first time. As circuits get more complex, sometimes things don't work as expected. This then needs testing to find the cause of the problem. This is the electronics equivalent of debugging software. There are two tools covered here. The most important tool is the multimeter, which is an essential piece of equipment for an electronics toolkit. The second is a bit more advanced which is a Raspberry Pi–based digital oscilloscope.

Multimeter

A multimeter is a test tool that can take a number of different measurements on an electronic circuit. Multimeters can vary in price considerably depending upon the required functionality and accuracy. My primary multimeter is a mid-range meter shown in Figure 12-10. A less expensive meter should be sufficient for most purposes, although I recommend looking for one with an audible connectivity tester, which is sometimes missing from the cheaper ones. It is not essential but can make it a little easier when you don't have to look at the screen when testing for a broken connection.

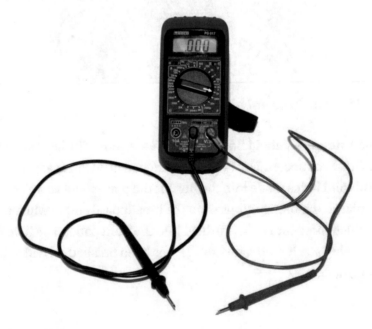

Figure 12-10. *Multimeter*

Across the bottom of the meter are three connectors for connecting the test leads. Two of these have test leads connected which is the most common setting. The black lead is connected to the central common connector and the red to the VΩmA (voltage resistance and milliamps). Most of the testing can be done with the probes in the positions, with the red wire being moved to the left connector if measuring large currents.

The rotary selector is then used to choose the appropriate measurement. The most common settings are as follows.

Voltage

Connect the black lead to the ground of a circuit and then use the red lead to measure the temperature at a certain point. The circuit needs to be connected to a power supply when testing the voltage.

Current

To measure the current involves making a break in the circuit and connecting the red and black leads across the break. The current will then flow through the ammeter where it is measured. For small currents, the leads are used in the normal positions, but for larger currents (above 200mA for this model), the other lead position should be used. There is often a fuse which may blow if you exceed the current rating.

Resistance

To measure the resistance of a component or wire, first disconnect the power and place the probes across the component. If the component is in a circuit, then other components may affect the measured value. Do not use the resistance setting on a live circuit.

Continuity

On many multimeters, the lowest resistance range (typically 200Ω) includes an audible connectivity tester. This can be useful for testing for short circuits or breaks in a connection as you don't need to watch the display.

Other Measurements

Some multimeters also include additional features. The multimeter shown in Figure 12-10 includes a transistor tester, capacitor measurement, and frequency setting.

For some of the measurements, there are several different positions with the maximum rating on them. When measuring voltage and current, you should not exceed the value selected. If you are not sure, then start on a higher value and then move the selector to a lower setting until you are in the correct range.

On this multimeter, there is a separate switch for use on AC and DC circuits, although for other multimeters this may be part of the rotary selector.

Oscilloscope

A limitation of a multimeter is that it can only show a single value for the voltage and cannot show how that changes over time or at least only when the changes are slow. An oscilloscope (or scope for short) is a measurement tool that can be used to show how the voltage at a point in the circuit changes over time. It used to be that these were too expensive for electronic hobbyists, but computer-based scopes have been introduced that are more affordable. In particular, the BitScope Micro is a low-cost scope that can be connected directly to a Raspberry Pi. The BitScope connects to a USB port providing a way to connect two standard oscilloscope channels or up to eight connections when used as a logic analyzer. The BitScope is shown in Figure 12-11.

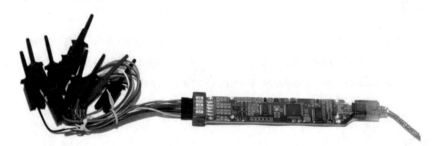

Figure 12-11. *BitScope Micro with test leads*

The software that runs on the Raspberry Pi is shown in Figure 12-12. In this case, it shows a square wave signal.

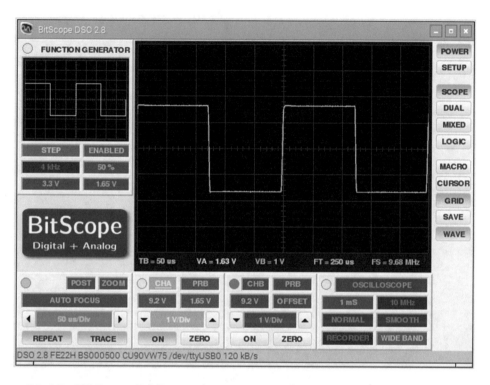

Figure 12-12. *BitScope DSO running on a Raspberry Pi*

More Project Making

This chapter has looked at how to use soldering to turn the temporary breadboard circuits into a permanent circuit. When getting started, stripboard is a good way to build circuits without the expense of a custom printed circuit board.

It then covered how to make the circuit more practical and look more professional by putting it into an enclosure. Finally, it has explained some test tools which are useful when the circuit doesn't work as expected.

The next chapter will cover designing and making your own circuits including how to design a circuit in Fritzing that could be made into a custom printed circuit board.

## CHAPTER 13

Let the Innovation Begin: Designing Your Own Circuits

This chapter will cover how you would go about designing your own circuits. It will show you where to find information about components and circuits, some tools for designing circuits, and how they can be used to create circuits, including custom printed circuit boards (PCBs). Finally, it will explain about creating a power supply suitable for powering a Raspberry Pi.

How to Design a Circuit

Designing a circuit is usually a multi-step process. First, you start with the idea, next research the available components, and then having decided on the components, design it into a circuit showing how they will be connected. You can then prototype the circuit, making a temporary circuit before creating the final finished circuit. The final circuit could be built on an off-the-shelf board such as stripboard or made into a complete printed circuit board depending upon your budget and the complexity of the circuit.

Each of these stages can be repeated as necessary until you come to the final design. As you move through the stages, the potential cost increases both in terms of money and the time taken, so the earlier you identify any potential problems, the less it will cost. Don't be afraid to go back to the start rather than trying to continue with a design that isn't working.

The prototyping stage is a useful stage as this is when you get to see if the circuit you have designed is likely to work. This is often done using a breadboard. You don't necessarily need to test every single component at this level, but you should test all the

© Stewart Watkiss 2020
S. Watkiss, *Learn Electronics with Raspberry Pi*, https://doi.org/10.1007/978-1-4842-6348-8_13

basic blocks. For example, when designing the four-light disco lights, I only tested one of the MOSFET switches, and the other three followed the same design, so I did not need to test them separately. The more comprehensive your testing, the better the chance of identifying any potential problems.

There is one additional step that is used in professional circuit design, which is to perform a circuit simulation. Circuit simulation involves computer modeling of the behavior between components to see how they will work together. It can be a complicated process and should not be required for the type of circuits you will be making at this stage.

The idea is something you can come up with yourself, although hopefully some of the ideas in this book may help with getting the inspiration. This will look at some of the sources of information, and the tools you can use help design a circuit.

Datasheets

When designing circuits, you need to understand the particular characteristics of the components we use. Components that look similar to each can behave in different ways when used in practice. To get this information, manufacturers provide a datasheet which explains the characteristics of their components. Interpreting the information from a datasheet is one of the key skills when designing your own circuit.

Datasheets for different types of components may be completely different, but there are a number of sections that are often included. Rather than covering just one type, I have created a few examples of the sort of thing that you may see on a datasheet. I suggest you download some real datasheets so that you get familiar with their content. The best place to download the datasheets is normally from your component supplier. Some companies such as Farnell/Element 14 provide links to the datasheets in the component listings, some other suppliers may include practical examples and tutorials, but some suppliers do not provide any information. If you don't find what you are looking for, then search for datasheet followed by the component name using an Internet search engine.

The first thing in a datasheet is a descriptive title, the component model number, and the name of the manufacturer. This is normally followed by a paragraph explaining what the component is and where it is useful. In some cases, a single datasheet may include multiple components (such as the TSOP2438 infrared receiver which shares a single datasheet with 23 other similar receivers).

There is often a diagram showing the pin layout. Obviously, this will look different for a discrete component such as a transistor compared to an integrated circuit. For a transistor or similar, it may be a 3D picture labeling the leads, or in the case of an integrated circuit, it may look like the example shown in Figure 13-1.

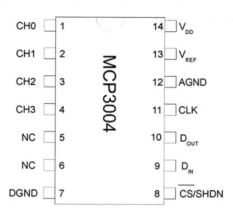

Figure 13-1. Pin layout for the MCP3004

This is the MCP3004 analog-to-digital integrated circuit that we used in Chapter 6. This has been chosen as it is a good example of the different types of pin labels that you may come across.

The numbers on the inside of the IC are the pin numbers. Pin 1 is indicated at the top left which is normally physically identified on the chip by a semicircle or small dot on the side with pin 1. CH0–CH3 are the input channels (analog inputs). NC means not connected; this normally means that it is not used and so the pin should be left without physically connecting to the rest of the circuit. Normally, GND is used to signify the pin that needs to be connected to the 0V ground part of the circuit. In this case, it has a separate ground connection for the digital and analog parts of the circuit indicated by DGND and AGND, respectively. An alternative is V_{SS} which is used by some manufacturers to refer to ground instead.

The pin marked CS/SHDN is used for chip select or to shut down the input. An alternative that you may see for some components is EN which stands for enable and normally means the same as chip select. You will see that there is a line above CS. This indicates that it is inverted, so a high input has the opposite meaning as the wording. In this case, "chip select" happens when it receives a low signal rather than a high signal.

The pins labeled as D_{IN} and D_{OUT} are the data in and out pins used to communicate with the Raspberry Pi using I²C. CLK stands for clock where a timing signal is required.

The V_{REF} pin is used for the analog part of the circuit as a reference voltage that the input is compared against. Finally, the V_{DD} pin is connected to the positive power supply; on some circuits, this may be V_{CC} instead.

The pin layout may also show different variants of the component. This may include an option for a surface mount device (SMD) or through the hole device. You will normally want to avoid the SMD components when first creating your own circuits as they can be difficult to solder.

The next part of the datasheet is often a table of absolute maximum ratings, which are values that should not be exceeded. Going outside of these ranges will mean that the component may not operate correctly or may cause permanent damage to the component.

The following example in Figure 13-2 shows part of the information for the IRL520 MOSFET.

ABSOLUTE MAXIMIM RATINGS (T_C = 25°C unless otherwise noted)			SYMBOL	LIMIT	UNIT
PARAMETER					
Drain-Source Voltage			V_{DS}	100	V
Gate-Source Voltage			V_{GS}	± 10	
Continous Drain Current	V_{GS} at 5V	T_C = 25°C	I_p	9.2	
		T_C = 100°C		6.5	A
Pulsed Drain Current			I_{DM}	36	

Figure 13-2. *Absolute maximum ratings for the IRL520 MOSFET*

This shows the maximum voltages between different pairs of pins as well as the continuous and pulsed currents. Exceeding these values is likely to damage the MOSFET. Also note that some values may depend upon certain conditions, and in this case, the maximum drain current is less as the temperature increases.

There are then often several tables providing more information about the behavior of the component under certain conditions. For logic circuits, this will include the valid voltage ranges for a signal to be considered as a true or false; for a transistor, it will include the typical gain; and for an LED, it may include the luminous intensity. There may be other information that is useful under certain circumstances such as timing information or effective capacitance.

Sometimes it is not possible to put the information into a table as the information may vary depending upon the input, temperature, or other characteristic. In this case, the information may be presented as graphs or timing diagrams.

Another common section is a circuit diagram showing the internal characteristics of the inputs or outputs. These are used when deciding what additional components may be needed to connect the circuit to another component. For instance, if a circuit has an open collector output as shown in Figure 13-3 and then if connecting to a logic circuit, then it would need a pull-up resistor to ensure that the input to the next stage was not floating when the transistor was switched off.

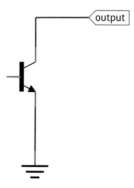

Figure 13-3. *Open collector used on certain ICs*

Another example is the diagram in Figure 13-4 which is from the SN754410 H-bridge IC, showing the effective output circuit from the chip, including the protection diodes.

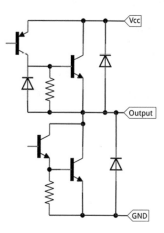

Figure 13-4. *Datasheet representation of output from SN754410 H-bridge IC*

The datasheet may also include examples of how the component can be used in a circuit and often includes the dimensions of the component and how it connects to a printed circuit board.

Some datasheets will be more useful than others, but as you can see, it can be an invaluable source of information when designing a circuit.

Introduction to Fritzing

Having read this far, you may be wondering how the circuit diagrams and breadboard images were created. The majority of these were created using a program called Fritzing, although I also created some myself using a drawing program. Fritzing is open source software available for Linux, Mac OS X, and Windows, which can help create circuit diagrams (schematics), breadboard layouts, and printed circuit board designs. You can download Fritzing from `http://fritzing.org/download/`. Although open source, the site does request payment to fund further development of the software. You can however download the source code for free, and it can be installed on a Raspberry Pi for free using

```
sudo apt install fritzing
```

If you want to run Fritzing on something other than a Raspberry Pi, then you can pay to download the software, which will allow you to download the latest version and to help support future development of the software.

Designing a Circuit Diagram/Schematic

The breadboard view is the first tab for designing circuits in Fritzing, although I recommend starting with a circuit diagram, which is called a schematic in Fritzing. This allows you to design the circuit as you would like it to connect logically, and it will then guide you to creating the physical layout for a breadboard or PCB. The initial schematic view is shown in Figure 13-5.

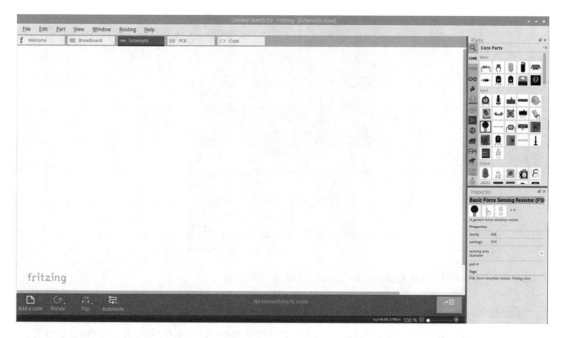

Figure 13-5. *Fritzing schematic view*

The main part of the screen contains an editor area, which is a white background with a grid for laying out the circuit design. The area to the top right is labeled parts which contains the available components and circuit boards, and the inspector area at the bottom right will allow you to change any of the parameters relating to the current component.

In the parts selector, most of the standard components are included under the CORE tab. This includes common components such as a resistor and PCB, but also labels, wires, and even an entire computer in the form of the Raspberry Pi. The components can be dragged across to the edit area. If the component has some options available, then these can be selected in the inspector area. This can be used to select values such as resistor values and different component types such as THT (through-hole technology) or SMD (surface mount devices). When presented with the choice of THT and SMD, you will usually want to choose the THT components, which are components with leads that can pass through a printed circuit board or mounted into a breadboard. SMDs are very small components that are mounted to only one side of a PCB and are very difficult to solder by hand without additional tools. The inspector panel for a resistor is shown in Figure 13-6.

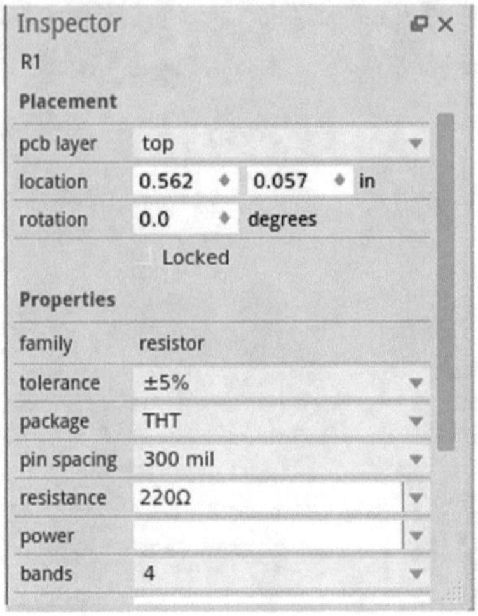

Figure 13-6. Fritzing inspector panel for a resistor

The components are then connected together by dragging the mouse from the lead of one component to the other. Each time you create a connection between the components, it is called a net. You can connect more components to the same net by right-clicking a connection and choosing add bendpoint. You could also connect to a net label (under the core components), and any other net labels with the same name are connected together. A complete circuit for the basic transistor LED circuit is included in Figure 13-7.

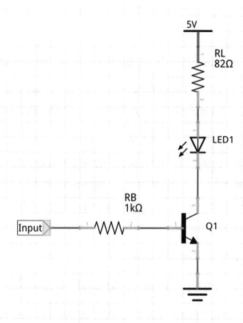

Figure 13-7. *Transistor LED circuit schematic view*

I haven't included the Raspberry Pi on this diagram, although you can include one by dragging it from the core components. In this case, I have used a net label at the point where the circuit connects to the GPIO, instead of showing the Raspberry Pi on the diagram.

Rules when Designing a Circuit

When creating a circuit diagram (in Fritzing or otherwise), there are a few standard conventions which are followed where possible. These are not fixed rules, but should be followed where possible. Some common rules are

- The positive supply is usually placed at the top of the diagram.

- The ground (0V) supply is normally placed at the bottom of the diagram.

- Inputs are normally positioned toward the left and outputs toward the right.

    - As a result, the data signals normally flow from left to right.

- If a battery is being used, then this may be displayed using the battery symbol, but often the supply is shown by marking the appropriate lines instead.

- Lines are normally drawn horizontally or vertically straight. A change in direction is normally through a 90-degree turn. In Fritzing, the connections will normally take the shortest path, but can be dragged out to form 90-degree turns.

- Avoid crossing lines where possible.

    - Where lines join, a dot (filled circle) is used to indicate a join.

    - Where lines cross but don't join, they normally pass in a straight line.

- Each component is normally given a reference. This is prefixed with a letter or few letters to denote the type of component. Examples include

    - R for resistor

    - D for diode

    - Q for transistor

    - BT for battery

    - C for capacitor

Creating a Breadboard Layout

Now that we have a circuit diagram, we can convert this to a breadboard layout by switching to the breadboard tab. If you do so, then it will likely look a bit of a mess, such as the diagram in Figure 13-8.

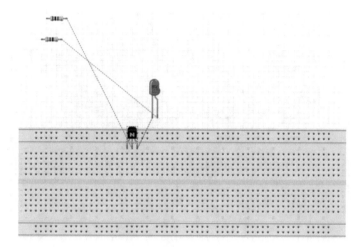

Figure 13-8. *Fritzing initial breadboard view*

Not only does this look a mess, but for some circuits, components will be on top of each other hiding those below them. First, you should click the breadboard and use the inspector to set it to the appropriate type of breadboard. The most common breadboard is the half+ breadboard.

You can now drag the components to an appropriate position, rotating them as necessary. When you place a component onto the breadboard, the row of pins that it will connect to will change to green. The dashed lines represent the nets that we created in the circuit diagram. Clicking one of these will turn it into a wire that you can place as appropriate. You will also need to add connections for the positive and ground power supplies, which are normally connected to one of the appropriate red or blue strips along the breadboard (not all breadboards include the colored lines). The final layout is shown in Figure 13-9.

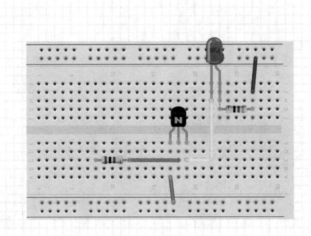

Figure 13-9. *Fritzing updated breadboard view*

The resistor going to the base of the transistor would normally connect to the Raspberry Pi, but I have not shown the Raspberry Pi in this view.

Creating a Stripboard Layout

If you would like to create a layout for a stripboard, then that is done using the same breadboard view. You will lose the view of the breadboard, so you may want to save that with a different name first. Click the breadboard and choose delete and then drag the stripboard part from the core parts. There are only a couple of different types of stripboard included, but you can adjust the number of columns and rows. You can also create breaks in the rows by clicking the stripboard between a pair of holes.

Designing a PCB

Fritzing can also be used for creating a professional printed circuit board (PCB). In the past, it was expensive to get custom PCBs made, but it has come down considerably in price and can provide a professional look for your project. The price for PCBs varies depending upon manufacturer, lead time, and quantity. The quantity is an important factor as buying in bulk can be much cheaper, but you will want to test your PCB design first.

This is a very simple circuit, so it doesn't really need its own PCB, but it is useful for illustrating the process of designing a PCB. Clicking the PCB tab shows a gray area for the PCB board. You will find all your components stacked up on the top corner which will need to be moved around.

First, set the size of the PCB and move the components to appropriate positions on the board. Before you go about working out how the copper will be laid out, you need to add some way of connecting to the power supply and to the Raspberry Pi. For the power supply, you can use one of the included power connectors, and for the Raspberry Pi, you may want to include a 30-way connector, but both these would be overkill for such a simple design, so I instead used three terminals, two for the power supply and one for the GPIO connection. I used the part for a terminal connector, but you could just solder wires directly to the pins rather than using a physical connector.

Under the core parts, look for connections and "Generic Female Header – 2 pins". The number of pins can then be changed in the inspector tab. The PCB so far is shown in Figure 13-10.

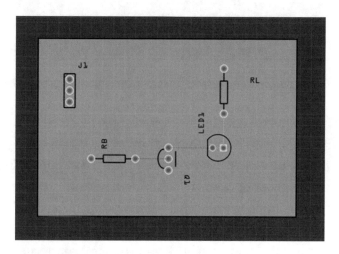

Figure 13-10. *Initial PCB layout without routing*

The next stage is to add the copper tracks which go between each component. There is an Autoroute option, but you can do this manually similar to the breadboard layout using the dotted lines as a guide. There will be no connections shown to the connector terminal, so you will need to add these as well. Before you start dragging out the connections, you may want to specify which layer to run the connections on. While technically it doesn't really matter whether these are on the top or the bottom, I normally prefer to put as many on the bottom as possible; this is more from my experience creating single layer boards in the past. To do this, look for the icon on the bottom that says "Both Layers" and choose "set bottom layer clickable". Any tracks you draw will be orange, indicating that they are on the bottom; if you change it to the top layer, then they will be colored yellow.

Once the tracks are connected, you should have something looking similar to Figure 13-11.

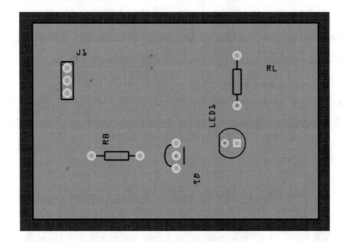

Figure 13-11. *PCB layout with copper tracks between the components*

If you now switch to the schematic view, you will see that the connector component has been added and that it has dashed connections to the power supply and resistor RB. This is one of the features of Fritzing as you can add a component in any of the different views, and it is added to all the others. You may want to tidy the other diagrams up by repositioning the connector and wires. Alternatively, if you didn't want to show the wires, you can use the "Delete ratsnest line" to hide the dashed line. Take care when using this option as it is a useful way to check that you have connected up your circuits correctly.

It's a good idea to rearrange the text labels for the components at this point and then label up the connections for J1. You can add text using the logo part, which can be used for adding any kind of text, not just logos. The updated PCB is shown in Figure 13-12.

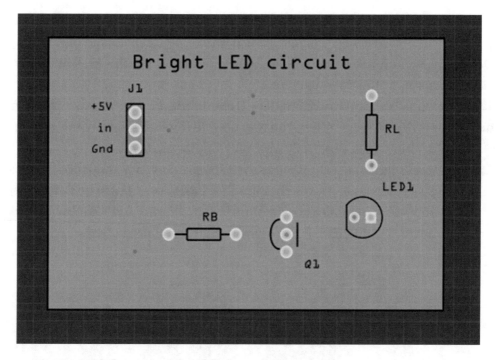

Figure 13-12. *PCB layout with added text information*

This is almost ready to have made up as a printed circuit board. The final thing you should do to the design is to add a ground or copper fill. This will fill most of the PCB with copper, and in the case of a ground fill, it will be connected to ground which can help with avoiding electromagnetic interference. To add a ground fill, right-click the Gnd connection and choose Set Ground Fill Seed, and then from the Routing menu, choose to apply a ground fill. The entire board will then be filled in with copper, except for a gap around each of the connections. If you look at the bottom layer, you should see that the ground connection from the connector to Q1 is merged into the ground fill.

The PCB is now ready to be sent for manufacturing. Before actually sending it off, it is a good idea to perform some checks on the finished layout. First, run the Design Rules Check (DRC) from the routing menu, which will check for any common problems. Then export the PCB layout using the File ➤ Export for Production and choosing PDF. Print off the component layout and check that the components fit. Double-check that all the components oriented correctly on the PCB layout.

Once you've checked everything twice, check it once more before you send the files to the manufacturer. Remember the extra cost and time if there is a mistake. If you want to use the Fritzing lab (which funds the development of Fritzing software), then you can use the Fabricate button which will load a web page for submission. There are a couple of advantages to using Fritzing. The first is that you can just send the Fritzing file as it is, and the second is that they will perform some additional checks. It can be more expensive than some other manufacturers.

If you would rather send to a different PCB manufacturer, then you can export for production as extended Gerber files. You may need to fine-tune some of these files and check the submission rules, especially what files they expect to receive.

I didn't actually have that circuit made as a PCB as it was easy enough to create on stripboard, but I have created a more complex PCB that I have used in one of my own projects. Figure 13-13 is a circuit that combines the disco lights and NeoPixel circuits onto a single board. This is a circuit that I have made up and used at a disco.

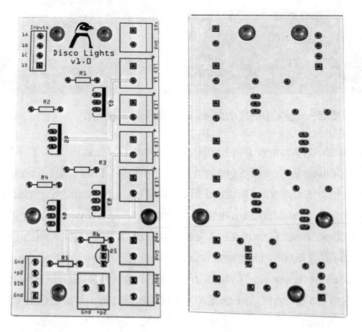

Figure 13-13. *Manufactured PCB for disco lights and NeoPixels*

Powering the Raspberry Pi

The Raspberry Pi is normally powered from a dedicated power supply through either a USB-C or micro-USB connector. This is fine for normal use, but what if you want to include the Raspberry Pi into a complete project that already has a power supply? When I created the disco light project which runs on 12V, I didn't want to have to add a second power supply for the 5V needed by the Raspberry Pi. You can make a power supply yourself; this is useful to understand how you can add a power supply directly into your own circuit. You can however buy more efficient solution that can be easily connected into the circuit.

78xx Linear Voltage Regulator

The 78xx series of voltage regulators are small components that can be easily included directly onto a PCB or stripboard circuit. The regulators take a higher voltage on their input and provide a constant lower voltage for their output. In this case, from 12V on the input to 5V for the output. The only extra components required are a capacitor at both the input and output to smooth out any noise. The circuit diagram is included in Figure 13-14.

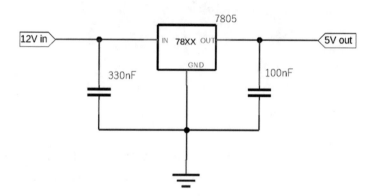

Figure 13-14. *7805 voltage regulator circuit*

The voltage regulator comes with a variety of different output voltages, which are denoted by the last two digits. For example, the 5V regulator suitable for the Raspberry Pi is the 7805. The input voltage needs to be higher than the output voltage and in the case of the 7805 needs to be at least 7.3V.

One disadvantage of a linear regulator is that the voltage difference between the input and output is turned into heat which wastes power. If this is supplying 600mA (a typical current draw for a Raspberry Pi 3) using a 12V power supply, then the amount of power lost would be 4.2 watts (7V dropped x 0.6A). This is quite a significant amount of heat, and a heat sink would be required to prevent the regulator overheating.

Buck Converter

A more efficient way of powering the Raspberry Pi from a 12V power supply is a buck converter, also known as a DC-DC converter or a DC switching regulator. I used one of these to power the Raspberry Pi used in the disco light project. The buck converter is normally bought pre-built on a printed circuit board. The output voltage can sometimes be changed using a trimmer built onto the PCB. You would need to use a multimeter to check the output voltage. A buck converter is shown in Figure 13-15.

Figure 13-15. *Buck converter*

A buck converter is available through various suppliers such as Amazon Marketplace or eBay. These are more expensive than the linear voltage regulator, and they take up more space but are better where power efficiency is concerned.

Caution   Always check the output from a buck converter before connecting it to your Raspberry Pi. I learned this from experience when the one I purchased gave too high a voltage, damaging the Raspberry Pi.

Designing More Circuits

In this chapter, you have looked at the information needed to design your own circuits. This has shown how datasheets provide the information needed when designing a circuit and how to extract the relevant information. It then looked at Fritzing and how it can be used to design circuits, including creating a schematic layout, designing a breadboard and stripboard layout, and finally creating a professional printed circuit board.

This chapter provides the basics for getting started with Fritzing, but only scratches the surface of what Fritzing can do. I encourage you to spend more time learning about Fritzing. There are also other circuit design software such as KiCad (which is open source software) and EAGLE PCB design software which is a commercial product but free to use for small circuits. Neither of these provides the ease of use and breadboard layouts that Fritzing does.

Through this book, you have learned about electronic circuits, about how to connect them to the Raspberry Pi, and the steps involved in designing your own circuit. With this information, you can now design your own electronic circuits to have the Raspberry Pi interact with the real world.

Look around at what others have made, come up with your own ideas, and design your own electronic circuits.

APPENDIX A

Required Tools and Components

Here, I have listed the most common components and tools you will need for each of the projects in the book. There are suggested design alternatives for some of the projects, so you may want to explore other components. I've also given suggested sizes or types for some of the tools, which should be considered as a guide only. It is often a good idea to start with a small set of basic tools and then expand that collection or add better quality tools as you gain more experience.

For the tools, I have listed these in a few groups of tools, which allow you to add to your tools as you progress. For the components, I've listed the components for each of the projects, although some of which may have already been used by other projects.

You can buy the components separately, or you can buy a beginner electronics starter kit. The starter kits often come with a breadboard and selection of components for wiring up your first kit, which can then be expanded as you need more specialized components.

Tools Required
Basic Breadboard Circuits

These are the recommended tools for Chapters 1–9:

- Raspberry Pi (preferably Raspberry Pi 3B or 4B)

- Breadboard (half size)

- Side cutters (small wire cutters)

- Crocodile clips with wires

© Stewart Watkiss 2020
S. Watkiss, *Learn Electronics with Raspberry Pi*, https://doi.org/10.1007/978-1-4842-6348-8

- Jumper wires and/or solid core wire

- Small screwdriver (cross-head and straight, or multi-head)

- Board to mount the Raspberry Pi and breadboard (optional)

Crimping and Soldering Tools

A crimping tool is useful for Chapters 8 and 17, and the rest of the tools are used for Chapters 12 and 13:

- Wire strippers

- Crimp tool SN-48B (for button/micro-switch connections)

- Crimp tool SN-2 (for Dupont-style connectors)

- Soldering iron with suitable tip (usually a small chisel tip)

- Soldering iron stand and cleaner

- Solder (normally lead-free)

- Stranded wire (not essential, but more flexible than the solid core used for breadboards)

- Heat shrink tubing

- Stripboard

- Spot face/stripboard cutter

Manufacturing Tools for Enclosures

Most of these circuits are designed to be made up and then taken apart. The exception is the arcade game in Chapter 10. You may also find that you do want to make a permanent version of some of the projects such as the True or False game in Chapter 6. Ultimately, these will be useful when you go on to create your own projects in future:

- Safety glasses or goggles

- Electric drill

- Small hacksaw

- Small files (needle files)

- Permanent marker pen

- Rotary tool (optional)

Meters and Test Equipment

Although not essential, an inexpensive multimeter can be very useful for all types of circuits. A BitScope would be considered a luxury at this stage, but may be useful in future. Chapter 12 includes use of these tools:

- Multimeter

- BitScope (optional)

Components for Each Project

Chapter 1 – Simple LED Circuit

- 9V PP3 battery

- 9V battery clip (with wires)

- LED (5mm any color)

- Miniature push-button switch (SPST)

- 470Ω resistor

Chapter 3 – LED Circuit

- 5mm red LED

- 220Ω resistor

Chapter 3 – Switch Input Circuit

This is required in addition to the parts in the LED circuit:

- 12mm push-to-make push-button switch
- Optional switch cap

Chapter 3 – Robot Soccer

These are a list of all the components needed, excluding those listed in the breadboard list at the start of this appendix:

- 5mm red LED
- 5mm green LED
- 2 x 220Ω resistors
- 2 x 12mm push-to-make push-button switch
- Optional 2 x switch caps

Chapter 4 – Brighter LED

- 10mm white LED
- Transistor – 2n2222 or BC548
- 82Ω resistor
- 1kΩ resistor

Chapter 4 – Brighter LEDs with Darlington Transistors

- USB LED light
- 5V USB power supply with suitable connector
- BD681 Darlington transistor
- 220Ω resistor
- 12mm push-to-make push-button switch

Chapter 4 – Disco Lights

- 4 x PAR 16 Theatre Lights

- 4 x MR16 LED bulbs

- 12V power brick with suitable connector

- 4 x IRL520 MOSFET transistors

- 4 x 470Ω resistors

- 5A fuse with holder or polyfuse

Chapter 5 – PIR Sensor

- PIR motion sensor (HC-SR501)

Chapter 5 – Light Sensor with LDR

- Light-dependent resistor

- 1μF capacitor

Chapter 5 – Infrared Transmitter and Receiver

- TSOP238 infrared receiver

- TSAL6400 infrared emitter

- 2N2222 transistor

- 68Ω resistor

- 100Ω resistor

- 220Ω resistor

- 0.1μF capacitor

- Infrared color-changing LED and remote control

Chapter 6 – I²C LCD Display True or False Game

- Bidirectional level shifter (Adafruit/SparkFun)
- LCD display
- I²C LCD display backpack
- 3 x push-to-make switches

Chapter 6 – LED Brightness Adjustment

- MCP3008 SPI ADC
- 1μF capacitor
- Potentiometer (variable resistor) – 10kΩ or similar
- LED
- 220Ω resistor

Chapter 6 – Motor Controller

- SN754410 quad half H-bridge driver IC
- DC motor (or two motors)

Chapter 7 – Light Sequences

- 4 x LEDs
- 4 x 220Ω resistors

Chapter 7 – Model Train Control

- 2KBP04 bridge rectifier (or 4 x 1N4002 rectifier diodes)
- L289N motor controller board
- Reed switch and magnet
- Model train set

Chapter 7 – NeoPixels

- 5V power supply and connector
- 470Ω resistor
- 2.2kΩ resistor
- 2N70000 MOSFET
- NeoPixels (2 x breadboard NeoPixels or strip of NeoPixels)

Chapter 8 – Video Capture

- Raspberry Pi camera module
- Push-button switch
- Selection of Lego figures or similar characters
- Background pictures

Chapter 8 – Pan and Tilt Camera

- Raspberry Pi camera module
- Pan and tilt module with HAT
- RGBW NeoPixel strip (optional)

Chapter 9 – CamJam Robot

- CamJam Education Kit 3 (Robotics)
- Raspberry Pi Zero WH (preferable)

Chapter 9 – STS-Pi Robot

- STS-Pi robot kit
- Explorer HAT or Explorer HAT Pro
- USB battery pack

Chapter 9 – T200 Robot

- T200 robot chassis

- L289N motor controller board

- Buck converter

Chapter 9 – Mecanum Robot

- 3D printed base (or handmade base)

- 3D printed motor mounts (or bought ones)

- Mecanum wheels

- Motors with 298:1 ratio gearbox (preferably with headers)

- 2 x TB6612FNG motor controllers

- 4 x AA battery holder with wires and batteries

- Raspberry Pi Zero WH (preferable)

Chapter 9 – Robot with Ultrasonic Range Sensor

- Any of the robot kits listed earlier

- Ultrasonic range sensor

- 39kΩ resistor

- 68kΩ resistor

Chapter 9 – Robot with Line Following Sensor

- Any of the robot kits listed earlier

- Three-light line following sensor

Chapter 9 – Robot with Wireless Controller

- Any of the robot kits listed earlier

- Wireless USB controller

Chapter 10 – Minecraft Hardware

- Sturdy box to mount the switches to (such as Really Useful Box 4 liters)

- Joystick (micro-switch)

- Large button switch

- Arcade button switches (five used in example)

- 2.5mm PCB mounts with screws

- Crimp terminals (uninsulated 4.8mm female spades)

- Crimp terminals (female Dupont style)

Chapter 11 – Bar Graph Display

- TPIC6B595 shift register IC

- LED bar graph or 8 x LEDs

- 220Ω resistor network (or 8 x 220Ω resistors)

Chapter 11 – 7-Segment Display

- 2 x SN74HC595 shift register ICs

- 2 x ULN2803 Darlington driver ICs

- 16 x 220Ω resistors

- 2 x LED 7-segment displays

- X-large breadboard

Chapter 12 – Permanent Circuits

The additional tools required are listed at the top of this appendix:

- Perma-Proto Pi HAT or similar Raspberry Pi prototyping board

- PCB terminal connectors (optional)

To create a permanent circuit also requires the components listed under any appropriate project earlier in the book. Good examples are the NeoPixel controller and infrared transmitter and receiver circuits.

Chapter 12 – True or False Game

The following are in addition to the components from the True or False game in Chapter 6:

- Enclosure/box

- PCB mounting screws and spacers

Chapter 13 – Powering the Raspberry Pi

You can use either a buck converter or create your own voltage regulator circuit with the following components.

- 7805 voltage regulator

- 330nF capacitor (also known as 0.33µF)

- 100nF capacitor (also known as 0.1µF)

- Heat sink (depending upon the power requirements)

Electronic Components Quick Reference

These are some of the common electronic components provided as a quick reference. Some technical details have been included for the common components, but these depend upon the model. Check the datasheets for more details.

Resistors

A resistor is normally used to reduce the amount of current that can flow through a circuit. This is particularly important to protect a component from being damaged due to too much current flowing through. They can also be used for dropping the voltage at a point in the circuit by creating a voltage divider.

The size of the resistor is measured in ohms "Ω" which is marked on the side of the resistor using a color code (see Appendix C). The resistors are available in certain values (depending upon the resistor series) and so the nearest common value is usually selected.

Variable Resistors

As its name suggests, a variable resistor is a resistor whose value can change. They normally have three terminals, two providing the specified value of the resistance and a third which can be adjusted to provide a resistance value between the other two.

The variable resistors can be accessible to the user such as the volume control buttons on a speaker or can be small components that are hidden inside an enclosure away from the user. The ones that are accessible to the user often have a control knob

© Stewart Watkiss 2020
S. Watkiss, *Learn Electronics with Raspberry Pi*, https://doi.org/10.1007/978-1-4842-6348-8

355

and are often called potentiometers. The smaller variable resistors that are not accessible to the user and are often used to calibrate a circuit are commonly called trimmers.

Light-Dependent Resistor (LDR)

A light-dependent resistor or photoresistor is a special type of resistor that changes resistance based on the amount of light received. It is normally cylindrical with a glass window. The more light that enters through the window, the lower the resistor.

This is often used to detect the amount of light in a room or outside to determine if additional lighting should be turned on.

Switches

Switches create a break in a circuit or join two parts of a circuit together. This can be used to turn a circuit off by creating a break in the circuit or to direct the current through a different part of the circuit.

These are most commonly available as push-button switches, toggle or rocker switches, rotary switches (such as a key switch), or micro-switches.

The switches are known by the number of poles (individual switches within the package) and the number of throws (number of positions which are switched by each pole). Common examples are

SPST, single pole single throw – On/off

SPDT, single pole double throw – Switch between A and B outputs

DPST, double pole double throw – Two on/off switches

Push-button switches are also known by whether the switch makes or breaks the circuit. The most common form is the momentary push-to-make where the switch closes (completing the circuit) when it is pressed and then open when the button is released; this is how a doorbell switch works. They are also available as push-to-break which is the opposite or locking/latching where one press closes the switch and a second opens the switch.

Diode

A diode is a component that allows current to flow in one direction, but not in the other. It effectively acts like a one-way valve. There is normally a white line around the body of the diode positioned nearest to the negative end (cathode), and the other end (anode) should be connected at the positive end of the circuit.

Light-Emitting Diode (LED)

An LED is a specific type of diode that gives out a light when an electric current passes through it. An important thing about an LED is that like any other diode it needs to be inserted the correct way around in the circuit. The diode has an anode which should be connected to the more positive end of the connection and a cathode which goes to the other side.

You can tell which end is the anode (the positive terminal) as it normally has a longer lead. There is often a flat area on the plastic casing which indicates the cathode (negative terminal).

An LED does not limit the current flowing through, so a resistor is normally required to protect the LED.

Bipolar Transistor

A transistor is an electronic component that is used to switch a larger current compared to its input. The bipolar transistor has three connections known as the collector, base, and emitter (represented by the letters C, B, and E on diagrams). When a small current flows between the base and emitter, then it allows a much larger current to flow between the collector and the emitter. The transistor is an analog component; varying the base current changes the corresponding collector current.

The bipolar transistor comes in two types: one called NPN and the other PNP. The name is based upon the way that the transistor is made. The NPN needs an input voltage that is higher than the emitter voltage to allow it to conduct, whereas the PNP needs an input voltage that is lower than the base voltage for it to conduct.

Darlington Transistor

A bipolar transistor increases the amount of current that can flow, but sometimes a second stage is required to increase the current further. This could be achieved by connecting two transistors with the output of the first stage used to drive the input of the second stage. This is known as a Darlington pair.

It is also possible to have both inside a single component, which is usually known as a Darlington transistor. This can be used in place of a standard transistor, but with a much higher gain.

MOSFET Transistor

A MOSFET transistor is different type of transistor which increases the signal based on the input voltage rather than the input current. They have three connections, known as the drain, gate, and source (represented by the letters d, g, and s). MOSFETs are available as an N-channel and a P-channel component. For the N-channel MOSFET, a small voltage at the gate will allow a current to flow from the drain to the source. A P-channel MOSFET works in an opposite manner; when a negative voltage is applied to the gate, a current can flow from the source to the drain.

Capacitor

A capacitor is a device for storing electrical charge. It is a bit like a small rechargeable battery that can charge and discharge while connected in a circuit. The capacitor has a variety of uses in analog circuits, including acting as a filter to remove signals outside of a specific frequency.

In digital circuits, capacitors are often used to smooth a power supply or signal removing any stray electrical noise.

Capacitance is measured in farads (F), but a farad is a really large value, so they are often denoted in microfarads (µF) which is 0.000001 of a farad, nanofarads (0.000000001 of a farad), or picofarads (0.000000000001 of a farad).

Thyristor

A thyristor is a component that only allows current to flow in one direction and only then when it receives a signal on the gate terminal. It is rather like a diode that needs to be turned on first. Once it has been turned on, it then stays on until the power supply is removed or goes negative. They are suitable for use in an AC circuit; as whilst a large reverse voltage would damage a MOSFET or transistor, the thyristor will work with a high reverse voltage. It does only allow for one half of the AC cycle to pass through, which is overcome using a TRIAC.

TRIAC

A TRIAC is effectively two thyristors connected in the opposite polarity but sharing the same three terminals. If a signal is applied to the gate, then it will switch on and allow current to flow. If the signal is removed, then it will stop conducting once the supply voltage reverses (on the opposite phase of the cycle).

APPENDIX C

Component Labeling

While many components have a part number written on them, some components instead use specific colors or special codes to denote their values. Color codes are often used on small components such as resistors, where it would be very difficult to read the value if it was printed in words. Some common component labels are explained in this appendix.

Resistor Color Codes

Resistors are normally labeled using four colored bands across the body of the resistor. This consists three bands together, indicating the resistance value of the resistor (ohms), and the fourth, further away than the first three, is used to indicate the tolerance (accuracy) of the resistor. This is shown in Figure C-1.

Figure C-1. *Resistor showing the color code*

The bands relate to the resistance as follows:

- First band – First significant figure of resistor value

- Second band – Second significant figure of resistor value

- Third band – Decimal multiplier (applied against the first two bands)

- Fourth band – Tolerance (if not present, tolerance is 20%)

© Stewart Watkiss 2020
S. Watkiss, *Learn Electronics with Raspberry Pi*, https://doi.org/10.1007/978-1-4842-6348-8

The first three bands can be one of ten different colors, which represent digits from 0 to 9. The tolerance is normally gold or silver, although other colors are sometimes used. The different colors are listed in Table C-1.

Table C-1. *Resistor color code meanings*

Color	Significant figures	Multiplier	Tolerance
Black	0	$\times 10^0$	–
Brown	1	$\times 10^1$	±1%
Red	2	$\times 10^2$	±2%
Orange	3	$\times 10^3$	–
Yellow	4	$\times 10^4$	–
Green	5	$\times 10^5$	±0.5%
Blue	6	$\times 10^6$	±0.25%
Violet	7	$\times 10^7$	±0.1%
Grey	8	$\times 10^8$	±0.05%
White	9	$\times 10^9$	–
Gold	–	$\times 10^{-1}$	±5%
Silver	–	$\times 10^{-2}$	±10%

The preceding example has colors: green, blue, black...gold.

This translates to 5 (green), 6 (blue), and $\times 10^0$ (black), with a tolerance of 5%.

This works out at 56Ω.

The tolerance is not normally a major consideration for most digital circuits, but if the exact value of the resistor is required, then that band should be considered as well.

Resistors are made in certain sizes. Normally, the nearest size can be selected, but in some circumstances, you may need to choose the nearest higher or lower as appropriate. For example, if you are calculating a resistor for the maximum current that can flow, then you should choose the next size up rather than a lower value.

A typical series is the E12 series which uses 12 equally spaced values across every multiple of 10. A common alternative is the E6 series which has six values per multiple of 10. If you intend to have some resistors in stock, then it is useful to have the E6 series as a minimum and then just buying any other specific size as required. The E6 resistor series is shown in Table C-2.

Table C-2. *E6 resistor series*

10Ω	15Ω	22Ω	33Ω	47Ω	68Ω
100Ω	150Ω	220Ω	330Ω	470Ω	680Ω
1kΩ	1.5kΩ	2.2kΩ	3.3kΩ	4.7kΩ	6.8kΩ
10kΩ	15kΩ	22kΩ	33kΩ	47kΩ	68kΩ
100kΩ	150kΩ	220kΩ	330kΩ	470kΩ	680kΩ
1MΩ					

The E12 resistor series with more resistor values is shown in Table C-3.

Table C-3. *E12 resistor series*

10Ω	12Ω	15Ω	18Ω	22Ω	27Ω	33Ω	39Ω	47Ω	56Ω	68Ω	82Ω
100Ω	120Ω	150Ω	180Ω	220Ω	270Ω	330Ω	390Ω	470Ω	560Ω	680Ω	820Ω
1kΩ	1.2kΩ	1.5kΩ	1.8kΩ	2.2kΩ	2.7kΩ	3.3kΩ	3.9kΩ	4.7kΩ	5.6kΩ	6.8kΩ	8.2kΩ
10kΩ	12kΩ	15kΩ	18kΩ	22kΩ	27kΩ	33kΩ	39kΩ	47kΩ	56kΩ	68kΩ	82kΩ
100kΩ	120kΩ	150kΩ	180kΩ	220kΩ	270kΩ	330kΩ	390kΩ	470kΩ	560kΩ	680kΩ	820kΩ
1MΩ											

SMD Resistors

While color codes are used for standard through-hole-technology resistors, surface mount resistors normally have a numeric code instead. There are different codes that are used; the most common code is a three-digit number code. The first two digits indicate the first and second significant figures and the third digit indicates the multiplier.

A resistor marked as 180 will be 18Ω, and a resistor marked 221 will be 220Ω.

Electrolytic Capacitors

Electrolytic capacitors are usually quite large both in physical size and their capacitance. They normally have the value of the capacitor written on them in microfarads (μF). An example of an electrolytic capacitor is shown in Figure C-2.

Figure C-2. *Electrolytic capacitor*

As well as showing the capacitance, the capacitor will also have the maximum voltage written on the body, which sometimes merges with the capacitance value. For example, a capacitor labeled

63V1000µF

can be used up to 63V and has a capacitance of 1000µF. Electrolytic capacitors are polarized and need to be connected the right way around. The negative terminal is normally denoted by an arrow marked with a 0 pointing toward it.

Polyester Capacitors

Polyester capacitors, such as the one in Figure C-3, normally have the value written directly on them. These may be missing the units, in which case they are normally in µF.

Figure C-3. *Polyester capacitor*

For example, a capacitor labeled as

`0.01`

will be 0.01µF, which is 10nF.

Ceramic Capacitors

Ceramic capacitors are normally the smallest in physical size, so often have a code instead of showing the actual value. A typical ceramic capacitor is shown in Figure C-4.

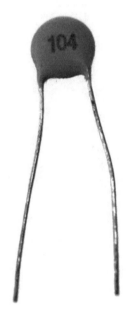

Figure C-4. *Ceramic capacitor*

The most common code is usually three digits. These give the value in pF (picofarads). The first two digits are the significant digits, and then the third digit is a factor of 10 multiplier.

The 104 capacitor is $10 \times 10^4 = 100,000$pF which is 100nF.

Some other capacitors are labeled with the letter n or p to denote nanofarads or picofarads, respectively. A capacitor labeled

`1n0`

has value of 1nF.

APPENDIX D

GPIO Quick Reference

This is a summary of the information about the GPIO pin layouts, provided for easy reference. The current Raspberry Pi models all use the 40-pin connector; the older 26-pin connectors are included for reference. Pin 1 is located nearest the SD card.

© Stewart Watkiss 2020
S. Watkiss, *Learn Electronics with Raspberry Pi*, https://doi.org/10.1007/978-1-4842-6348-8

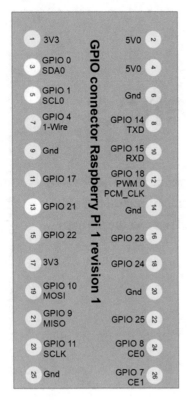

Figure D-1. *GPIO port numbers*

GPIO Ports with Alternative Functions

A summary of the ports and common alternative functions is provided in Table D-1. This is based on the 40-pin connector.

Table D-1. *GPIO pin reference*

Pin number	GPIO port	Alternative function	Comments
1		3.3V power supply	
2		5V power supply	
3	GPIO 2	SDA1 (I²C data)	Changed from revision 1 boards
4		5V power supply	
5	GPIO 3	SCL1 (I²C clock)	Changed from revision 1 boards
6		Ground	
7	GPIO 4		
8	GPIO 14	Serial/console TXD	Serial transmit
9		Ground	
10	GPIO 15	Serial/console RXD	Serial receive
11	GPIO 17		
12	GPIO 18	PWM	Pulse-width modulation
13	GPIO 27		Changed from revision 1 boards
14		Ground	
15	GPIO 22		
16	GPIO 23		
17		3.3V	
18	GPIO 24		
19	GPIO 10	MOSI (SPI)	SPI Master Output, Slave Input
20		Ground	

(*continued*)

Table D-1. (*continued*)

Pin number	GPIO port	Alternative function	Comments
21	GPIO 9	MISO (SPI)	SPI Master Input, Slave Output
22	GPIO 25		
23	GPIO 11	SCLK (SPI)	SPI clock
24	GPIO 8	CE0 (SPI)	Chip enable (slave select)
25		Ground	
26	GPIO 7	CE1 (SPI)	Chip enable (slave select)
27		ID_SD	For HAT EEPROM
28		ID_SC	For HAT EEPROM
29	GPIO 5		
30		Ground	
31	GPIO 6		
32	GPIO 12		
33	GPIO 13		
34		Ground	
35	GPIO 19	SPI1_MISO	
36	GPIO 16	CE2 (SPI)	Chip enable (slave select)
37	PIO 26		
38	GPIO 20	SPI1_MOSI	
39		Ground	
40	GPIO 21	SPI1_CLK	

For more details, see the schematics of the Raspberry Pi and related documentation at www.raspberrypi.org/documentation/hardware/raspberrypi/schematics/README.md.

Index

Symbols

A

B

C

© Stewart Watkiss 2020
S. Watkiss, *Learn Electronics with Raspberry Pi*, https://doi.org/10.1007/978-1-4842-6348-8

Q

R

Printed in the United States
By Bookmasters